William Wordsworth, Andrew Jackson George

The Prelude

growth of a poet's mind

William Wordsworth, Andrew Jackson George

The Prelude
growth of a poet's mind

ISBN/EAN: 9783744718189

Printed in Europe, USA, Canada, Australia, Japan

Cover: Foto ©Thomas Meinert / pixelio.de

More available books at **www.hansebooks.com**

THE PRELUDE,

OR

GROWTH OF A POET'S MIND;

An Autobiographical Poem.

By WILLIAM WORDSWORTH.

WITH NOTES

By A. J. GEORGE, A.M.,

ACTING PROFESSOR OF ENGLISH LITERATURE IN BOSTON UNIVERSITY;
INSTRUCTOR IN ENGLISH LITERATURE IN THE
NEWTON HIGH SCHOOL.

"The child is father of the man."

BOSTON:

D. C. HEATH & CO., PUBLISHERS.

1888.

TO THE MEMORY

OF

Henry Norman Hudson, LL.D.,

WHOSE RARE QUALITIES OF MIND AND HEART WERE REVEALED
TO ME IN A LONG AND LOVING INTIMACY, AND WHOSE
COUNSEL, ENCOURAGEMENT, AND FRIENDSHIP HAVE
BEEN AMONG THE BLESSINGS OF MY LIFE,
THIS SELECTION FROM HIS BELOVED
POET IS AFFECTIONATELY
INSCRIBED.

PREFACE.

The gods talk in the breath of the woods,
 They talk in the shaken pine,
And fill the long reach of the old seashore
 With dialogue divine.
And the poet who overhears
 Some random word they say,
Is the fated man of men
 Whom the ages must obey.[1]

It is interesting in our survey of the past to study the crises in the world's history, and notice how Providence has, by particular surroundings and education, prepared special men for special emergencies. Seers, prophets, and teachers have been divinely raised up to interpret the mind of God to men, the

Heroes, Sages, Bards sublime,
And all that fetched the flowing rhyme
 From genuine springs.

In one of these crises, — that of the last half of the eighteenth century, — there was a stirring of the depths in all departments of human life. Literature, the outcome of the whole life of a people, was consequently involved in the revolutionary conflagration which ran over all the European world, from the ashes of which arose new ideas of mankind.

Poetry had been removed from its natural home, the country, and was forced to do service in the artificial surroundings of city life. In the hands of Dryden and Pope it had been shorn of all

[1] Emerson.

its natural charms, and appeared in court dress with " ruffles and rapier." It dealt with the outside aspects and artificial manners of the people, and lost sight of the human heart, —

> The haunt and main region of song.

During this time, Providence was rearing amid the rural scenery of Cumberland and Westmoreland one who was to stand forth as the exponent and defender of the Beautiful, the True, and the Good in English poesy, and by whose heroic struggle the Muse was to be returned to her long-lost home.·

The face of English literature was changed by that infusion of new blood from the hearts of such men as constituted the new brotherhood. Out of the souls of Cowper, Wordsworth, and Coleridge the poetry of freedom, of equal rights and of universal brotherhood, sprang full-grown into a life of earnest protest against tyranny of all kinds, political, moral, or priestly, — into a life which was to endure no decay.

The pitiless storm of ribaldry and abuse which the leader of this new movement of a return to nature had to encounter, was such as would have discouraged any one but him who knew no fear save the fear to do wrong. Clad in the strength of a lofty and consecrated purpose, he stood through the long pelting, true to himself, and all the time calmly singing from his retirement at Rydal : —

> For thus I live remote
> From evil-speaking; rancor never sought
> Comes to me not; malignant truth, or lie.
> Hence have I genial seasons, hence have I
> Smooth passion, smooth discourse and joyous thought.

Not a note of querulousness or bitterness escaped him. This was not the calm of indifference, but the calm of a nature capable of storms of indignation, yet under the sway of a powerful will. The great Preceptress by whom he was educated did not allow him to remain in the quietude of Nature. The poet of Humanity must needs

> see ill sights
> Of madding passions mutually inflamed;

or

> hang
> Brooding above the fierce confederate storm
> Of sorrow, barricado'd evermore
> Within the walls of cities.

On his first entrance to London a new and truer idea of man arose within him, and in passing to that theatre where the first acts in the mighty drama of Revolution were being enacted, a revolution was produced in his own mind, and he was seized with those ideas which added to his enthusiasm for Nature that enthusiasm for Man which characterized all his work, and raised him to the imperial height of a poet of the first order, — a poet of the " moral depths of the human soul."

> Blessings be with them — and eternal praise,
> Who gave us nobler loves and nobler cares, —
> The Poets — who on earth have made us heirs
> Of truth and pure delight by heavenly lays!
> Oh! might my name be numbered among theirs;
> Then gladly would I end my mortal days.

Thus wrote Wordsworth in 1805, and long and patiently did he wait for the answer to his prayer. At last, in the summer of 1839, he was permitted to realize that for which he had labored so assiduously and prayed so earnestly, when, by the foremost university of his land and the world, he was honored as one of the chief glories of English poetry and the greatest name since Milton.

Keble, the professor of Poetry in the University, introduced him as being "one who had shed a celestial light upon the affections, the occupations, and the piety of the poor." The ovation which he received was such as had never been witnessed there before, except upon the occasion of the visit of the Duke of Wellington. The long battle had been patiently and courageously fought, and victory was at length achieved. Of this victory the Rev. Frederick Robertson says : —

"It was my lot, during a short university career, to witness a transition and a reaction, or revulsion, of public feeling with regard to two great men. The first of these was Arnold of Rugby; the second, Wordsworth. When he came forward to receive his honorary degree, scarcely had his name been pronounced than from three thousand voices at once there broke forth a burst of applause echoed and taken up again and again. There were young eyes then filled with an emotion of which they had no need to be ashamed; there were hearts beating with the proud feeling of triumph that at last the world had recognized the merit of the man they had loved so long and acknowledged as their teacher."

In 1843 a still greater honor was conferred upon him at the hands of the young Queen. He was urged to accept the Laureateship, but gratefully and respectfully declined, as he considered that his years unfitted him for the discharge of its duties. He was then in his seventy-fourth year. This brought a letter from the Prime Minister, Sir Robert Peel, urging his acceptance of the appointment, saying, "As the Queen can select for this honorable appointment no one whose claims for respect and honor, on account of eminence as a poet, can be placed in competition with you, I trust that you will no longer hesitate to accept it. There is but one unanimous feeling on the part of all who have heard of the proposal.

"The offer was made not for the purpose of imposing upon you any onerous task or disagreeable duties, but in order to pay you that tribute of respect which is justly due to the first of living poets."

This letter removed his scruples, and the laurel wreath was placed upon the brows " of him who uttered nothing base." He produced but little poetry after this date; but there is one poem, written in 1846 upon the fly-leaf of a gift copy of his poems, presented to the Royal Library at Windsor Castle, which is of special interest (in this Jubilee Year), as connected with his Laureateship.

As it does not appear in any edition of his works, I give it entire : —

> Deign, Sovereign Mistress! to accept a lay,
>   No Laureate offering of elaborate art;
> But salutation, taking its glad way
>   From deep recesses of a loyal heart.
>
> Queen, wife, and mother! may all-judging Heaven
>   Shower with a bounteous hand on thee and thine
> Felicity, that only can be given
>   On earth to goodness blessed by grace divine.
>
> Lady! devoutly honored and beloved
>   Through every realm confided to thy sway;
> May'st thou pursue thy course by God approved,
>   And he will teach thy people to obey.
>
> As thou art wont thy sovereignty adorn
>   With woman's gentleness, yet firm and staid;
> So shall that earthly crown thy brows have worn
>   Be changed to one whose glory cannot fade.
>
> And now, by duty urged, I lay this book
>   Before thy Majesty in humble trust,
> That on its simplest pages thou wilt look
>   With a benign indulgence, more than just.
>
> Nor wilt thou blame an aged poet's prayer,
>   That, issuing hence, may steal into thy mind,
> Some solace under weight of royal care,
>   Or grief, the inheritance of human kind.
>
> For know we not that from celestial spheres
>   When time was young an inspiration came,
> (O were it mine!) to hallow saddest tears
>   And help life onward in its noblest aim?

W. W.

RYDAL MOUNT, 9th January, 1846.

He had sung his *nunc dimittis*, and composed no longer. His mission was completed. The bright dream of his boyhood was fulfilled, and that spirit singled out for holy services, after the discipline of sadness and suffering, entered into its rest.

His body lies, as he had requested, in the churchyard at Grasmere, in the bosom of that dear vale where he had lived and loved and sung; surrounded by the Dalesmen whom he honored; beneath the shade of those yews planted by his own hands, in sound of Rotha murmuring her plaintive strain that

> "few or none
> Hear her voice right now he is gone."

While round about in phalanx firm stand the mountains old, faithful guardians of the sacred spot. Earth has no more fitting resting-place for the dust of William Wordsworth.

> Plain is the stone that marks the Poet's rest;
> Not marble worked beneath Italian skies —
> A grey slate headstone tells where Wordsworth lies,
> Cleft from the native hills he loved the best.
> No heavier thing upon his gentle breast
> Than turf starred o'er in spring with daisy eyes,
> Nor richer music makes him lullabies
> Than Rotha fresh from yonder mountain crest.
> His name, his date, the years he lived to sing,
> Are deep incised and eloquently terse;
> But Fancy hears the graver's hammer ring,
> And sees mid lines of much remembered verse
> These words in gold beneath his title wrought —
> "Singer of Humble Themes and Noble Thought." [1]

There was but one thing more which his countrymen could do for him, and this was not long left undone, for in the Venerable Abbey, surrounded by the medallion of Keble and the busts of Kingsley and Maurice, may be seen the life-size statue of the poet in white marble: he is represented seated in the attitude of contemplation, the characteristic of all his portraits being thus strikingly reproduced in the marble. Underneath are engraved

[1] H. D. Rawnsley.

the words above quoted, " Blessings be with them and eternal praise," etc.

The world has not often seen a life so well rounded and symmetrical, a soul so strong and lofty, consecrate itself to a single purpose. Few poets have bequeathed to the world such a legacy of lofty thought and ennobling feeling which will cause all who love it to think the more deeply and feel the more tenderly, thus making men " wiser, better, and happier."

Professor Shairp says : " No poet of modern times has had in him so much of the prophet. What earth's far-off, lonely mountains do for the plains and cities, that Wordsworth has done and will do for literature, and through literature for society ; sending down great streams of higher truth, fresh, purifying winds of feeling to those who least dream from what quarter they came. The more thoughtful of each generation will draw nearer and observe him more closely, will ascend his imaginative heights and sit under the shadow of his profound meditations, and in proportion as they do so will they become more noble and pure in heart."

> The sunrise on his breezy lake,
> The rosy tints his sunset caught,
> World seen are gladdening all the vales
> And mountain peaks of thought.[1]

Accepting these estimates of the work and influence of Wordsworth, my aim is to bring before the reader this simple narrative of the ways in which his childhood walked and of what first led him to the love of rivers, woods, and hills, and how the love of nature led him up to the love of man. Goethe said, if you would understand an author, you must understand his age. There can be no more interesting or profitable study than that which seeks to determine by what principles, methods, chances, and changes, by what impulses of the mind and heart, a great personality impresses itself upon the intellectual history of a nation, and feeds it with moral truth and human passion.

[1] Whittier.

It is to William Wordsworth that we owe the nineteenth century renaissance in English poetry, because he led it a step farther than it had gone before, and penetrated the heart of man where it seemed that all were known and explored; he gave it a style which found itself the style of everybody, — a style at once new and antique because contemporary with all the ages. In a word, he gave to poetry a "vital soul."

> He found us when the age had bound
> Our souls in its benumbing round;
> He spoke and loosed our heart in tears.
>
> *   *   *   *   *   *
>
> Our youth returned; for there was shed,
> On spirits that had long been dead,
> Spirits dried up and closely furled,
> The freshness of the early world.[1]

It is the element of personality in Wordsworth's poetry which gives it its influence over the minds of those who enter into vital relations with it. He everywhere speaks to man's entire being. His profound thoughts, his vivid illustration, his ennobling sensibility, and his wise reflection have to do with the "here and now," — the sphere of our interests, duties, and dangers. He distinctly teaches that the sphere of motives is the sphere of morals; and that love of the true, the beautiful and the good in human action is a higher and worthier source of inspiration than the hatred of their opposites. He thus grounds his moral teaching upon the spirit of the Founder of Christianity, and in the *Ode to Duty* and *Character of the Happy Warrior* we find the highest manifestation of it.

> Serene will be our days and bright,
> And happy will our nature be,
> When love is an unerring light
> And joy its own security.

[1] Matthew Arnold.

—'Tis finally, the man who, lifted high,
Conspicuous object in a Nation's eye,
Or left unthought of in obscurity,—
Who, with a toward or untoward lot,
Prosperous or adverse, to his wish or not,
Plays in the many games of life, that one
Where what he most doth value must be won.
Who, not content that former worth stand fast,
Looks forward, persevering to the last,
From well to better, daily self-surpast;
Who, whether praise of him must walk the earth
Forever, and to nobler deeds give birth,
Or he must go to dust without his fame,
And leave a dead, unprofitable name,
Finds comfort in himself and in his cause;
And, while the mortal mist is gathering, draws
His breath in confidence of Heaven's applause:
This is the Happy Warrior; this is he
Whom every man in arms should wish to be.

Believing that the poet's function was to

Help life onward in its noblest aim,

he wrote to Sir George Beaumont: "The poet is a teacher; I wish to be considered as a teacher or as nothing." But his method is not that of the Doctrinaires and Examining Boards, for he had learned that the aim of education is the development of all the faculties, — body, soul, and spirit. He has severe words of condemnation for the method which produces that intellectual monstrosity, who

Can string you names of countries, cities, towns,
The whole world over, tight as beads of dew
Upon a gossamer thread.   *   *   *
*   *   *   Who must live,
Knowing that he grows wiser every day,
Or else not live at all.
For this unnatural growth the trainer blame,
Pity the tree.

He offers words of encouragement to those of us who believe that we should teach as Nature teaches, and that the original and poetic spirit in children should be encouraged rather than crushed out by cramming them to the throat with mere instruction. Grandeur of character has its roots in a freedom to drink in other lessons than those which may be *recited*.

> Thy art be Nature, the live current quaff,
> And let the groveller sip his stagnant pool,
> In fear that else when Critics, grave and cool,
> Have killed him, Scorn should write his epitaph.
> * * * * * * *
> How does the meadow-flower its bloom unfold?
> Because the lovely little flower is free
> Down to its root, and in that freedom bold;
> And so the grandeur of the forest tree
> Comes not by casting in a formal mould,
> But by its *own* divine vitality.

Wordsworth was a patriot as well as a poet, and in the school of citizenship, too, he proves our wisest teacher, insisting that good citizenship cannot exist without true manhood, — that the good citizen is the good man. This is the lesson of the French Revolution, and in this school Wordsworth was a pupil of the first rank. He was the first in England to honor the lives of men in all ranks, with the glory and the wealth and the beauty of song. He was the first to assert the right of every man to the best education which the State can give, and to protection from that greed which would oppress them with unremitting toil. He teaches that the only safety for a Nation is in that spirit of Fraternity which binds together the rich and the poor; that the liberty and true greatness of a nation are in its agreement with the laws of righteousness.

> By the soul
> Only the nations shall be great and free;

not from

> Fleets and armies, and external wealth,
> But from within proceeds a nation's strength.

With youthful ardor he championed the cause of suffering humanity in France, when the nation seemed

> Standing on the top of golden hours.

But when he saw the career of Napoleon begin, and France turn oppressor, in wrath and pity he espoused the interests of the oppressed nations. In a noble outburst of indignation he expressed his hatred of the cruel attack upon the liberties of Switzerland, of St. Domingo, and of the Venetian Republic.

After the imprisonment of the patriot Toussaint L'Ouverture. he wrote : —

> Thou hast left behind
> Powers that will work for thee; air, earth, and skies;
> There's not a breathing of the common wind
> That will forget thee; thou hast great allies;
> Thy friends are exultations, agonies,
> And love, and man's unconquerable mind.

When at last the dreadful contest ended and the tyrant was overthrown at Waterloo, in humble gratitude he pours forth his enthusiasm and his joy that the fate of nations is knit to the government of God.

> To Thee, to Thee,
> Just God of Christianised Humanity,
> Shall praise be poured forth, and thanks ascend,
> That thou hast brought our warfare to an end,
> And that we need no second victory!
> *   *   *   *   *   *
> Blest, above measure blest,
> If on thy love our Land her hopes shall rest,
> And all the nations labor to fulfil
> Thy law, and live henceforth in peace, in pure good will.

From his retirement at Rydal he issued poem and pamphlet in which he discussed

> the end
> Of civil government, and its wisest forms :

also education and the duty of the State to insist upon a high standard of citizenship; the poor laws; the relation of capital to labor, and the rights of workmen congregated in manufactories.

Strange themes for a poet! They were not strange for a poet who had imbibed the old Teutonic spirit of the people and the people's rights.

> We must be free or die, who speak the tongue
> That Shakespeare spake, the faith and morals hold
> Which Milton held.

One of the wisest of our public men has said: —

"I do not think that anybody of his time — statesman, philosopher, or poet — saw with such unerring insight into the great moral forces that determine the currents of history."[1]

As far back as 1820 he foresaw with remarkable penetration the movement which we designate as "Home Rule," and in a letter to Mrs. Hemans he said: —

"These two islands will reap the fruit of their own folly and madness, in becoming for the present generation the two most unquiet and miserable spots upon the earth."

He must have had in perspective the great English Liberal when he wrote: —

> Blest statesman he, whose mind's unselfish will
> Leaves her at ease among grand thoughts; whose eye
> Sees that apart from Magnanimity
> Wisdom exists not.

Americans should claim a close relationship to Wordsworth, for he is spiritually akin to these patriots who stood by the side of Washington, and felt his great arm lean on them for support. His burning words upon the fate of nations which build upon other principles than those of truth and justice have inspired many of our noblest statesmen.

In the rustic simplicity and delightful domesticity of that

---

[1] Hon. George F. Hoar.

Grasmere Cottage where, in manly independence, peace, and happy poverty, a practical example of "plain living and high thinking" was given to the world, we have a picture not uncommon in the rural villages of New England.

In his sorrow at the worldliness and materialism of those who live in luxury and frivolity, he exclaims : —

> Which way shall I look
> For comfort, being as I am, opprest,
> To think that now our life is only drest
> For show ; mean handiwork of craftsman, cook
> Or groom — we must run glittering like a brook
> In the open sunshine, or we are unblest ;
> The richest man among us is the best.
> *   *   *   *   Rapine, Avarice, Expense.
> This is idolatry, and these we adore ;
> Plain living and high thinking are no more.

There has been some alarm caused by the attitude of Science toward literary studies, and fears have been entertained that Poetry would be relegated to the sphere of mere pastime and amusement, — a subject no longer needed in our education, the human mind having outgrown it. Aware of the arrogance and dogmatism with which Science is claiming the exclusive right to our intellectual estate, aware also of her boast that she has banished the Muse from her birthright, we have no fears that either the claim or the boast can be substantiated so long as human nature remains what it is.

> True it is Nature hides
> Her treasures less and less. Man now presides
> In power, where once he trembled in his weakness ;
> Science advances with gigantic strides :
> But are we aught enriched in love and meekness ?
> Can aught be found in us of pure and wise
> More than in humble times graced human story ?
> That makes our heart more apt to sympathize ?

The claims of Science to "sovereign sway and masterdom" should be met in the spirit of candor and fair dealing, and the claims of Poetry pressed with earnestness.

This will help much in determining the sphere of each and to what place in our system of education each is entitled. If the aim of education be a harmonious development of all the faculties, we assuredly need other aids than those which Science furnishes. When we consider what treatment Poetry has received in the house of its friends, and upon what weak arguments it has often rested its claim, there can be no wonder that it has received but a contemptuous toleration.

The domain of Science is in no wise similar to that of Poetry, and the two ought never to antagonize one another. Science deals with the forces, e'ements, qualities, and operations of the material world; it is mainly the field of acquirement; its organ is the understanding, and that alone; in the abstractions of the intellect it finds its food and life. Involving but one side of our complex nature, it has no elevating or purifying effect; it does not reach the sphere of motives.

Poetry, on the other hand, deals with the facts of our moral and spiritual life and develops the ethical imaginative and emotional sides of our nature: its truths are those of the heart, the conscience, the imagination, and those are quite as essential as any with which Science has to deal. Remove duty, love, gratitude, admiration, reverence, and sympathy from life, and what a blank would be left! Where then would be the "vision and faculty divine"?

From what source is the heart to receive its warmth, the soul its inspiration, and life its beauty, if Science is to have supreme control of our mental furnishing? We certainly are in as great need, at the present time, of high moral character as of enlightened understanding. "A nation which exhausts all its power in developing steam engines and mill privileges will, in the end, learn that soul power is greater than steam power."

> We live by admiration, hope and love,
> And even as these are well and wisely fixed
> In dignity of being we ascend.

While Science is developing the perfect machine and pushing the division of labor to the extreme, literature must look to it that this movement which is "scientific in method, rationalistic in spirit, and utilitarian in purpose," shall not result in making man "a tool or implement."

An eminent French critic has said that, owing to the specializing tendency and the all-devouring force of Science, poetry would cease to be read in fifty years. After the severity with which Science was for so long time treated by Literature, there is no wonder that now, in the moment of her mighty exaltation, she should retaliate.

Of the relative claims of Science and Literature, the great Dr. Arnold said: "If one might wish for impossibilities, I might then wish that my children might be well versed in physical science, but in due subordination to the fulness and freshness of their knowledge on moral subjects."[1]

In order that we may lay a deep and sure foundation for character, we must insist that poetry be used for its power to elevate and refine: we must not divert it to the use of teaching logic, rhetoric, and the rules of poetic architecture; if we do, we must not complain that we "dwindle as we pore." Let the scientist dive into the earth, and the philosopher soar into the sky; but let us keep our feet upon the sure facts of experience,

> True to the kindred points of Heaven and Home.

That poetry will assist us even though we be scientists, we cannot doubt when we view the lives of such men as Newton, Kepler, and Agassiz — men who considered every new insight into Nature as bringing them so much nearer the mind of God. They

---

[1] Stanley's Life of Arnold.

recognized a logic of the heart no less than of the head, and that
it gave them truths that wake

> to perish never;
> Which neither listlessness nor mad endeavor,
> Nor man, nor boy,
> Nor all that is at enmity with joy,
> Can utterly abolish or destroy.

Thus we see that, instead of being antagonistic, Science and
Poetry may be mutually helpful. Every new field won for Science
may be entered and possessed by Poetry, and until the dull eye
of the scientist is lighted up and his cold heart warmed by the
vivifying influence of imagination,

> A primrose by the river's brim
> A yellow primrose is to him,
> And it is nothing more.

Mr. Ruskin has told us that the difference between a tyro and
a master is, that the one stops in details while the other refers all
the details to a final purpose,

> By which sense is made
> Subservient still to moral purposes
> Auxiliar to divine.

So long as we view all objects "in disconnection dull and spiritless," we are dealing with nature as a mere grammarian deals
with a poem, and are waging

> An impious warfare with the very life
> Of our own souls.

We believe that there is no poet who will, if rightly used, do so
much toward counteracting the utilitarian theories of our time,
and to bring poetry and science into harmony, as will Wordsworth. Although living in a pre-scientific age he had clear views
upon the tendency of exclusively scientific studies, and he sought
to counteract it by teaching us not to centre our life upon the

petty and the transient, but to rise to the higher fields beyond the realm of sense to the realm of spirit, where there are facts to be gained and relations to be adjusted, as truly as in the physical world, and where the consequences of neglect are more fatal. He looks upon both sides of the shield.

> When soothing darkness spreads
> O'er hill and vale *   *   *
> *   *   *   And the punctual stars
> Glitter, undisturbing, undisturbed;
> *   *   *   *   *   *
> Then in full many a region, once like this,
> The assured domain of calm simplicity
> And pensive quiet, an unnatural light
> Breaks forth from a many windowed fabric huge;
> And at the appointed hour a bell is heard,
> A local summons to unceasing toil!
> *   *   *   Men, maidens, youths,
> Mother and little children, boys and girls,
> Enter, and each the wonted task resumes
> Within this temple where is offered up
> To Gain, the master idol of the realm,
> Perpetual sacrifice.

He does not hate Science because some of its votaries see nothing beyond it, nor decry it because of the many abuses attendant upon its practical application.

> Yet do I exult
> Casting reserve away, exult to see
> An intellectual mastery exercised
> O'er the blind elements; a purpose given,
> A perseverance fed; almost a soul
> Imparted — to brute matter.

In his *Principles of Poetry* he says: "If the time shall ever come when what is now called science shall be ready to put on, as it were, the form of flesh and blood, the poet will lend his divine spirit to aid in the transformation, and will welcome the being thus produced as a dear and genuine inmate of the household of man."

That Wordsworth's poetry will purify, dignify, and inspire human life we have the testimony of a Positivist, John Stuart Mill. When in a great mental crisis, after seeing all his schèmes for social renovation fail, and when he was being driven to the verge of fatalism and despondency, he was led to the study of Wordsworth, and he says: " What made Wordsworth's poems a medicine for my state of mind was that they seemed to be the very culture of the feelings which I was in quest of. In them I seemed to draw from a source of inward joy, of sympathetic and imaginative pleasure which could be shared by all human beings, and I felt myself at once better and happier as I came under their influence." [1]

The growth of a poet's mind, as seen in the Prelude, developing itself serene and lofty amid the quiet and sublime influences of Nature, or bewildered amid those convulsions attendant upon the French Revolution, affords us the key to all of his later work. This poem was not published until the year after the author's death, and consequently is less known, even to students of Wordsworth, than almost any other of his works.

Professor Knight has pronounced it the greatest poem of its kind ever contributed to literature. Mr. Myers has said that there is hardly any biography which can be read with such implicit confidence. The Rev. Frederick Robertson said of it: " The diction is always pure and clear, like an atmosphere of crystal pellucidness, through which you can see all objects without being diverted aside to consider the medium through which they are seen." Mrs. Oliphant says: " The value of the poem as a picture of the mental history of the period can scarcely be over-estimated. It is full of the freshness of the mountains and the thrill of simple life and nature." In Professor Shairp's most admirable lectures upon the Poetic Interpretation of Nature we find the following: " There were many who knew Wordsworth's poetry well while he was still alive, who felt its power, and the

---

[1] Autobiography.

new light it threw upon the material world. But though they half guessed, they did not know the secret of it. They got glimpses of part, but could not grasp the philosophy on which it was based. But when, after his death, the Prelude was published, they were let into the secret; they saw the hidden foundations on which it rests as they had never seen them before. The smaller poems were more beautiful, more delightful, but the Prelude revealed the secret of their beauty. It showed that all Wordsworth's impassioned feeling toward Nature was no mere fantastic dream, but based on sanity, on a most assured and reasonable philosophy. It was as though one who had been long gazing on some building grand and fair, admiring the vast sweep of its walls and the strength of its battlements, without understanding their principle of coherence, were at length to be admitted inside · by the master-builder, and given a view of the whole plan from within, the principles of architecture, and the hidden substructures upon which it was built. This is what the Prelude does for the rest of Wordsworth's poetry."

In every man whose life is life in any true sense of the word there are some central principles which move and control the rest, and if we are to come into a living relation with his individuality we must ascertain what these principles are. In such a study we pass through the creation to the mind of the creator.

No finer estimate of Wordsworth has ever been given than that of Coleridge in his *Biographia Literaria*, the chief points of which are: "*First*, an austere purity of language, a perfect appropriateness of the words to the meaning. . . . *Second*, a corresponding weight and sanity of the thoughts and sentiments, won not from books, but from the poet's own meditative observation. . . . They are fresh and have the dew upon them. . . . *Third*, the sinewy strength and originality of single lines and paragraphs. . . . *Fourth*, the perfect truth of nature in his images and descriptions. *Fifth*, a meditative pathos. a union of deep and subtle thought with sensibility, a sympathy with man as man. . . . In this mild and philosophic pathos

Wordsworth appears to me without a compeer. . . . *Last,* and pre-eminently, I challenge for this poet the gift of imagination in the highest and strictest sense of the word. . . . In imaginative power he stands nearest of all modern writers to Shakespeare and Milton ; and yet in a kind perfectly unborrowed and his own." Dr. Moir, the Scottish author and critic, says: "Never, perhaps, in the whole range of literary history, from Homer downwards, did any individual, throughout the course of a long life, dedicate himself to poetry with a devotion so pure, so perfect, and so uninterrupted as he did. It was not his amusement, his recreation, his mere pleasure. It was the main, the serious, the solemn business of his being. It was his morning, noon, and evening thought, the object of his out-door rambles, the subject of his in-door reflections ; and, as an art, he studied it as severely as ever Canova did sculpture, or Michael Angelo painting."[1]

The inscription upon the memorial in Grasmere church is sc just and so comprehensive that I give it entire.

TO THE MEMORY OF
WILLIAM WORDSWORTH.
A TRUE PHILOSOPHER AND POET,
WHO BY THE SPECIAL GIFT AND CALLING OF
ALMIGHTY GOD,
WHETHER HE DISCOURSED ON MAN OR NATURE,
FAILED NOT TO LIFT UP THE HEART
TO HOLY THINGS,
TIRED NOT OF MAINTAINING THE CAUSE
OF THE POOR AND SIMPLE:
AND SO IN PERILOUS TIMES WAS RAISED UP
TO BE A CHIEF MINISTER
NOT ONLY OF NOBLEST POESY,
BUT OF HIGH AND SACRED TRUTH.
THIS MEMORIAL
IS PLACED HERE BY HIS FRIENDS AND NEIGHBORS
IN TESTIMONY OF
RESPECT, AFFECTION, AND GRATITUDE.
ANNO 1851.

[1] The Poetical Literature of the Last Half-Century.

Wordsworth's poems are so intimately connected with the Lake country that they are the only guide needed to that ground which he has rendered classic. Most of his verses were murmured in the open air, while he sat upon the mountain side and

> beheld the Sun
> Rise up and bathe the world in light;

or as he followed the path of the brook hurrying to its resting-place in the bosom of the lake; or, in company with some loved friend, paced the terraced walk at Rydal, as the sun was sinking behind Loughrigg, and the clouds of evening began to gather upon the breast of Wansfell.

The Prelude was mostly composed at Under Lancrigg, a terrace on the side of Helm Crag, overlooking Grasmere Vale. As he walked to and fro repeating the verses, they were taken down by his sympathetic scribes, — his wife and sister.

The Prelude is connected with all that is greatest in the poetical achievement of Wordsworth; with all that makes for his immortality as a poet. For more than forty years it was suppressed, and there is no doubt but that he intended it should remain so for all time. How can this fact be reconciled with much of the current criticism which declares that he was over-anxious for fame? In the interval between 1799 and 1806, when the yoke of the Prelude rested heavily upon him, and he was weary of tracing

> "Home to its cloud the lightning of his mind,"

he found rest and recreation in those divine poems, *The Brothers*, *Tintern Abbey*, the *Platonic Ode*, and those shorter gems of song which reveal his genius at its loftiest pitch of energy, — poems all the sweeter, perhaps, because the time devoted to them was stolen from the Prelude. "In writing them he was like an Eton boy out of bounds; he was a truant from the Prelude; he was shirking school; he was dodging his tutor."[1] At a time when

---

[1] Sir Francis Doyle in Oxford Lectures.

he had passed on to the enjoyment of other sights and sounds, other beauties and melodies than those of earth, his disciples rescued the work from oblivion, and by so doing revealed to us all the stormy hopes, all the struggling energies, all the solemn deliberations, and all the tumultuous yearnings of his lofty, capacious, and impassioned soul.

We readily admit the existence of lines which are faulty in execution and obscure in meaning, but it must be remembered that the work was left in the rough and never received the final touches which a revision for publication would have given it. Had it been given to the world in the poet's time he would, no doubt, have pruned it and improved it in many respects. The pure, transparent, and beautiful English; the grace and melody of versification; the sinewy strength of single lines; the treasures of imagination and the general poetic power displayed; the mingling of genius and common sense; the spirit of candor and conscientiousness which pervades the whole, — these stamp it as one of the most remarkable poetic productions in the language, and constitute it one of the brightest flowers in his unfading coronal.

"It appears to me that the memorials of a great soul have at least as much claim upon our indulgence as *The Memorials of a Quiet Life*, in two volumes of somewhat humdrum prose." [1]

In the notes I have endeavored to furnish such assistance — historical, geographical, and explanatory — as the reader would not be likely to get elsewhere. The localities have been carefully studied in the light of the poem itself, and with the assistance of those local historians — the dalesmen.

It is well known to what extent and with what success the late Professor Hudson made use of Wordsworth in his classes, and that he contemplated doing for Wordsworth what he had done for Shakespeare. Although aware of how far this work falls short of what his mature judgment and ripe scholarship would have produced, I nevertheless hope that it may prove a help to

[1] Sir Francis Doyle in Oxford Lectures.

those who are desirous of understanding the mind of the great poet.

Grateful acknowledgments are here tendered to Hon. George F. Hoar, for permission to quote from a letter of his to the late Dr. Hudson; to the Rev. H. D. Rawnsley, Crosthwaite, Keswick, for his *Sonnets at the English Lakes*, one of which I have quoted entire; to Mr. R. Mitchell, Jr., Wordsworth's House, Cockermouth, for assistance in studying the poet's birthplace; to Professor William Knight, of the University of St. Andrews, for the privilege of using material from his edition of Wordsworth's poems; and also to Mrs. William Wordsworth, of the Stepping Stones, Ambleside, for her interest in the work and her efforts to render the editor's visits to the homes and haunts of the poet both pleasant and profitable. Whoever writes upon the genius of Wordsworth must, almost of necessity, be under obligation to previous writers. I am especially indebted to the works of Professor Shairp and the Rev. Stopford Brooke; these were my earliest and most helpful guides in the study of that poet

> " of the cloud, the cataract, the lake,
> Who on Helvellyn's summit wide awake,
> Catches his freshness from Archangels' wing.
> He of the rose, the violet, the spring,
> The social smile, the chain for freedom's sake."

The Prelude will be followed by the publication of other of Wordsworth's poems.

A. J. G.

BROOKLINE, MASS., November, 1887.

CONTENTS.

[The following lines were composed by Coleridge after listening to the recitation of the Prelude by its author at Coleorton, Leicestershire, where the Wordsworths were living in the winter of 1806.]

———∞°⚬°∞———

TO WILLIAM WORDSWORTH.

———◆———

FRIEND of the wise ! and teacher of the good !
Into my heart have I received that lay
More than historic, that prophetic lay
Wherein (high theme by thee first sung aright)
Of the foundations and the building up
Of a Human Spirit thou hast dared to tell
What may be told, to the understanding mind
Revealable ; and what within the mind
By vital breathings secret as the soul
Of vernal growth, oft quickens in the heart
Thoughts all too deep for words ! —
                    Theme hard as high,
Of smiles spontaneous, and mysterious fears
(The first-born they of Reason and twin birth),
Of tides obedient to external force,
And currents self-determined, as might seem,
Or by some inner power : of moments awful,
Now in thy inner life, and now abroad,
When power streamed from thee, and thy soul received
The Light reflected, as a light bestowed —
Of fancies fair, and milder hours of youth,
Hyblean murmurs of poetic thought

Industrious in its joy, in vales and glens,
Native or outland, lakes and famous hills !
Or on the lonely high-road, when the stars
Were rising ; or by secret mountain-streams,
The guides and the companions of thy way !
Of more than Fancy, of the Social Sense
Distending wide, and man beloved as man,
Where France in all her towns lay vibrating
Like some becalmed bark beneath the burst
Of Heaven's immediate thunder, when no cloud
Is visible, or shadow on the main.
For thou wert there, thine own brows garlanded,
Amid the tremor of a realm aglow,
Amid a mighty nation jubilant,
When from the general heart of humankind
Hope sprang forth like a full-born Deity !
— Of that dear Hope afflicted and struck down,
So summoned homeward, thenceforth calm and sure,
From the dread watch-tower of man's absolute self,
With light unwaning on her eyes, to look
Far on — herself a glory to behold.
The Angel of the vision !   Then (last strain)
Of Duty, chosen laws controlling choice,
Action and joy ! — An Orphic song indeed,
A song divine of high and passionate thoughts
To their own music chanted !
                       O great Bard !
Ere yet that last strain dying awed the air,
With steadfast eye I viewed thee in the choir
Of ever-enduring men.   The truly great
Have all one age, and from one visible space

Shed influence !   They, both in power and act,
Are permanent, and Time is not with them,
Save as it worketh for them, they in it.
Nor less a sacred roll, than those of old,
And to be placed, as they, with gradual fame
Among the archives of mankind, thy work
Makes audible a linked lay of Truth,
Of Truth profound a sweet continuous lay,
Not learnt, but native, her own natural notes !
Ah ! as I listened with a heart forlorn,
The pulses of my being beat anew :
And even as life returns upon the drowned,
Life's joy rekindling roused a throng of pains —
Keen pangs of Love, awakening as a babe
Turbulent, with an outcry in the heart ;
And fears self-willed, that shunned the eye of hope ;
And hope that scarce would know itself from fear ;
Sense of past youth, and manhood come in vain,
And genius given, and knowledge won in vain ;
And all which I had culled in wood-walks wild,
And all which patient toil had reared, and all,
Commune with thee had opened out — but flowers
Strewed on my corse, and borne upon my bier,
In the same coffin, for the self-same grave !
.   .   .   .   Eve following eve,
Dear tranquil time, when the sweet sense of Home
Is sweetest ! moments for their own sake hailed,
And more desired, more precious for thy song,
In silence listening, like a devout child,
My soul lay passive, by thy various strain
Driven as in surges now beneath the stars,

With momentary stars of my own birth,
Fair constellated foam, still darting off
Into the darkness ; now a tranquil sea,·
Outspread and bright, yet swelling to the moon.
And when ! O Friend ! my comforter and guide !
Strong in thyself and powerful to give strength ! —
Thy long-sustained Song finally closed,
And thy deep voice had ceased — yet thou thyself
Wert still before my eyes, and round us both
That happy vision of beloved faces —
Scarce conscious, and yet conscious of its close
I sate, my being blended in one thought
(Thought was it ? or aspiration ? or resolve ?)
Absorbed, yet hanging still upon the sound —
And when I rose I found myself in prayer.

THE PRELUDE,

OR GROWTH OF A POET'S MIND;

AN AUTOBIOGRAPHICAL POEM.

———o·o·:·o·:·oo———

ADVERTISEMENT.

THE following Poem was commenced in the beginning of the year 1799, and completed in the summer of 1805.

The design and occasion of the work are described by the Author in his Preface to the EXCURSION, first published in 1814, where he thus speaks : —

" Several years ago, when the Author retired to his native mountains with the hope of being enabled to construct a literary work that might live, it was a reasonable thing that he should take a review of his own mind, and examine how far Nature and Education had qualified him for such an employment.

" As subsidiary to this preparation, he undertook to record, in verse, the origin and progress of his own powers, as far as he was acquainted with them.

" That work, addressed to a dear friend, most distinguished for his knowledge and genius, and to whom the Author's intellect is deeply indebted, has been long finished, and the result of the investigation which gave rise to it, was a determination to compose a philosophical Poem, containing views of Man, Nature, and Society, and to be entitled the 'Recluse'; as having for its principal subject the sensations and opinions of a poet living in retirement.

"The preparatory Poem is biographical, and conducts the history of the Author's mind to the point when he was emboldened to hope that his faculties were sufficiently matured for entering upon the arduous labor which he had proposed to himself; and the two works have the same kind of relation to each other, if he may so express himself, as the Ante-chapel has to the body of a Gothic church. Continuing this allusion, he may be permitted to add, that his minor pieces, which have been long before the public, when they shall be properly arranged, will be found by the attentive reader to have such connection with the main work as may give them claim to be likened to the little cells, oratories, and sepulchral recesses, ordinarily included in those edifices."

Such was the Author's language in the year 1814.

It will thence be seen, that the present Poem was intended to be introductory to the RECLUSE, and that the RECLUSE, if completed, would have consisted of Three Parts. Of these, the Second Part alone, viz., the EXCURSION, was finished, and given to the world by the Author.

The First Book of the First Part of the RECLUSE still remains in manuscript, but the Third Part was only planned. The materials of which it would have been formed have, however, been incorporated, for the most part, in the Author's other Publications, written subsequently to the EXCURSION.

The Friend, to whom the present Poem is addressed, was the late SAMUEL TAYLOR COLERIDGE, who was resident in Malta, for the restoration of his health, when the greater part of it was composed.

RYDAL MOUNT, *July* 13, 1850.

BOOK FIRST.

————◦◦◦————

INTRODUCTION. — CHILDHOOD AND SCHOOL-TIME.

O THERE is blessing in this gentle breeze,
A visitant that while it fans my cheek
Doth seem half-conscious of the joy it brings
From the green fields, and from yon azure sky,
Whate'er its mission, the soft breeze can come
To none more grateful than to me ; escaped
From the vast city, where I long had pined
A discontented sojourner ; now free,
Free as a bird to settle where I will.
What dwelling shall receive me ? in what vale   10
Shall be my harbor ? underneath what grove
Shall I take up my home ? and what clear stream
Shall with its murmur lull me into rest ?
The earth is all before me.   With a heart
Joyous, nor scared at its own liberty,
I look about ; and should the chosen guide
Be nothing better than a wandering cloud,
I cannot miss my way.   I breathe again !
Trances of thought and mountings of the mind
Come fast upon me : it is shaken off,   20
That burthen of my own unnatural self,

The heavy weight of many a weary day
Not mine, and such as were not made for me.
Long months of peace (if such bold word accord
With any promises of human life),
Long months of ease and undisturbed delight
Are mine in prospect; whither shall I turn,
By road or pathway, or through trackless field,
Up hill or down, or shall some floating thing
Upon the river point me out my course?   30

   Dear Liberty!   Yet what would it avail
But for a gift that consecrates the joy?
For I, methought, while the sweet breath of heaven
Was blowing on my body, felt within
A correspondent breeze, that gently moved
With quickening virtue, but is now become
A tempest, a redundant energy,
Vexing its own creation.   Thanks to both,
And their congenial powers, that, while they join
In breaking up a long-continued frost,   40
Bring with them vernal promises, the hope
Of active days urged on by flying hours, —
Days of sweet leisure, taxed with patient thought .
Abstruse, nor wanting punctual service high,
Matins and vespers of harmonious verse!

   Thus far, O Friend! did I, not used to make
A present joy the matter of a song,
Pour forth that day my soul in measured strains
That would not be forgotten, and are here
Recorded; to the open fields I told   50

A prophecy: poetic numbers came
Spontaneously to clothe in priestly robe
·A renovated spirit singled out,
Such hope was mine, for holy services.
My own voice cheered me, and, far more, the mind's
Internal echo of the imperfect sound;
To both I listened, drawing from them both
A cheerful confidence in things to come.

Content and not unwilling now to give
A respite to this passion, I paced on   60
With brisk and eager steps; and came, at length,
To a green shady place, where down I sate
Beneath a tree, slackening my thoughts by choice,
And settling into gentler happiness.
'Twas autumn, and a clear and placid day,
With warmth, as much as needed, from a sun
Two hours declined towards the west; a day
With silver clouds, and sunshine on the grass,
And in the sheltered and the sheltering grove
A perfect stillness.   Many were the thoughts   70
Encouraged and dismissed, till choice was made
Of a known Vale, whither my feet should turn,
Nor rest till they had reached the very door
Of the one cottage which methought I saw.
No picture of mere memory ever looked
So fair; and while upon the fancied scene
I gazed with growing love, a higher power
Than Fancy gave assurance of some work
Of glory there forthwith to be begun,
Perhaps too there performed.   Thus long I mused,   80

Nor e'er lost sight of what I mused upon,
Save when, amid the stately grove of oaks,
Now here, now there, an acorn, from its cup
Dislodged, through sere leaves rustled, or at once
To the bare earth dropped with a startling sound.
From that soft couch I rose not, till the sun
Had almost touched the horizon ; casting then
A backward glance upon the curling cloud
Of city smoke, by distance ruralized ;
Keen as a Truant or a Fugitive,   90
But as a Pilgrim resolute, I took,
Even with the chance equipment of that hour,
The road that pointed toward the chosen Vale.
It was a splendid evening, and my soul
Once more made trial of her strength, nor lacked
Æolian visitations ; but the harp
Was soon defrauded, and the banded host
Of harmony dispersed in straggling sounds
And lastly utter silence !   " Be it so ;
Why think of anything but present good? "   100
So, like a home-bound laborer I pursued
My way beneath the mellowing sun, that shed
Mild influence ; nor left in me one wish
Again to bend the Sabbath of that time
To a servile yoke.   What need of many words?
A pleasant loitering journey, through three days
Continued, brought me to my hermitage.
I spare to tell of what ensued, the life
In common things — the endless store of things,
Rare, or at least so seeming, every day   110
Found all about me in one neighborhood —

The self-congratulation, and, from morn
To night, unbroken cheerfulness serene.
But speedily an earnest longing rose
To brace myself to some determined aim,
Reading or thinking ; either to lay up
New stores, or rescue from decay the old
By timely interference : and therewith
Came hopes still higher, that with outward life
I might endue some airy phantasies   120
That had been floating loose about for years,
And to such beings temperately deal forth
The many feelings that oppressed my heart.
That hope hath been discouraged ; welcome light
Dawns from the east, but dawns to disappear
And mock me with a sky that ripens not
Into a steady morning : if my mind,
Remembering the bold promise of the past,
Would gladly grapple with some noble theme,
Vain is her wish ; where'er she turns she finds   130
Impediments from day to day renewed.

And now it would content me to yield up
Those lofty hopes awhile, for present gifts
Of humbler industry.   But, oh, dear Friend !
The Poet, gentle creature as he is,
Hath, like the Lover, his unruly times ;
His fits when he is neither sick nor well,
Though no distress be near him but his own
Unmanageable thoughts : his mind, best pleased
While she as duteous as the mother dove   140
Sits brooding, lives not always to that end,

But like the innocent bird, hath goadings on
That drive her as in trouble through the groves;
With me is now such passion, to be blamed
No otherwise than as it lasts too long.

When, as becomes a man who would prepare
For such an arduous work, I through myself
Make rigorous inquisition, the report
Is often cheering; for I neither seem
To lack that first great gift, the vital soul,   150
Nor general Truths, which are themselves a sort
Of Elements and Agents, Under-powers,
Subordinate helpers of the living mind :
Nor am I naked of external things,
Forms, images, nor numerous other aids
Of less regard, though won perhaps with toil
And needful to build up a Poet's praise.
Time, place, and manners do I seek, and these
Are found in plenteous store, but nowhere such
As may be singled out with steady choice;   160
No little band of yet remembered names
Whom I, in perfect confidence, might hope
To summon back from lonesome banishment,
And make them dwellers in the hearts of men
Now living, or to live in future years.
Sometimes the ambitious Power of choice, mistaking
Proud spring-tide swellings for a regular sea,
Will settle on some British theme, some old
Romantic tale by Milton left unsung;
More often turning to some gentle place   170
Within the groves of Chivalry, I pipe

To shepherd swains, or seated harp in hand,
Amid reposing knights by a river side
Or fountain, listen to the grave reports
Of dire enchantments faced and overcome
By the strong mind, and tales of warlike feats,
Where spear encountered spear, and sword with sword
Fought, as if conscious of the blazonry
That the shield bore, so glorious was the strife ;
Whence inspiration for a song that winds   180
Through ever changing scenes of votive quest
Wrongs to redress, harmonious tribute paid
To patient courage, and unblemished truth,
To firm devotion, zeal unquenchable,
And Christian meekness hallowing faithful loves.
Sometimes, more sternly moved, I would relate
How vanquished Mithridates northward passed,
And, hidden in the cloud of years, became
Odin, the Father of a race by whom
Perished the Roman Empire ; how the friends   190
And followers of Sertorious, out of Spain,
Flying, found shelter in the Fortunate Isles,
And left their usages, their arts and laws,
To disappear by a slow gradual death,
To dwindle and to perish one by one,
Starved in those narrow bounds : but not the soul
Of Liberty, which fifteen hundred years
Survived, and, when the European came
With skill and power that might not be withstood,
Did, like a pestilence, maintain its hold   200
And wasted down by glorious death that race
Of natural heroes : or I would record

How, in tyrannic times, some high-souled man,
Unnamed among the chronicles of kings,
Suffered in silence for Truth's sake : or tell
How that one Frenchman, through continued force
Of meditation on the inhuman deeds
Of those who conquered first the Indian Isles,
Went single in his ministry across
The Ocean ; not to comfort the oppressed,   210
But, like a thirsty wind, to roam about
Withering the Oppressor ; how Gustavus sought
Help at his need in Dalecarlia's mines :
How Wallace fought for Scotland ; left the name
Of Wallace to be found, like a wild flower,
All over his dear Country ; left the deeds
Of Wallace, like a family of Ghosts,
To people the steep rocks and river banks,
Her natural sanctuaries, with a local soul
Of independence and stern liberty.   220
Sometimes it suits me better to invent
A tale from my own heart, more near akin
To my own passions and habitual thoughts ;
Some variegated story, in the main
Lofty, but the unsubstantial structure melts
Before the very sun that brightens it,
Mist into air dissolving ! then a wish,
My last and favorite aspiration, mounts
With yearning towards some philosophic song
Of Truth that cherishes our daily life ;   230
With meditations passionate from deep
Recesses in man's heart, immortal verse
Thoughtfully fitted to the Orphean lyre ;

But from this awful burthen I full soon
Take refuge and beguile myself with trust
That mellower years will bring a riper mind
And clearer insight.   Thus my days are past
In contradiction ; with no skill to part
Vague longing, haply bred by want of power,
From paramount impulse not to be withstood,   240
A timorous capacity from prudence,
From circumspection, infinite delay.
Humility and modest awe themselves
Betray me, serving often for a cloak
To a more subtle selfishness ; that now
Locks every function up in blank reserve,
Now dupes me, trusting to an anxious eye
That with intrusive restlessness beats off
Simplicity and self-presented truth.
Ah ! better far than this, to stray about   250
Voluptuously through fields and rural walks,
And ask no record of the hours, resigned
To vacant musing, unreproved neglect
Of all things, and deliberate holiday.
Far better never to have heard the name
Of zeal and just ambition, than to live
Baffled and plagued by a mind that every hour
Turns recreant to her task ; takes heart again,
Then feels immediately some hollow thought
Hang like an interdict upon her hopes.   260
This is my lot ; for either still I find
Some imperfection in the chosen theme,
Or see of absolute accomplishment
Much wanting, so much wanting, in myself,

That I recoil and droop, and seek repose
In listlessness from vain perplexity,
Unprofitably travelling toward the grave,
Like a false steward who hath much received
And renders nothing back.

                 Was it for this
That one, the fairest of all rivers, loved   270
To blend his murmurs with my nurse's song,
And, from his alder shades and rocky falls,
And from his fords and shallows, sent a voice
That flowed along my dreams? For this, didst thou,
O Derwent! winding among grassy holms
Where I was looking on, a babe in arms,
Make ceaseless music that composed my thoughts
To more than infant softness, giving me
Amid the fretful dwellings of mankind
A foretaste, a dim earnest, of the calm   280
That Nature breathes among the hills and groves?
When he had left the mountains and received
On his smooth breast the shadow of those towers
That yet survive, a shattered monument
Of feudal sway, the bright blue river passed
Along the margin of our terrace walk ;
A tempting playmate whom we dearly loved.
Oh, many a time have I, a five years' child,
In a small mill-race severed from his stream,
Made one long bathing of a summer's day ;   290
Basked in the sun, and plunged and basked again
Alternate, all a summer's day, or scoured
The sandy fields, leaping through flowery groves
Of yellow ragwort ; or when rock and hill,

The woods, and distant Skiddaw's lofty height,
Were bronzed with deepest radiance, stood alone
Beneath the sky, as if I had been born
On Indian plains, and from my mother's hut
Had run abroad in wantonness, to sport
A naked savage, in the thunder shower.   300

   Fair seed-time had my soul, and I grew up
Fostered alike by beauty and by fear
Much favored in my birth-place, and no less
In that beloved Vale to which ere long
We were transplanted — there were we let loose
For sports of wider range.   Ere I had told
Ten birth-days, when among the mountain slopes
Frost, and the breath of frosty wind, had snapped
The last autumnal crocus, 'twas my joy
With store of springes o'er my shoulder hung   310
To range the open heights where woodcocks run
Along the smooth green turf.   Through half the night,
Scudding away from snare to snare, I plied
That anxious visitation ; — moon and stars
Were shining o'er my head.   I was alone,
And seemed to be a trouble to the peace
That dwelt among them.   Sometimes it befell
In these night wanderings, that a strong desire
O'erpowered my better reason, and the bird
Which was the captive of another's toil   320
Became my prey ; and when the deed was done
I heard among the solitary hills
Low breathings coming after me, and sounds

Of undistinguishable motion, steps
Almost as silent as the turf they trod.

Nor less when spring had warmed the cultured Vale,
Moved we as plunderers where the mother-bird
Had in high places built her lodge ; though mean
Our object and inglorious, yet the end
Was not ignoble.   Oh ! when I have hung   330
Above the raven's nest, by knots of grass
And half-inch fissures in the slippery rock
But ill sustained, and almost (so it seemed)
Suspended by the blast that blew amain,
Shouldering the naked crag, oh, at that time
While on the perilous ridge I hung alone,
With what strange utterance did the loud dry wind
Blow through my ear ! the sky seemed not a sky
Of earth — and with what motion moved the clouds !

Dust as we are, the immortal spirit grows   340
Like harmony in music ; there is a dark
Inscrutable workmanship that reconciles
Discordant elements, makes them cling together
In one society.   How strange that all
The terrors, pains, and early miseries,
Regrets, vexations, lassitudes interfused
Within my mind, should e'er have borne a part,
And that a needful part, in making up
The calm existence that is mine when I
Am worthy of myself !   Praise to the end !   350
Thanks to the means which Nature deigned to employ ;
Whether her fearless visitings, or those

That came with soft alarm, like hurtless light
Opening the peaceful clouds; or she may use
Severer interventions, ministry
More palpable, as best might suit her aim.

One summer evening (led by her) I found
A little boat tied to a willow tree
Within a rocky cove, its usual home.
Straight I unloosed her chain, and stepping in   360
Pushed from the shore.   It was an act of stealth
And troubled pleasure, nor without the voice
Of mountain-echoes did my boat move on ;
Leaving behind her still, on either side,
Small circles glittering idly in the moon,
Until they melted all into one track
Of sparkling light.   But now, like one who rows,
Proud of his skill, to reach a chosen point
With an unswerving line, I fixed my view
Upon the summit of a craggy ridge,   370
The horizon's utmost boundary ; far above
Was nothing but the stars and the gray sky.
She was an elfin pinnace ; lustily
I dipped my oars into the silent lake,
And, as I rose upon the stroke, my boat
Went heaving through the water like a swan ;
When, from behind that craggy steep till then
The horizon's bound, a huge peak, black and huge,
As if with voluntary power instinct
Upreared its head.   I struck and struck again,   380
And growing still in stature the grim shape
Towered up between me and the stars, and still,

For so it seemed, with purpose of its own
And measured motion like a living thing,
Strode after me.   With trembling oars I turned,
And through the silent water stole my way
Back to the covert of the willow tree ;
There in her mooring-place I left my bark, —
And through the meadows homeward went, in grave
And serious mood ; but after I had seen   390
That spectacle, for many days, my brain
Worked with a dim and undetermined sense
Of unknown modes of being ; o'er my thoughts
There hung a darkness, call it solitude
Or blank desertion.   No familiar shapes
Remained, no pleasant images of trees,
Of sea or sky, no colors of green fields ;
But huge and mighty forms, that do not live
Like living men, moved slowly through the mind
By day, and were a trouble to my dreams.   400

Wisdom and Spirit of the universe !
Thou Soul that art the eternity of thought,
That givest to forms and images a breath
And everlasting motion, not in vain
By day or star-light thus from my first dawn
Of childhood didst thou intertwine for me
The passions that build up our human soul ;
Not with the mean and vulgar works of man,
But with high objects, with enduring things —
With life and nature — purifying thus   410
The elements of feeling and of thought,
And sanctifying, by such discipline,

Both pain and fear, until we recognize
A grandeur in the beatings of the heart.
Nor was this fellowship vouchsafed to me
With stinted kindness.   In November days,
When vapors rolling down the valley made
A lonely scene more lonesome, among woods,
At noon and 'mid the calm of summer nights,
When, by the margin of the trembling lake,   420
Beneath the gloomy hills homeward I went
In solitude, such intercourse was mine ;
Mine was it in the fields both day and night,
And by the waters, all the summer long.

      And in the frosty season, when the sun
Was set, and visible for many a mile
The cottage windows blazed through twilight gloom,
I heeded not their summons : happy time
It was indeed for all of us — for me
It was a time of rapture !   Clear and loud   430
The village clock tolled six, — I wheeled about,
Proud and exulting like an untired horse
That cares not for his home.   All shod with steel,
We hissed along the polished ice in games
Confederate, imitative of the chase
And woodland pleasures, — the resounding horn,
The pack loud chiming, and the hunted hare.
So through the darkness and the cold we flew,
And not a voice was idle ; with the din
Smitten, the precipices rang aloud ;   440
The leafless trees and every icy crag
Tinkled like iron ; while far distant hills

Into the tumult sent an alien sound
Of melancholy not unnoticed, while the stars
Eastward were sparkling clear, and in the west
The orange sky of evening died away.
Not seldom from the uproar I retired
Into a silent bay, or sportively
Glanced sideway, leaving the tumultuous throng,
To cut across the reflex of a star   450
That fled, and, flying still before me, gleamed
Upon the glassy plain; and oftentimes,
When we had given our bodies to the wind,
And all the shadowy banks on either side
Came sweeping through the darkness, spinning still
The rapid line of motion, then at once
Have I, reclining back upon my heels,
Stopped short; yet still the solitary cliffs
Wheeled by me — even as if the earth had rolled
With visible motion her diurnal round!   460
Behind me did they stretch in solemn train,
Feebler and feebler, and I stood and watched
Till all was tranquil as a dreamless sleep.

          Ye Presences of Nature in the sky
And on the earth!   Ye visions of the hills!
And Souls of lonely places! can I think
A vulgar hope was yours when ye employed
Such ministry, when ye through many a year
Haunting me thus among my boyish sports,   ·
On caves and trees, upon the woods and hills,   470
Impressed upon all forms the characters
Of danger or desire; and thus did make

The surface of the universal earth
With triumph and delight, with hope and fear,
Work like a sea?
                    Not uselessly employed,
Might I pursue this theme through every change
Of exercise and play, to which the year
Did summon us in his delightful round.

We were a noisy crew; the sun in heaven
Beheld not vales more beautiful than ours;   480
Nor saw a band in happiness and joy
Richer, or worthier of the ground they trod.
I could record with no reluctant voice
The woods of autumn, and their hazel bowers
With milk-white clusters hung; the rod and line,
True symbol of hope's foolishness, whose strong
And unreproved enchantment led us on
By rocks and pools shut out from every star,
All the green summer, to forlorn cascades
Among the windings hid of mountain brooks,   490
— Unfading recollections! at this hour
The heart is almost mine with which I felt,
From some hill-top on sunny afternoons,
The paper kite high among fleecy clouds
Pull at her rein like an impetuous courser;
Or, from the meadows sent on gusty days,
Beheld her breast the wind, then suddenly
Dashed headlong, and rejected by the storm.

Ye lowly cottages wherein we dwelt,
A ministration of your own was yours;   500

Can I forget you, being as you were
So beautiful among the pleasant fields
In which ye stood? or can I here forget
The plain and seemly countenance with which
Ye dealt out your plain comforts?   Yet had ye
Delights and exultations of your own.
Eager and never weary we pursued
Our home-amusements by the warm peat-fire
At evening, when with pencil, and smooth slate
In square divisions parcelled out and all   510
With crosses and with cyphers scribbled o'er,
We schemed and puzzled, head opposed to head
In strife too humble to be named in verse ;
Or round the naked table, snow-white deal,
Cherry or maple, sate in close array,
And to the combat, Loo or Whist, led on
A thick-ribbed army ; not, as in the world,
Neglected and ungratefully thrown by
Even for the very service they had wrought,
But husbanded through many a long campaign.   520
Uncouth assemblage was it, where no few
Had changed their functions ; some, plebeian cards
Which Fate, beyond the promise of their birth,
Had dignified, and called to represent
The persons of departed potentates.
Oh, with what echoes on the board they fell !
Ironic diamonds, — clubs, hearts, diamonds, spades,
A congregation piteously akin !
Cheap matter offered they to boyish wit,
Those sooty knaves, precipitated down   530
With scoffs and taunts, like Vulcan out of heaven :

The paramount ace, a moon in her eclipse,
Queens gleaming through their splendor's last decay,
And monarchs surly at the wrongs sustained
By royal visages.   Meanwhile abroad
Incessant rain was falling, or the frost
Raged bitterly, with keen and silent tooth ;
And, interrupting oft that eager game,
From under Esthwaite's splitting fields of ice
The pent-up air, struggling to free itself,   540
Gave out to meadow grounds and hills a loud
Protracted yelling, like the noise of wolves
Howling in troops along the Bothnic Main.

Nor, sedulous as I have been to trace
How Nature by extrinsic passion first
Peopled the mind with forms sublime or fair,
And made me love them, may I here omit
How other pleasures have been mine, and joys
Of subtler origin ; how I have felt,
Not seldom even in that tempestuous time,   550
Those hallowed and pure motions of the sense
Which seem, in their simplicity, to own
An intellectual charm ; that calm delight
Which, if I err not, surely must belong
To those first-born affinities that fit
Our new existence to existing things,
And, in our dawn of being, constitute
The bond of union between life and joy.

Yes, I remember when the changeful earth
And twice five summers on my mind had stamped   560

The faces of the moving year, even then
I held unconscious intercourse with beauty
Old as creation, drinking in a pure
Organic pleasure from the silver wreaths
Of curling mist, or from the level plain
Of waters colored by impending clouds.

    The sands of Westmoreland, the creeks and bays
Of Cumbria's rocky limits, they can tell
How, when the Sea threw off his evening shade,
And to the shepherd's hut on distant hills   570
Sent welcome notice of the rising moon,
How I have stood, to fancies such as these
A stranger, linking with the spectacle
No conscious memory of a kindred sight,
And bringing with me no peculiar sense
Of quietness or peace ; yet have I stood,
Even while mine eye hath moved o'er many a league
Of shining water, gathering as it seemed
Through every hair-breadth in that field of light
New pleasure like a bee among the flowers.   580

    Thus oft amid those fits of vulgar joy
Which, through all seasons, on a child's pursuits
Are prompt attendants, 'mid that giddy bliss
Which, like a tempest, works along the blood
And is forgotten ; even then I felt
Gleams like the flashing of a shield ; — the earth
And common face of Nature spake to me
Rememberable things ; sometimes, 'tis true,
By chance collisions and quaint accidents

(Like those ill-sorted unions, work supposed   590
Of evil-minded fairies), yet not vain
Nor profitless, if haply they impressed
Collateral objects and appearances,   .
Albeit lifeless then, and doomed to sleep
Until maturer seasons called them forth
To impregnate and to elevate the mind.
— And if the vulgar joy by its own weight
Wearied itself out of the memory,
The scenes which were a witness of that joy
Remained in their substantial lineaments   600
Depicted on the brain, and to the eye
Were visible, a daily sight ; and thus
By the impressive discipline of fear,
By pleasure and repeated happiness,
So frequently repeated, and by force
Of obscure feelings representative
Of things forgotten, these same scenes so bright,   .
So beautiful, so majestic in themselves,
Though yet the day was distant, did become
Habitually dear, and all their forms   610
And changeful colors by invisible links
Were fastened to the affections.

                                        I began
My story early — not misled, I trust,
By an infirmity of love for days
Disowned by memory — ere the breath of spring
Planting my snowdrops among winter snows :
Nor will it seem to thee, O Friend ! so prompt
In sympathy, that I have lengthened out

With fond and feeble tongue a tedious tale.
Meanwhile, my hope has been that I might fetch   620
Invigorating thoughts from former years ;
Might fix the wavering balance of my mind,
And haply meet reproaches too, whose power
May spur me on, in manhood now mature
To honorable toil.   Yet should these hopes
Prove vain, and thus should neither I be taught
To understand myself, nor thou to know
With better knowledge how the heart was framed
Of him thou lovest : need I dread from thee
Harsh judgments, if the song be loth to quit   630
Those recollected hours that have the charm
Of visionary things, those lovely forms
And sweet sensations that throw back our life,
And almost make remotest infancy
A visible scene, on which the sun is shining?

    One end at least hath been attained ; my mind
Hath been revived, and if this genial mood
Desert me not, forthwith shall be brought down
Through later years the story of my life.
The road lies plain before me ; — 'tis a theme   640
Single and of determined bounds ; and hence
I choose it rather at this time, than work
Of ampler or more varied argument,
Where I might be discomfited and lost :
And certain hopes are with me, that to thee
This labor will be welcome, honored Friend !

BOOK SECOND.

THUS far, O Friend ! have we, though leaving much
Unvisited, endeavored to retrace
The simple ways in which my childhood walked :
Those chiefly that first led me to the love
Of rivers, woods, and fields.   The passion yet
Was in its birth, sustained as might befall
By nourishment that came unsought ; for still
From week to week, from month to month, we lived
A round of tumult.   Duly were our games
Prolonged in summer till the day-light failed :   10
No chair remained before the door ; the bench
And threshold steps were empty ; fast asleep
The laborer, and the old man who had sate
A later lingerer, yet the revelry
Continued and the loud uproar : at last,
When all the ground was dark, and twinkling stars
Edged the black clouds, home and to bed we went,
Feverish with weary joints and beating minds.
Ah ! is there one who ever has been young,
Nor needs a warning voice to tame the pride   20
Of intellect and virtue's self-esteem !

One is there, though the wisest and the best
Of all mankind, who covets not at times
Union that cannot be ; — who would not give,
If so he might, to duty and to truth
The eagerness of infantine desire ?
A tranquillizing spirit presses now
On my corporeal frame, so wide appears
The vacancy between me and those days
Which yet have such self-presence in my mind   30
That, musing on them, often do I seem
Two consciousnesses, conscious of myself
And of some other Being.   A rude mass
Of native rock, left midway in the square
Of our small market village, was the goal
Or centre of these sports ; and when, returned
After long absence, thither I repaired,
Gone was the old gray stone, and in its place
A smart Assembly-room usurped the ground
That hath been ours.   There let the fiddle scream,   40
And be ye happy !   Yet, my Friends ! I know
That more than one of you will think with me
Of those soft starry nights, and that old Dame
From whom the stone was named, who there had sate,
And watched her table with its huckster's wares
Assiduous, through the length of sixty years.

We ran a boisterous course : the year span round
With giddy motion.   But the time approached
That brought with it a regular desire
For calmer pleasures, when the winning forms   50
Of nature were collaterally attached

To every scheme of holiday delight,
And every boyish sport, less grateful else
And languidly pursued.
    When summer came,
Our pastime was, on bright half-holidays,
To sweep along the plain of Windermere
With rival oars ; and the selected bourne
Was now an Island musical with Birds
That sang and ceased not ; now a sister Isle
Beneath the oaks' umbrageous covert, sown   60
With lilies of the valley like a field ;
And now a third small Island where survived
In solitude the ruins of a shrine
Once to Our Lady dedicate, and served
Daily with chaunted rites. In such a race
So ended, disappointment could be none,
Uneasiness, or pain, or jealousy :
We rested in the shade, all pleased alike,
Conquered and conqueror. Thus the pride of strength,
And the vain-glory of superior skill,   70
Were tempered ; thus was gradually produced
A quiet independence of the heart ;
And to my Friend who knows me 1 may add,
Fearless of blame, that hence for future days
Ensued a diffidence and modesty,
And I was taught to feel, perhaps too much,
The self-sufficing power of Solitude.

 Our daily meals were frugal, Sabine fare !
More than we wished we knew the blessing then
Of vigorous hunger — hence corporeal strength   80

Unsapped by delicate viands; for, exclude
A little weekly stipend, and we lived
Through three divisions of the quartered year
In penniless poverty.   But now to school
From the half-yearly holidays returned,
We came with weightier purses, that sufficed
To furnish treats more costly than the Dame
Of the old gray stone, from her scant board, supplied.
Hence rustic dinners on the cool green-ground,
Or in the woods, or by a river side,   90
Or shady fountains, while among the leaves
Soft airs were stirring, and the mid-day sun
Unfelt shone brightly round us in our joy.
Nor is my aim neglected if I tell
How sometimes, in the length of those half-years,
We from our funds drew largely; — proud to curb,
And eager to spur on, the galloping steed;
And with the courteous inn-keeper, whose stud
Supplied our want, we haply might employ
Sly subterfuge, if the adventure's bound   100
Were distant: some famed temple where of yore
The Druids worshipped, or the antique walls
Of that large Abbey where within the Vale
Of Nightshade, to St. Mary's honor built,
Stands yet a mouldering pile with fractured arch,
Belfry, and images, and living trees;
A holy scene! — Along the smooth green turf
Our horses grazed.   To more than inland peace,
Left by the west wind sweeping overhead
From a tumultuous ocean, trees and towers   110
In that sequestered valley may be seen,

Both silent and both motionless alike :
Such the deep shelter that is there, and such
The safeguard for repose and quietness.

    Our steeds remounted and the summons given,
With whip and spur we through the chauntry flew
In uncouth race, and left the cross-legged knight,
And the stone-abbot, and that single wren
Which one day sang so sweetly in the nave
Of the old church, that — though from recent showers 120
The earth was comfortless, and, touched by faint
Internal breezes, sobbings of the place
And respirations, from the roofless walls
The shuddering ivy dripped large drops — yet still
So sweetly 'mid the gloom the invisible bird
Sang to herself, that there I could have made
My dwelling-place, and lived forever there
To hear such music. Through the walls we flew
And down the valley, and, a circuit made
In wantonness of heart, through rough and smooth 130
We scampered homewards. Oh, ye rocks and streams,
And that still spirit shed from evening air !
Even in this joyous time I sometimes felt
Your presence, when with slackened step we breathed
Along the sides of the steep hills, or when
Lighted by gleams of moonlight from the sea
We beat with thundering hoofs the level sand.

    Midway on long Winander's eastern shore,
Within the crescent of a pleasant bay,
A tavern stood ; no homely-featured house,   140
Primeval like its neighboring cottages,

But, 'twas a splendid place, the door beset
With chaises, grooms, and liveries, and within
Decanters, glasses, and the blood-red wine.
In ancient times, and ere the Hall was built
On the large island, had this dwelling been
More worthy of a poet's love, a hut,
Proud of its own bright fire and sycamore shade.
But—though the rhymes were gone that once inscribed
The threshold, and large golden characters,   150
Spread o'er the spangled sign-board, had dislodged
The old Lion and usurped his place, in slight
And mockery of the rustic painter's hand —
Yet, to this hour, the spot to me is dear
With all its foolish pomp.   The garden lay
Upon a slope surmounted by a plain
Of a small bowling-green ; beneath us stood
A grove, with gleams of water through the trees
And over the treetops ; nor did we want
Refreshment, strawberries and mellow cream.   160
There, while through half an afternoon we played
On the smooth platform, whether skill prevailed
Or happy blunder triumphed, bursts of glee
Made all the mountains ring.   But, ere nightfall,
When in our pinnace we returned at leisure
Over the shadowy lake, and to the beach
Of some small island steered our course with one,
The Minstrel of the Troop, and left him there,
And rowed off gently, while he blew his flute
Alone upon the rock — oh, then, the calm   170
And dead still water lay upon my mind
Even with a weight of pleasure, and the sky,

Never before so beautiful, sank down
Into my heart, and held me like a dream !
Thus were my sympathies enlarged, and thus
Daily the common range of visible things
Grew dear to me : already I began
To love the sun ; a boy I loved the sun,
Not as I since have loved him, as a pledge
And surety of our earthly life, a light   180
Which we behold and feel we are alive ;
Nor for his bounty to so many worlds —
But for this cause, that I had seen him lay
His beauty on the morning hills, had seen
The western mountain touch his setting orb,
In many a thoughtless hour, when, from excess
Of happiness, my blood appeared to flow
For its own pleasure, and I breathed with joy.
And, from like feelings, humble though intense,
To patriotic and domestic love   190
Analogous, the moon to me was dear :
For I could dream away my purposes,
Standing to gaze upon her while she hung
Midway between the hills, as if she knew
No other region, but belonged to thee,
Yea, appertained by a peculiar right
To thee and thy gray huts, thou one dear Vale !

Those incidental charms which first attached
My heart to rural objects, day by day
Grew weaker, and I hasten on to tell   200
How Nature, intervenient till this time
And secondary, now at length was sought

For her own sake.   But who shall parcel out
His intellect by geometric rules,
Split like a province into round and square?
Who knows the individual hour in which
His habits were first sown, even as a seed?
Who that shall point as with a wand and say
"This portion of the river of my mind
Came from yon fountain?" Thou, my Friend! art one 210
More deeply read in thy own thoughts; to thee
Science appears but what in truth she is,
Not as our glory and our absolute boast,
But as a succedaneum, and a prop
To our infirmity.   No officious slave
Art thou of that false secondary power
By which we multiply distinctions, then
Deem that our puny boundaries are things
That we perceive, and not that we have made.
To thee, unblinded by these formal arts,   220
The unity of all hath been revealed,
And thou wilt doubt, with me less aptly skilled
Than many are to range the faculties
In scale and order, class the cabinet
Of their sensations, and in voluble phrase
Run through the history and birth of each
As of a single independent thing.
Hard task, vain hope, to analyze the mind,
If each most obvious and particular thought,
Not in a mystical and idle sense,   230
But in the words of Reason deeply weighed,
Hath no beginning.
                    Blest the infant Babe,

(For with my best conjecture I would trace
Our Being's earthly progress), blest the Babe,
Nursed in his Mother's arms, who sinks to sleep
Rocked on his Mother's breast ; who with his soul
Drinks in the feelings of his Mother's eye !
For him, in one dear Presence, there exists
A virtue which irradiates and exalts
Objects through widest intercourse of sense,   240
No outcast he, bewildered and depressed :
Along his infant veins are interfused
The gravitation and the filial bond
Of nature that connect him with the world.
Is there a flower, to which he points with hand
Too weak to gather it, already love
Drawn from love's purest earthly fount for him
Hath beautified that flower ; already shades
Of pity cast from inward tenderness
Do fall around him upon aught that bears   250
Unsightly marks of violence or harm.
Emphatically such a Being lives,
Frail creature as he is, helpless as frail,
An inmate of this active universe :
For feeling has to him imparted power
That through the growing faculties of sense
Doth like an agent of the one great Mind
Create, creator and receiver both,
Working but in alliance with the works
Which it beholds. — Such, verily, is the first   260
Poetic spirit of our human life,
By uniform control of after years,
In most, abated or suppressed ; in some,

Through every change of growth and of decay,
Pre-eminent till death.
                        From early days,
Beginning not long after that first time
In which, a Babe, by intercourse of touch
I held mute dialogues with my Mother's heart,
I have endeavored to display the means
Whereby this infant sensibility,   270
Great birthright of our being, was in me
Augmented and sustained.   Yet is a path
More difficult before me ; and I fear
That in its broken windings we shall need
The chamois' sinews, and the eagle's wing,
For now a trouble came into my mind
From unknown causes.   I was left alone
Seeking the visible world, nor knowing why.
The props of my affection were removed,
And yet the building stood, as if sustained   280
By its own spirit !   All that I beheld
Was dear, and hence to finer influxes
The mind lay open to a more exact
And close communion.   Many are our joys
In youth, but oh ! what happiness to live
When every hour brings palpable access
Of knowledge, when all knowledge is delight,
And sorrow is not there !   The seasons came,
And every season wheresoe'er I moved
Unfolded transitory qualities,   290
Which, but for this most watchful power of love,
Had been neglected ; left a register
Of permanent relations, else unknown.

Hence life, and change, and beauty, solitude
More active even than " best society " —
Society made sweet as solitude
By silent inobtrusive sympathies,
And gentle agitations of the mind
From manifold distinctions, difference
Perceived in things, where, to the unwatchful eye,   300
No difference is, and hence, from the same source,
Sublimer joy ; for I would walk alone,
Under the quiet stars, and at that time
Have felt whate'er there is of power in sound
To breathe an elevated mood, by form
Or image unprofaned ; and I would stand,
If the night blackened with a coming storm,
Beneath some rock, listening to notes that are
The ghostly language of the ancient earth,
Or make their dim abode in distant winds.   310
Thence did I drink the visionary power :
And deem not profitless those fleeting moods
Of shadowy exultation : not for this
That they are kindred to our purer mind
And intellectual life ; but that the soul,
Remembering how she felt, but what she felt
Remembering not, retains an obscure sense
Of possible sublimity, whereto
With growing faculties she doth aspire,
With faculties still growing, feeling still   320
That whatsoever point they gain, they yet
Have something to pursue.
                And not alone,
'Mid gloom and tumult, but no less 'mid fair

And tranquil scenes, that universal power
And fitness in the latent qualities
And essences of things, by which the mind
Is moved with feelings of delight, to me
Came strengthened with a superadded soul,
A virtue not its own.   My morning walks
Were early ; — oft before the hours of school   330
I travelled round our little lake, five miles
Of pleasant wandering.   Happy time ! more dear
For this, that one was by my side, a Friend,
Then passionately loved ; with heart how full
Would he peruse these lines !   For many years
Have since flowed in between us, and, our minds
Both silent to each other, at this time
We live as if those hours had never been.
Nor seldom did I lift our cottage latch
Far earlier, ere one smoke-wreath had risen   340
From human dwelling, or the vernal thrush
Was audible : and sate among the woods
Alone upon some jutting eminence,
At the first gleam of dawn-light, when the Vale,
Yet slumbering, lay in utter solitude.
How shall I seek the origin? where find
Faith in the marvellous things which then I felt?
Oft in these moments such a holy calm
Would overspread my soul that bodily eyes
Were utterly forgotten, and what I saw   350
Appeared like something in myself, a dream,
A prospect in the mind.
                    'Twere long to tell
What spring and autumn, what the winter snows,

And what the summer shade, what day and night,
Evening and morning, sleep and waking, thought
From sources inexhaustible, poured forth
To feed the spirit of religious love
In which I walked with Nature.   But let this
Be not forgotten, that I still retained
My first creative sensibility ;   360
That by the regular action of the world
My soul was unsubdued.   A plastic power
Abode with me ; a forming hand, at times
Rebellious, acting in a devious mood ;
A local spirit of his own, at war
With general tendency, but, for the most,
Subservient strictly to external things
With which it communed.   An auxiliar light
Came from my mind, which on the setting sun
Bestowed new splendor ; the melodious birds,   370
The fluttering breezes, fountains that run on
Murmuring so sweetly in themselves, obeyed
A like dominion, and the midnight storm
Grew darker in the presence of my eye :
Hence my obeisance, my devotion hence,
And hence my transport.
      Nor should this, perchance,
Pass unrecorded, that I still had loved
The exercise and produce of a toil,
That analytic industry to me
More pleasing, and whose character I deem   380
Is more poetic as resembling more
Creative agency.   The song would speak
Of that interminable building reared

By observation of affinities
In objects where no brotherhood exists
To passive minds.   My seventeenth year was come ;
And, whether from this habit rooted now
So deeply in my mind, or from excess
In the great social principle of life
Coercing all things into sympathy,   390
To unorganic natures were transferred
My own enjoyments ; or the power of truth
Coming in revelation, did converse
With things that really are ; I, at this time,
Saw blessings spread around me like a sea.
Thus while the days flew by and years passed on,
From Nature and her overflowing soul,
I had received so much that all my thoughts
Were steeped in feeling ; I was only then
Contented, when with bliss ineffable   400
I felt the sentiment of Being spread
O'er all that moves and all that seemeth still ;
O'er all that, lost beyond the reach of thought
And human knowledge, to the human eye
Invisible, yet liveth to the heart :
O'er all that leaps and runs, and shouts and sings,
Or beats the gladsome air ; o'er all that glides
Beneath the wave, yea, in the wave itself,
And mighty depth of waters.   Wonder not
If high the transport, great the joy I felt,   410
Communing in this sort through earth and heaven
With every form of creature, as it looked
Towards the Uncreated with a countenance
Of adoration, with an eye of love.

One song they sang, and it was audible,
Most audible then when the fleshly ear
O'ercome by humblest prelude of that strain
Forgot her functions, and slept undisturbed.

    If this be error, and another faith
Find easier access to the pious mind,   420
Yet were I grossly destitute of all
Those human sentiments that make this earth
So dear, if I should fail with grateful voice
To speak of you, ye mountains, and ye lakes
And sounding cataracts, ye mists and winds
That dwell among the hills where I was born.
If in my youth I have been pure in heart,
If, mingling with the world, I am content
With my own modest pleasures, and have lived
With God and Nature communing, removed   430
From little enmities and low desires,
The gift is yours : if in these times of fear,
This melancholy waste of hopes o'erthrown,
If, 'mid indifference and apathy,
And wicked exultation when good men
On every side fall off, we know not how,
To selfishness, disguised in gentle names
Of peace and quiet and domestic love,
Yet mingled not unwillingly with sneers
On visionary minds ; if, in this time   440
Of dereliction and dismay, I yet
Despair not of our nature, but retain
A more than Roman confidence, a faith
That fails not, in all sorrow my support,

The blessing of my life ; the gift of yours,
Ye winds and sounding cataracts ! 'tis yours,
Ye mountains ! thine, O Nature !　Thou hast fed
My lofty speculations ; and in thee,
For this uneasy heart of ours, I find
A never-failing principle of joy　　　　　　　450
And purest passion.
　　　　　　　　Thou, my Friend ! wert reared
In the great city, 'mid far other scenes ;
But we, by different roads, at length have gained
The self-same bourne.　And for this cause to thee
I speak, unapprehensive of contempt,
The insinuated scoff of coward tongues,
And all that silent language which so oft
In conversation between man and man
Blots from the human countenance all trace
Of beauty and of love.　For thou hast sought　　460
The truth in solitude, and since the days
That gave liberty, full long desired,
To serve in Nature's Temple, thou hast been
The most assiduous of her ministers ;
In many things my brother, chiefly here
In this our deep devotion.
　　　　　　　　　　Fare thee well !
Health and the quiet of a healthful mind
Attend thee ! seeking oft the haunts of men,
And yet more often living with thyself,
And for thyself, so happily shall thy days .　　470
Be many, and a blessing to mankind.

BOOK THIRD.

It was a dreary morning when the wheels
Rolled over a wide plain o'erhung with clouds,
And nothing cheered our way till first we saw
The long-roofed chapel of King's College lift
Turrets and pinnacles in answering files,
Extended high above a dusky grove.

Advancing, we espied upon the road
A student clothed in gown and tasselled cap
Striding along as if o'ertasked by Time,
Or covetous of exercise and air;   10
He passed — nor was I master of my eyes
Till he was left an arrow's flight behind.
As near and nearer to the spot we drew,
It seemed to suck us in with an eddy's force.
Onward we drove beneath the Castle; caught,
While crossing Magdalene Bridge, a glimpse of Cam;
And at the *Hoop* alighted, famous Inn.

My spirit was up, my thoughts were full of hope;
Some friends I had, acquaintances who there

Seemed friends, poor simple school-boys, now hung round
With honor and importance : in a world   21
Of welcome faces up and down I roved ;
Questions, directions, warnings and advice,
Flowed in upon me, from all sides ; fresh day
Of pride and pleasure ! to myself I seemed
A man of business and expense, and went
From shop to shop about my own affairs,
To Tutor or to Tailor, as befell,
From street to street with loose and careless mind.

    I was the dreamer, they the dream ; I roamed   30
Delighted through the motley spectacle ;
Gowns grave, or gaudy, doctors, students, streets,
Courts, cloisters, flocks of churches, gateways, towers :
Migration strange for a stripling of the hills,
A northern villager.
                As if the change
Had waited on some Fairy's wand, at once
Behold me rich in monies, and attired
A splendid garb, with hose of silk, and hair
Powdered like rimy trees, when frost is keen.
My lordly dressing-gown, I pass it by,   40
With other signs of manhood that supplied
The lack of beard. — The weeks went roundly on,
With invitations, suppers, wine and fruit,
Smooth housekeeping within, and all without
Liberal, and suiting gentleman's array.

    The Evangelist St. John my patron was ;
Three Gothic courts are his, and in the first

Was my abiding-place, a nook obscure ;
Right underneath, the College kitchens made
A humming sound, less tunable than bees,   50
But hardly less industrious ; with shrill notes
Of sharp command and scolding intermixed.
Near me hung Trinity's loquacious clock,
Who never let the quarters, night or day,
Slip by him unproclaimed, and told the hours
Twice over with a male and female voice.
Her pealing organ was my neighbor too ;
And from my pillow, looking forth by light
Of moon or favoring stars, I could behold
The antechapel where the statue stood   60
Of Newton with his prism and silent face,
The marble index of a mind forever
Voyaging through strange seas of Thought alone.

Of College labors, of the Lecturer's room
All studded round, as thick as chairs could stand,
With loyal students, faithful to their books,
Half-and-half idlers, hardy recusants,
And honest dunces — of important days,
Examinations, when the man was weighed
As in a balance ! of excessive hopes,   70
Tremblings withal and commendable fears,
Small jealousies, and triumphs good or bad —
Let others that know more speak as they know.
Such glory was but little sought by me,
And little won.   Yet from the first crude days
Of settling time in this untried abode,
I was disturbed at times by prudent thoughts

Wishing to hope without a hope, some fear,
About my future worldly maintenance,
And, more than all, a strangeness in the mind,   80
A feeling that I was not for that hour,
Nor for that place.   But wherefore be cast down?
For (not to speak of Reason and her pure
Reflective acts to fix the moral law
Deep in the conscience, nor of Christian Hope,
Bowing her head before her sister Faith
As one far mightier), hither I had come,
Bear witness Truth, endowed with holy powers
And faculties, whether to work or feel.
Oft when the dazzling show, no longer new,   90
Had ceased to dazzle, ofttimes did I quit
My comrades, leave the crowd, buildings and groves,
And as I paced alone the level fields
Far from those lovely sights and sounds sublime
With which I had been conversant, the mind
Drooped not ; but there into herself returning,
With prompt rebound seemed fresh as heretofore.
At least I more distinctly recognized
Her native instincts : let me dare to speak
A higher language, say that now I felt   100
What independent solaces were mine,
To mitigate the injurious sway of place
Or circumstance, how far soever changed
In youth, or to be changed in after years.
As, if awakened, summoned, roused, constrained,
I looked for universal things ; perused
The common countenance of earth and sky :
Earth, nowhere unembellished by some trace

Of that first Paradise whence man was driven;
And sky, whose beauty and bounty are expressed 110
By the proud name she bears — the name of Heaven.
I called on both to teach me what they might;
Or, turning the mind in upon herself,
Pored, watched, expected, listened, spread my thoughts
And spread them with a wider creeping; felt
Incumbencies more awful, visitings
Of the Upholder of the tranquil soul
That tolerates the indignities of Time,
And from the centre of Eternity
All finite motions overruling, lives 120
In glory immutable. But peace! enough
Here to record that I was mounting now
To such community with highest truth —
A track pursuing, not untrod before,
From strict analogies by thought supplied
Or consciousnesses not to be subdued.
To every natural form, rock, fruit or flower,
Even the loose stones that cover the highway,
I gave a moral life: I saw them feel,
Or linked them to some feeling: the great mass 130
Lay bedded in a quickening soul, and all
That I beheld respired with inward meaning.
Add that whate'er of Terror or of Love
Or Beauty Nature's daily face put on
From transitory passion, unto this
I was as sensitive as waters are
To the sky's influence in a kindred mood
Of passion; was obedient as a lute,
That waits upon the touches of the wind.

Unknown, unthought of, yet I was most rich —   140
I had a world about me — 'twas my own;
I made it, for it only lived to me,
And to the God who sees into the heart.
Such sympathies, though rarely, were betrayed
By outward gestures and by visible looks;
Some called it madness — so indeed it was,
If child-like fruitfulness in passing joy,
If steady moods of thoughtfulness matured
To inspiration, sort with such a name;
If prophecy be madness; if things viewed   150
By poets in old time, and higher up
By the first men, earth's first inhabitants,
May in these tutored days no more be seen
With undisordered sight.   But leaving this,
It was no madness, for the bodily eye
Amid my strongest workings evermore
Was searching out the lines of difference
As they lie hid in all external forms,
Near or remote, minute or vast; an eye
Which, from a tree, a stone, a withered leaf,   160
To the broad ocean and the azure heavens
Spangled with kindred multitudes of stars,
Could find no surface where its power might sleep:
Which spake perpetual logic to my soul,
And by an unrelenting agency
Did bind my feelings even as in a chain.

    And here, O Friend! have I retraced my life
Up to an eminence, and told a tale
Of matters which not falsely may be called

The glory of my youth. Of genius, power,   170
Creation, and divinity itself,
I have been speaking, for my theme has been
What passed within me.   Not of outward things
Done visibly for other minds, words, signs,
Symbols or actions, but of my own heart
Have I been speaking, and my youthful mind.
O Heavens ! how awful is the might of souls,
And what they do within themselves while yet
The yoke of earth is new to them, the world
Nothing but a wild field where they were sown.   180
This is, in truth, heroic argument,
This genuine prowess, which I wished to touch
With hand however weak, but in the main
It lies far hidden from the reach of words.
Points have we all of us within our souls
Where all stand single ; this I feel, and make
Breathings for incommunicable powers ;
But is not each a memory to himself?
And, therefore, now that we must quit this theme,
I am not heartless, for there's not a man   190
That lives who hath not known his god-like hours,
And feels not what an empire we inherit
As natural beings in the strength of Nature.

  No more ; for now into a populous plain
We must descend.   A Traveller I am,
Whose tale is only of himself; even so,
So be it, if the pure of heart be prompt
To follow and if thou, my honored Friend !

Who in these thoughts art ever at my side,
Support, as heretofore, my fainting steps.   200

   It hath been told, that when the first delight
That flashed upon me from this novel show
Had failed, the mind returned into herself;
Yet true it is, that I had made a change
In climate, and my nature's outward coat
Changed also slowly and insensibly.
Full oft the quiet and exalted thoughts
Of loneliness gave way to empty noise
And superficial pastimes ; now and then
Forced labor, and more frequently forced hopes ;   210
And, worst of all, a treasonable growth
Of indecisive judgment, that impaired
And shook the mind's simplicity — And yet
This was a gladsome time.   Could I behold —
Who, less insensible than sodden clay
In a sea-river's bed at ebb of tide,
Could have beheld — with undelighted heart,
So many happy youths, so wide and fair
A congregation in its budding-time
Of health and hope, and beauty, all at once   220
So many divers samples from the growth
Of life's sweet season — could have seen unmoved
That miscellaneous garland of wild flowers
Decking the matron temples of a place
So famous through the world?   To me, at least,
It was a goodly prospect ; for, in sooth,
Though I had learnt betimes to stand unpropped,
And independent musing pleased me so

That spells seemed on me when I was alone,
Yet could I only cleave to solitude 230
In lonely places : if a throng was near,
That way I leaned by nature, for my heart
Was social, and loved idleness and joy.

Not seeking those who might participate
My deeper pleasures (nay, I had not once,
Though not unused to mutter lonesome songs,
Even with myself divided such delight,
Or looked that way for aught that might be clothed
In human language), easily I passed
From the remembrances of better things, 240
And slipped into the ordinary works
Of careless youth, unburthened, unalarmed.
Caverns there were within my mind which sun
Could never penetrate, yet did there not
Want store of leafy *arbors* where the light
Might enter in at will. Companionships,
Friendships, acquaintances, were welcome all.
We sauntered, played, or rioted, we talked
Unprofitable talk at morning hours ;
Drifted about along the streets and walks, 250
Read lazily in trivial books, went forth
To gallop through the country in blind zeal
Of senseless horsemanship, or on the breast
Of Cam sailed boisterously, and let the stars
Come forth, perhaps without one quiet thought.

Such was the tenor of the second act
In this new life. Imagination slept,
And yet not utterly. I could not print

Ground where the grass had yielded to the steps
Of generations of illustrious men,   260
Unmoved.   I could not always lightly pass
Through the same gateways, sleep where they had slept,
Wake where they waked, range that inclosure old,
That garden of great intellects, undisturbed,
Place also by the side of this dark sense
Of noble feeling that those spiritual men,
Even the great Newton's own ethereal self,
Seemed humbled in these precincts thence to be
The more endeared.   Their several memories here
(Even like their persons in their portraits clothed   270
With the accustomed garb of daily life)
Put on a lowly and a touching grace
Of more distinct humanity, that left
All genuine admiration unimpaired.

Beside the pleasant Mill of Trompington
I laughed with Chaucer in the hawthorn shade ;
Heard him, while birds were warbling, tell his tales
Of amorous passion.   And that gentle Bard,
Chosen by the Muses for their Page of State —
Sweet Spenser, moving through his clouded heaven   280
With the moon's beauty and the moon's soft pace,
I called him Brother, Englishman, and Friend !
Yea, our blind Poet, who, in his later day,
Stood almost single, uttering odious truth —
Darkness before, and danger's voice behind,
Soul awful — if the earth has ever lodged
An awful soul — I seemed to see him here
Familiarly, and in his scholar's dress

Bounding before me, yet a stripling youth —
A boy, no better, with his rosy cheeks   290
Angelical, keen eye, courageous look,
And conscious step of purity and pride.
Among the band of my compeers was one
Whom chance had stationed in the very room
Honored by Milton's name.   O temperate Bard !
Be it confest that, for the first time, seated
Within thy innocent lodge and oratory,   -
One of a festive circle, I poured out
Libations, to thy memory drank, till pride
And gratitude grew dizzy in a brain   300
Never excited by the fumes of wine
Before that hour, or since.   Then, forth I ran
From the assembly ; through a length of streets,
Ran, ostrich-like, to reach our chapel door
In not a desperate or opprobrious time,
Albeit long after the importunate bell
Had stopped, with wearisome Cassandra voice
No longer haunting the dark winter night.
Call back, O Friend ! a moment to thy mind,
The place itself and fashion of the rites.   310
With careless ostentation shouldering up
My surplice, through the inferior throng I clove
Of the plain Burghers, who in audience stood
On the last skirts of their permitted ground,
Under the pealing organ.   Empty thoughts !
I am ashamed of them : and that great Bard,
And thou, O Friend ! who in thy ample mind
Hast placed me high above my best deserts,
Ye will forgive the weakness of that hour,

In some of its unworthy vanities,
Brother to many more.
                            In this mixed sort
The months passed on, remissly, not given up
To wilful alienation from the right,
Or walks of open scandal, but in vague
And loose indifference, easy likings, aims
Of a low pitch — duty and zeal dismissed,
Yet Nature, or a happy course of things
Not doing in their stead the needful work.
The memory languidly revolved, the heart
Reposed in noontide rest, the inner pulse
Of contemplation almost failed to beat.
Such life might not inaptly be compared
To a floating island, an amphibious spot
Unsound, of spongy texture, yet withal
Not wanting a fair face of water weeds
And pleasant flowers.   The thirst of living praise,
Fit reverence for the glorious Dead, the sight
Of those long vistas, sacred catacombs,
Where mighty *minds* lie visibly entombed,
Have often stirred the heart of youth, and bred
A fervent love of rigorous discipline —
Alas ! such high emotions touched not me.
Look was there none within these walls to shame
My easy spirits, and discountenance
Their light composure, far less to instil
A calm resolve of mind, firmly addressed
To puissant efforts.   Nor was this the blame
Of others, but my own ; I should, in truth,
As far as doth concern my single self,

Misdeem most widely, lodging it elsewhere : 350
For I, bred up 'mid Nature's luxuries,
Was a spoiled child, and rambling like the wind,
As I had done in daily intercourse
With those crystalline rivers, solemn heights,
And mountains, ranging like a fowl of the air,
I was ill-tutored for captivity ;
To quit my pleasure, and, from month to month,
Take up a station calmly on the perch
Of sedentary peace. Those lovely forms
Had also left less space within my mind, 360
Which, wrought upon instinctively, had found
A freshness in those objects of her love,
A winning power, beyond all other power.
Not that I slighted books, — that were to lack
All sense, — but other passions in me ruled,
Passions more fervent, making me less prompt
To in-door study than was wise or well,
Or suited to those years. Yet I, though used
In magisterial liberty to rove,
Culling such flowers of learning as might tempt 370
A random choice, could shadow forth a place
(If now I yield not to a flattering dream)
Whose studious aspect should have bent me down
To instantaneous service, should at once
Have made me pay to science and to arts
And written lore, acknowledged my liege lord,
A homage frankly offered up, like that
Which I had paid to Nature. Toil and pains
In this recess, by thoughtful Fancy built,
Should spread from heart to heart ; and stately groves,

Majestic edifices, should not want   381
A corresponding dignity within.
The congregating temper that pervades
Our unripe years, not wasted, should be taught
To minister to works of high attempt —
Works which the enthusiast would perform with love.
Youth should be awed, religiously possessed
With a conviction of the power that waits
On knowledge, when sincerely sought and prized
For its own sake, on glory and on praise   390
If but by labor won, and fit to endure
The passing day; should learn to put aside
Her trappings here, should strip them off abashed
Before antiquity and steadfast truth
And strong book-mindedness; and over all
A healthy sound simplicity should reign,
A seemly plainness, name it what you will,
Republican or pious.

               If these thoughts
Are a gratuitous emblazonry
That mocks the recreant age *we* live in, then   400
Be Folly and False-seeming free to affect
Whatever formal gait of discipline
Shall raise them highest in their own esteem —
Let them parade among the Schools at will,
But spare the House of God. Was ever known
The witless shepherd who persists to drive
A flock that thirsts not to a pool disliked?
A weight must surely hang on days begun
And ended with such mockery. Be wise,

Ye Presidents and Deans, and, till the spirit   410
Of ancient times revive, and youth be trained
At home in pious service, to your bells
Give seasonable rest, for 'tis a sound
Hollow as ever vexed the tranquil air,
And your officious doings bring disgrace
On the plain steeples of our English Church,
Whose worship, 'mid remotest village trees,
Suffers for this.   Even Science, too, at hand   .
In daily sight of this irreverence,
Is smitten thence with an unnatural taint,   420
Loses her just authority, falls beneath
Collateral suspicion, else unknown.
This truth escaped me not, and I confess,
That having 'mid my native hills given loose
To a schoolboy's vision, I had raised a pile
Upon the basis of the coming time,
That fell in ruins round me.   Oh, what joy
To see a sanctuary for our country's youth
Informed with such a spirit as might be
Its own protection ; a primeval grove,   430
Where, though the shades with cheerfulness were filled,
Nor indigent of songs warbled from crowds
In under-coverts, yet the countenance
Of the whole place should bear stamp of awe ;
A habitation sober and demure
For ruminating creatures, a domain
For quiet things to wander in ; a haunt
In which the heron should delight to feed
By the shy rivers, and the pelican   ′
Upon the cypress spire in lonely thought   440

Might sit and sun himself. — Alas ! Alas !
In vain for such solemnity I looked ;
Mine eyes were crossed by butterflies, ears vexed
By chattering popinjays ; the inner heart
Seemed trivial, and the impresses without
Of a too gaudy region.

                     Different sight
Those venerable Doctors saw of old,
When all who dwelt within these famous walls
Led in abstemiousness a studious life ;
When, in forlorn and naked chambers cooped   450
And crowded, o'er the ponderous books they hung
Like caterpillars eating out their way
In silence, or with keen devouring noise
Not to be tracked or fathered.   Princes then
At matins froze, and couched at curfew-time,
Trained up through piety and zeal to prize
Spare diet, patient labor, and plain weeds.
O seat of Arts ! renowned throughout the world !
Far different service in those homely days
The Muses' modest nurslings underwent   460
From their first childhood : in that glorious time
When Learning, like a stranger come from far,
Sounding through Christian lands her trumpet, roused
Peasant and king, when boys and youths, the growth
Of ragged villages and crazy huts,
Forsook their homes, and, errant in the quest
Of Patron, famous school or friendly nook,
Where, pensioned, they in shelter might sit down,
From town to town and through wide scattered realms

Journeyed with ponderous folios in their hands;   470
And often, starting from some covert place,
Saluted the chance comer on the road,
Crying, " An obulus, a penny give
To a poor scholar ! "— when illustrious men,
Lovers of truth, by penury constrained,
Bucer, Erasmus, or Melancthon, read
Before the doors or windows of their cells
By moonshine through mere lack of taper light.

   But peace to vain regrets ! We see but darkly
Even when we look behind us, and best things   480
Are not so pure by nature that they needs
Must keep to all, as fondly all believe,
Their highest promise.   If the mariner,
When at reluctant distance he hath passed
Some tempting island, could but know the ills
That must have fallen upon him had he brought
His bark to land upon the wished-for shore,
Good cause would oft be his to thank the surf
Whose white belt scared him thence, or wind that blew
Inexorably adverse : for myself   490
I grieve not ; happy is the gownèd youth
Who only misses what I missed, who falls
No lower than I fell.
               I did not love,
Judging not ill perhaps, the timid course
Of our scholastic studies ; could have wished
To see the river flow with ampler range
And freer pace ; but more, far more, I grieved
To see displayed among an eager few,

Who in the field of contest persevered,
Passions unworthy of youth's generous heart   500
And mounting spirit, pitiably repaid,
When so disturbed, whatever palms are won.
From these I turned to travel with the shoal
Of more unthinking natures, easy minds
And pillowy, yet not wanting love that makes
The day pass lightly on, when foresight sleeps,
And wisdom and the pledges interchanged
With our own inner being are forgot.

Yet was this deep vacation not given up
To utter waste.   Hitherto I had stood   510
In my own mind remote from social life,
(At least from what we commonly so name,)
Like a lone shepherd on a promontory
Who lacking occupation looks far forth
Into the boundless sea, and rather makes
Than finds what he beholds.   And sure it is,
That this first transit from the smooth delights
And wild outlandish walks of simple youth
To something that resembles an approach
Towards human business, to a privileged world   520
Within a world, a midway residence
With all its intervenient imagery,
Did better suit my visionary mind,
Far better, than to have been bolted forth,
Thrust out abruptly into Fortune's way
Among the conflicts of substantial life ;
By a more just gradation did lead on
To higher things ; more naturally matured,

For permanent possession, better fruits,
Whether of truth or virtue, to ensue.   530
In serious mood, but oftener, I confess,
With playful zest of fancy, did we note
(How could we less?) the manners and the ways
Of those who lived distinguished by the badge
Of good or ill report : or those with whom
By frame of Academic discipline
We were perforce connected, men whose sway
And known authority of office served
To set our minds on edge, and did no more.
Nor wanted we rich pastime of this kind,   540
Found everywhere, but chiefly in the ring
Of the grave Elders, men unscoured, grotesque
In character, tricked out like aged trees
Which through the lapse of their infirmity
Give ready place to any random seed
That chooses to be reared upon their trunks.

    Here on my view, confronting vividly
These shepherd swains whom I had lately left,
Appeared a different aspect of old age ;
How different ! yet both distinctly marked,   550
Objects embossed to catch the general eye,
Or portraitures for special use designed,
As some might seem, so aptly do they serve
To illustrate Nature's book of rudiments —
That book upheld as with maternal care
When she would enter on her tender scheme
Of teaching comprehension with delight,
And mingling playful with pathetic thoughts.

The surfaces of artificial life
And manners finely wrought, the delicate race   560
Of colors, lurking, gleaming up and down
Through that state arras woven with silk and gold:
This wily interchange of snaky hues,
Willingly or unwillingly revealed,
I neither knew nor cared for; and as such
Were wanting here, I took what might be found
Of less elaborate fabric.   At this day
I smile, in many a mountain solitude
Conjuring up scenes as obsolete in freaks
Of character, in points of wit as broad,   570
As aught by wooden images performed
For entertainment of the gaping crowd
At wake or fair.   And oftentimes do flit
Remembrances before me of old men —
Old humorists, who have been long in their graves,
And having almost in my mind put off
Their human names, have into phantoms passed
Of texture midway between life and books.

I play the loiterer: 'tis enough to note
That here in dwarf proportions were expressed   580
The limbs of the great world; its eager strifes
Collaterally portrayed, as in mock fight,
A tournament of blows, some hardly dealt
Though short of mortal combat; and whate'er
Might in this pageant be supposed to hit
An artless rustic's notice, this way less,
More that way, was not wasted upon me.
And yet the spectacle may well demand

A more substantial name, no mimic show,
Itself a living part of a live whole, 590
A creek in the vast sea ; for all degrees
And shapes of spurious fame and short-lived praise
Here sate in state, and fed with daily alms
Retainers won away from solid good ;
And here was Labor, his own bond-slave ; Hope,
That never set the pains against the prize ;
Idleness halting with his weary clog,
And poor misguided Shame, and witless Fear,
And simple Pleasure foraging for Death ;
Honor misplaced, and Dignity astray ; 600
Feuds, factions, flatteries, enmity, and guile
Murmuring submission, and bald government,
(The idol weak as the idolater,)
And Decency and Custom starving Truth,
And blind Authority beating with his staff
The child that might have led him ; Emptiness
Followed as of good omen, and meek Worth
Left to herself unheard of and unknown.

Of these and other kindred notices
I cannot say what portion is in truth 610
The naked recollection of that time,
And what may rather have been called to life
By after meditation. But delight
That, in an easy temper lulled asleep,
Is still with Innocence its own reward,
This was not wanting. Carelessly I roamed
As through a wide museum from whose stores
A casual rarity is singled out

And has its brief perusal, then gives way
To others, all supplanted in their turn ;   620
Till 'mid this crowded neighborhood of things
That are by nature most unneighborly,
The head turns round and cannot right itself ;
And though an aching and a barren sense
Of gay confusion still be uppermost,
With few wise longings and but little love,
Yet to the memory something cleaves at last,
Whence profit may be drawn in times to come.

Thus in submissive idleness, my Friend !
The laboring time of autumn, winter, spring,   630
Eight months ! rolled pleasingly away ; the ninth
Came and returned me to my native hills.

BOOK FOURTH.

SUMMER VACATION.

BRIGHT was the summer's noon when quickening steps
Followed each other till a dreary moor
Was crossed, a bare ridge clomb, upon whose top
Standing alone, as from a rampart's edge,
I overlooked the bed of Windermere,
Like a vast river, stretching in the sun.
With exultation, at my feet I saw
Lake, islands, promontories, gleaming bays,
A universe of Nature's fairest forms
Proudly revealed with instantaneous burst,   10
Magnificent, and beautiful, and gay.
I bounded down the hill shouting amain
For the old Ferryman; to the shout the rocks
Replied, and when the Charon of the flood
Had stayed his oars, and touched the jutting pier,
I did not step into the well-known boat
Without a cordial greeting. Thence with speed
Up the familiar hill I took my way
Towards that sweet Valley where I had been reared;
'Twas but a short hour's walk ere veering round   20
I saw the snow-white church upon her hill
Sit like a thronèd Lady, sending out

A gracious look all over her domain.
Yon azure smoke betrays the lurking town ;
With eager footsteps I advance and reach
The cottage threshold where my journey closed.
Glad welcome had I, with some tears, perhaps,
From my old Dame, so kind and motherly,
While she perused me with a parent's pride.
The thoughts of gratitude shall fall like dew   30
Upon thy grave, good creature !   While my heart
Can beat never will I forget thy name.
Heaven's blessing be upon thee where thou liest
After thy innocent and busy stir
In narrow cares, thy little daily growth
Of calm enjoyments, after eighty years,
And more than eighty, of untroubled life,
Childless, yet by the strangers to thy blood
Honored with little less than filial love.
What joy was mine to see thee once again,   40
Thee and thy dwelling, and a crowd of things
About its narrow precincts all beloved,
And many of them seeming yet my own !
Why should I speak of what a thousand hearts
Have felt, and every man alive can guess?
The rooms, the court, the garden were not left
Long unsaluted, nor the sunny seat
Round the stone table under the dark pine,
Friendly to studious or to festive hours ;
Nor that unruly child of mountain birth,   50
The famous brook, who, soon as he was boxed
Within our garden, found himself at once,
As if by trick insidious and unkind,

Stripped of his voice and left to dimple down
(Without an effort and without a will)
A channel paved by man's officious care.
I looked at him and smiled, and smiled again,
And in the press of twenty thousand thoughts,
" Ha," quoth I, " pretty prisoner, are you there ! "
Well might sarcastic fancy then have whispered,   60
"An emblem here behold of thy own life ;
In its late course of even days with all
Their smooth enthralment ; " but the heart was full,
Too full for that reproach.   My aged Dame
Walked proudly at my side : she guided me ;
I willing, nay — nay, wishing to be led.
The face of every neighbor whom I met
Was like a volume to me ; some were hailed
Upon the road, some busy at their work,
Unceremonious greetings interchanged   70
With half the length of a long field between.
Among my schoolfellows, I scattered round
Like recognitions, but with some constraint
Attended, doubtless, with a little pride,
But with more shame, for my habiliments,
The transformation wrought by gay attire.
Not less delighted did I take my place
At our domestic table : and, dear Friend !
In this endeavor simply to relate
A Poet's history, may I leave untold   80
The thankfulness with which I laid me down
In my accustomed bed, more welcome now
Perhaps than if it had been more desired
Or been more often thought of with regret ;

That lowly bed whence I had heard the wind
Roar, and the rain beat hard; where I so oft
Had lain awake on summer nights to watch
The moon in splendor couched among the leaves
Of a tall ash, that near our cottage stood;
Had watched her with fixed eyes while to and fro   90
In the dark summit of the wavering tree
She rocked with every impulse of the breeze.

    Among the favorites whom it pleased me well
To see again, was one by ancient right
Our inmate, a rough terrier of the hills;
The birth and call of nature pre-ordained
To hunt the badger and unearth the fox
Among the impervious crags, but having been
From youth our own adopted, he had passed
Into a gentler service.   And when first   100
The boyish spirit flagged, and day by day
Along my veins I kindled with the stir,
The fermentation, and the vernal heat
Of poesy, affecting private shades
Like a sick Lover, then this dog was used
To watch me, an attendant and a friend,
Obsequious to my steps early and late,
Though often of such dilatory walk
Tired, and uneasy at the halts I made.
A hundred times when, roving high and low,   110
I have been harassed with the toil of verse,
Much pains and little progress, and at once
Some lovely Image in the song rose up
Full-formed, like Venus rising from the sea;

Then have I darted forwards to let loose
My hand upon his back with stormy joy,
Caressing him again and yet again.
And when at evening on the public way
I sauntered, like a river murmuring
And talking to itself when all things else   120
Are still, the creature trotted on before ;
Such was his custom ; but whene'er he met
A passenger approaching, he would turn
To give me timely notice, and straightway,
Grateful for that admonishment, I hushed
My voice, composed my gait, and, with the air
And mien of one whose thoughts are free, advanced
To give and take a greeting that might save
My name from piteous rumors, such as wait
On men suspected to be crazed in brain.   130

Those walks well worthy to be prized and loved —
Regretted ! — that word, too, was on my tongue,
But they were richly laden with all good,
And cannot be remembered but with thanks
And gratitude, and perfect joy of heart —
Those walks in all their freshness now came back
Like a returning Spring.   When first I made
Once more the circuit of our little lake,
If ever happiness hath lodged with man,
That day consummate happiness was mine,   140
Wide-spreading, steady, calm, contemplative.
The sun was set, or setting, when I left
Our cottage door, and evening soon brought on
A sober hour, not winning or serene,

For cold and raw the air was, and untuned.
But as a face we love is sweetest then,
When sorrow damps it, or, whatever look
It chance to wear, is sweetest if the heart
Have fulness in herself; even so with me
It fared that evening.   Gently did my soul   150
Put off her veil, and, self-transmuted, stood
Naked, as in the presence of her God.
While on I walked, a comfort seemed to touch
A heart that had not been disconsolate:
Strength came where weakness was not known to be,
At least not felt; and restoration came
Like an intruder knocking at the door
Of unacknowledged weariness.   I took
The balance, and with firm hand weighed myself.
—Of that external scene which round me lay,   160
Little in this abstraction, did I see;
Remembered less; but I had inward hopes
And swellings of the spirit, was wrapped and soothed,
Conversed with promises, had glimmering views
How life pervades the undecaying mind;
How the immortal soul with God-like power
Informs, creates, and thaws the deepest sleep
That time can lay upon her; how on earth,
Man, if he do but live within the light
Of high endeavors, daily spreads abroad   170
His being, armed with strength that cannot fail.
Nor was there want of milder thoughts, of love,
Of innocence, and holiday repose;
And more than pastoral quiet, 'mid the stir
Of boldest projects, and a peaceful end

At last, or glorious, by endurance won.
Thus musing, in a wood I sate me down
Alone, continuing there to muse ; the slopes
And heights meanwhile were slowly overspread
With darkness, and before a rippling breeze   180
The long lake lengthened out its hoary line,
And in the sheltered coppice where I sate,
Around me from among the hazel leaves,
Now here, now there, moved by the straggling wind,
Came ever and anon a breath-like sound,
Quick as the pantings of a faithful dog,
The off and on companion of my walk ;
And such, at times, believing them to be,
I turned my head to look if he were there ;
Then into solemn thought I passed once more.   190

A freshness also found I at this time
In human Life, the daily life of those
Whose occupations really I loved ;
The peaceful scene oft filled me with surprise,
Changed like a garden in the heat of spring
After an eight-days' absence.   For (to omit
The things which were the same and yet appeared
Far otherwise) amid this rural solitude,
A narrow Vale where each was known to all,
'Twas not indifferent to a youthful mind   200
To mark some sheltering bower or sunny nook,
Where an old man had used to sit alone,
Now vacant ; pale-faced babes whom I had left
In arms, now rosy prattlers at the feet
Of a pleased grandame tottering up and down ;

And growing girls whose beauty, filched away
With all its pleasant promises, was gone
To deck some slighted playmate's homely cheek.

Yes, I had something of a subtler sense,
And often looking round was moved to smiles   210
Such as a delicate work of humor breeds;
I read, without design, the opinions, thoughts,
Of those plain-living people now observed
With clearer knowledge; with another eye
I saw the quiet woodman in the woods,
The shepherd roam the hills.   With new delight,
This chiefly, did I note my gray-haired Dame;
Saw her go forth to church or other work
Of state equipped in monumental trim;
Short velvet cloak (her bonnet of the like),   220
A mantle such as Spanish Cavaliers
Wore in old time.   Her smooth domestic life,
Affectionate without disquietude,
Her talk, her business, pleased me; and no less
Her clear though shallow stream of piety
That ran on Sabbath days a fresher course;
With thoughts unfelt till now I saw her read
Her Bible on hot Sunday afternoons,
And loved the book, when she had dropped asleep
And made of it a pillow for her head.   230

Nor less do I remember to have felt,
Distinctly manifested at this time,
A human-heartedness about my love
For objects hitherto the absolute wealth
Of my own private being and no more;

Which I had loved, even as a blessed spirit
Or Angel, if he were to dwell on earth,
Might love in individual happiness.
But now there opened on me other thoughts
Of change, congratulation or regret,   240
A pensive feeling !   It spread far and wide ;
The trees, the mountains shared it, and the brooks,
The stars of Heaven, now seen in their old haunts —
White Sirius glittering o'er the southern crags,
Orion with his belt, and those fair Seven,
Acquaintances of every little child,
And Jupiter, my own beloved star !
Whatever shadings of mortality,
Whatever imports from the world of death
Had come among these objects heretofore,   250
Were, in the main, of mood less tender : strong,
Deep, gloomy were they, and severe ; the scatterings
Of awe or tremulous dread, that had given way
In later youth to yearnings of a love
Enthusiastic, to delight and hope.

  As one who hangs down-bending from the side
Of a slow-moving boat, upon the breast
Of a still water, solacing himself
With such discoveries as his eye can make
Beneath him in the bottom of the deep,   260
Sees many beauteous sights — weeds, fishes, flowers,
Grots, pebbles, roots of trees, and fancies more,
Yet often is perplexed, and cannot part
The shadow from the substance, rocks and sky,
Mountains and clouds, reflected in the depth

Of the clear flood, from things which there abide
In their true dwelling; now is crossed by gleam
Of his own image, by a sunbeam now,
And wavering motions sent he knows not whence,
Impediments that make his task more sweet;   270
Such pleasant office have we long pursued
Incumbent o'er the surface of past time
With like success, nor often have appeared
Shapes fairer or less doubtfully discerned
Than these to which the Tale, indulgent Friend !
Would now direct thy notice.   Yet in spite
Of pleasure won, and knowledge not withheld,
There was an inner falling off — I loved,
Loved deeply all that had been loved before,
More deeply even than ever : but a swarm   280
Of heady schemes jostling each other, gawds,
And feast and dance, and public revelry,
And sports and games (too grateful in themselves,
Yet in themselves less grateful, I believe,
Than as they were a badge glossy and fresh
Of manliness and freedom) all conspired
To lure my mind from firm habitual quest
Of feeding pleasures, to depress the zeal
And damp those yearnings which had once been mine —
A wild, unworldly-minded youth, given up   290
To his own eager thoughts.   It would demand
Some skill, and longer time than may be spared,
To paint these vanities, and how they wrought
In haunts where they, till now, had been unknown.
It seemed the very garments that I wore
Preyed on my strength, and stopped the quiet stream

Of self-forgetfulness.

               Yes, that heartless chase
Of trivial pleasures was a poor exchange
For books and nature at that early age.
'Tis true, some casual knowledge might be gained   300
Of character or life ; but at that time,
Of manners put to school I took small note,
And all my deeper passions lay elsewhere.
Far better had it been to exalt the mind
By solitary study, to uphold
Intense desire through meditative peace ;
And yet, for chastisement of these regrets,
The memory of one particular hour
Doth here rise up against me. 'Mid a throng
Of maids and youths, old men, and matrons staid,   310
A medley of all tempers, I had passed
The night in dancing, gayety and mirth,
With din of instruments and shuffling feet,
And glancing forms, and tapers glittering,
And unaimed prattle flying up and down ;
Spirits upon the stretch, and here and there
Slight shocks of young love-liking interspersed,
Whose transient pleasure mounted to the head,
And tingled through the veins. Ere we retired,
The cock had crowed, and now the eastern sky   320
Was kindling, not unseen, from humble copse
And open field, through which the pathway wound,
And homeward led my steps. Magnificent
The morning rose, in memorable pomp,
Glorious as e'er I had beheld — in front,
The sea lay laughing at a distance ; near,

The solid mountains shone, bright as the clouds,
Grain-tinctured, drenched in empyrean light ;
And in the meadows and the lower grounds
Was all the sweetness of a common dawn —   330
Dews, vapors, and the melody of birds,
And laborers going forth to till the fields.
Ah ! need I say, dear Friend ! that to the brim
My heart was full ; I made no vows, but vows
Were then made for me ; bond unknown to me
Was given, that I should be, else sinning greatly,
A dedicated Spirit.   On I walked
In thankful blessedness, which yet survives.

  Strange rendezvous !   My mind was at that time
A parti-colored show of grave and gay,   340
Solid and light, short-sighted and profound ;
Of inconsiderate habits and sedate,
Consorting in one mansion unreproved.
The worth I knew of powers that I possessed,
Though slighted and too oft misused.   Besides,
That summer, swarming as it did with thoughts
Transient and idle, lacked not intervals
When Folly from the frown of fleeting Time
Shrunk, and the mind experienced in herself
Conformity as just as that of old   350
To the end and written spirit of God's works,
Whether held forth in Nature or in Man,
Through pregnant vision, separate or conjoined.

  When from our better selves we have too long
Been parted by the hurrying world, and droop,

Sick of its business, of its pleasures tired,
How gracious, how benign, is Solitude ;
How potent a mere image of her sway ;
Most potent when impressed upon the mind
With an appropriate human centre — hermit,   360
Deep in the bosom of the wilderness ;
Votary (in vast cathedral, where no foot
Is treading, where no other face is seen)
Kneeling at prayers, or watchman on the top
Of lighthouse, beaten by Atlantic waves ;
Or as the soul of that great Power is met
Sometimes embodied on a public road,
When, for the night deserted, it assumes
A character of quiet more profound
Than pathless wastes.

         Once, when those summer months 370
Were flown, and autumn brought its annual show
Of oars with oars contending, sails with sails,
Upon Winander's spacious breast, it chanced
That — after I had left a flower-decked room
(Whose in-door pastime, lighted up, survived
To a late hour), and spirits overwrought
Were making night do penance for a day
Spent in a round of strenuous idleness —
My homeward course led up a long ascent,
Where the road's watery surface, to the top   380
Of that sharp rising, glittered to' the moon
And bore the semblance of another stream
Stealing with silent lapse to join the brook
That murmured in the vale.   All else was still ;

No living thing appeared in earth or air,
And, save the flowing water's peaceful voice,
Sound there was none — but, lo ! an uncouth shape,
Shown by a sudden turning of the road,
So near that, slipping back into the shade
Of a thick hawthorn, I could mark him well,   390
Myself unseen.   He was of stature tall,
A span above man's common measure, tall,
Stiff, lank, and upright ; a more meagre man
Was never seen before by night or day.
Long were his arms, pallid his hands, his mouth
Looked ghastly in the moonlight : from behind,
A mile-stone propped him ; I could also ken
That he was clothed in military garb,
Though faded, yet entire.   Companionless,
No dog attending, by no staff sustained,   400
He stood, and in his very dress appeared
A desolation, a simplicity,
To which the trappings of a gaudy world
Make a strange back-ground.   From his lips, ere long,
Issued low muttered sounds, as if of pain
Or some uneasy thought ; yet still his form
Kept the same awful steadiness — at his feet
His shadow lay, and moved not.   From self-blame
Not wholly free, I watched him thus ; at length
Subduing my heart's specious cowardice,   410
I left the shady nook where I had stood
And hailed him.   Slowly from his resting-place
He rose, and with a lean and wasted arm
In measured gesture lifted to his head
Returned my salutation ; then resumed

His station as before ; and when I asked
His history, the veteran, in reply,
Was neither slow nor eager, but, unmoved,
And with a quiet uncomplaining voice,
A stately air of mild indifference,   420
He told in few plain words a soldier's tale —
That in the Tropic Islands he had served,
Whence he had landed scarcely three weeks past ;
That on his landing he had been dismissed,
And now was travelling towards his native home.
This heard, I said, in pity, " Come with me."
He stooped, and straightway from the ground took up
An oaken staff by me yet unobserved —
A staff which must have dropped from his slack hand
And lay till now neglected in the grass.   430
Though weak his step and cautious, he appeared
To travel without pain, and I beheld,
With an astonishment but ill suppressed,
His ghostly figure moving at my side ;
Nor could I, while we journeyed thus, forbear
To turn from present hardships to the past,
And speak of war, battle, and pestilence,
Sprinkling this talk with questions, better spared,
On what he might himself have seen or felt.
He all the while was in demeanor calm,   440
Concise in answer ; solemn and sublime
He might have seemed, but that in all he said
There was a strange half-absence, as of one
Knowing too well the importance of his theme,
But feeling it no longer.   Our discourse
Soon ended, and together on we passed

In silence through a wood gloomy and still.
Up-turning, then, along an open field,
We reached a cottage. At the door I knocked,
And earnestly to charitable care 450
Commended him as a poor friendless man,
Belated and by sickness overcome.
Assured that now the traveller would repose
In comfort, I entreated that henceforth
He would not linger in the public ways,
But ask for timely furtherance and help
Such as his state required. At this reproof,
With the same ghastly mildness in his look,
He said, " My trust is in the God of Heaven,
And in the eye of him who passes me ! " 460

The cottage door was speedily unbarred.
And now the soldier touched his hat once more
With his lean hand, and in a faltering voice,
Whose tone bespake reviving interests
Till then unfelt, he thanked me ; I returned
The farewell blessing of the patient man,
And so we parted. Back I cast a look,
And lingered near the door a little space,
Then sought with quiet heart my distant home.

BOOK FIFTH.

———◦◦◦———

BOOKS.

WHEN Contemplation, like the night-calm felt
Through earth and sky, spreads widely, and sends deep
Into the soul its tranquillizing power,
Even then I sometimes grieve for thee, O Man,
Earth's paramount Creature ! not so much for woes
That thou endurest ; heavy though that weight be,
Cloud-like it mounts, or touched with light divine
Doth melt away, but for those palms achieved,
Through length of time, by patient exercise
Of study and hard thought ; there, there, it is   10
That sadness finds its fuel.   Hitherto,
In progress through this Verse, my mind hath looked
Upon the speaking face of earth and heaven
As her prime teacher, intercourse with man
Established by the sovereign Intellect,
Who through that bodily image hath diffused,
As might appear to the eye of fleeting time,
A deathless spirit.   Thou also, man ! hast wrought,
For commerce of thy nature with herself,
Things that aspire to unconquerable life ;   20
And yet we feel — we cannot choose but feel —

That they must perish.   Tremblings of the heart
It gives, to think that our immortal being
No more shall need such garments ; and yet man,
As long as he shall be the child of earth,
Might almost " Weep to have " what he may lose,
Nor be himself extinguished, but survive,
Abject, depressed, forlorn, disconsolate.
A thought is with me sometimes, and I say, —
Should the whole frame of earth by inward throes
Be wrenched, or fire come down from far to scorch
Her pleasant habitations, and dry up
Old Ocean, in his bed left singed and bare,
Yet would the living Presence still subsist
Victorious, and composure would ensue,
And kindlings like the morning — presage sure
Of day returning and of life revived.
But all the meditations of mankind,
Yea, all the adamantine holds of truth
By reason built, or passion, which itself
Is highest reason in a soul sublime ;
The consecrated works of Bard and Sage,
Sensuous or intellectual, wrought by men,
Twin laborers and heirs of the same hopes ;
Where would they be?   Oh ! why hath not the Mind
Some element to stamp her image on
In nature somewhat nearer to her own?
Why, gifted with such powers to send abroad
Her spirit, must it lodge in shrines so frail?

One day, when from my lips a like complaint
Had fallen in presence of a studious friend,

He with a smile made answer, that in truth
'Twas going far to seek disquietude :
But on the front of his reproof confessed
That he himself had oftentimes given way
To kindred hauntings.   Whereupon I told,
That once in the stillness of a summer's noon,
While I was seated in a rocky cave
By the sea-side, perusing, so it chanced,
The famous history of the errant knight   60
Recorded by Cervantes, these same thoughts
Beset me, and to height unusual rose,
While listlessly I sate, and, having closed
The book, had turned my eyes towards the wide sea.
On poetry and geometric truth,
And their high privilege of lasting life,
From all internal injury exempt,
I mused ; upon these chiefly : and at length,
My senses yielding to the sultry air,
Sleep seized me, and I passed into a dream.   70
I saw before me stretched a boundless plain
Of sandy wilderness, all black and void,
And as I looked around, distress and fear
Came creeping over me, when at my side,
Close at my side, an uncouth shape appeared
Upon a dromedary, mounted high.
He seemed an Arab of the Bedouin tribes :
A lance he bore, and underneath one arm
A stone, and in the opposite hand a shell
Of a surpassing brightness.   At the sight   80
Much I rejoiced, not doubting but a guide
Was present, one who with unerring skill

Would through the desert lead me ; and while yet
I looked and looked, self-questioned what this freight
Which the new comer carried through the waste
Could mean, the Arab told me that the stone
(To give it in the language of the dream)
Was " Euclid's Elements ; " and " This," said he,
" Is something of more worth ; " and at the word
Stretched forth the shell, so beautiful in shape,   90
In color so resplendent, with command
That I should hold it to my ear.   I did so,
And heard that instant in an unknown tongue,
Which yet I understood, articulate sounds,
A loud prophetic blast of harmony ;
An Ode, in passion uttered, which foretold
Destruction to the children of the earth
By deluge, now at hand.   No sooner ceased
The song, than the Arab with calm look declared
That all would come to pass of which the voice   100
Had given forewarning, and that he himself
Was going then to bury those two books :
The one that held acquaintance with the stars,
And wedded soul to soul in purest bond
Of reason, undisturbed by space or time ;
The other that was a god, yea many gods,
Had voices more than all the winds, with power
To exhilarate the spirit, and to soothe,
Through every clime, the heart of human kind.
While this was uttering, strange as it may seem,   110
I wondered not, although I plainly saw
The one to be a stone, the other a shell ;
Nor doubted once but that they both were books,

Having a perfect faith in all that passed.
Far stronger, now, grew the desire I felt
To cleave unto this man ; but when I prayed
To share his enterprise, he hurried on
Reckless of me : I followed, not unseen,
For oftentimes he cast a backward look,
Grasping his twofold treasure. — Lance in rest,   120
He rode, I keeping pace with him ; and now
He, to my fancy, had become the knight
Whose tale Cervantes tells ; yet not the knight,
But as an Arab of the desert too ;
Of these was neither, and was both at once.
His countenance, meanwhile, grew more disturbed ;
And, looking backwards when he looked, mine eyes
Saw, over half the wilderness diffused,
A bed of glittering light : I asked the cause :
" It is," said he, " the waters of the deep   130
Gathering upon us ;" quickening then the pace
Of the unwieldy creature he bestrode,
He left me : I called after him aloud ;
He heeded not ; but, with his twofold charge
Still in his grasp, before me, full in view,
Went hurrying o'er the illimitable waste,
With the fleet waters of a drowning world
In chase of him ; whereat I waked in terror,
And saw the sea before me, and the book,
In which I had been reading, at my side.   140

   Full often, taking from the world of sleep
This Arab phantom, which I thus beheld,
This semi-Quixote, I to him have given

A substance, fancied him a living man,
A gentle dweller in the desert crazed
By love and feeling, and internal thought
Protracted among endless solitudes ;
Have shaped him wandering upon this quest !
Nor have I pitied him ; but rather felt
Reverence was due to a being thus employed ;   150
And thought that, in the blind and awful lair
Of such a madness, reason did lie couched.
Enow there are on earth to take in charge
Their wives, their children, and their virgin loves,
Or whatsoever else the heart holds dear ;
Enow to stir for these ; yea, will I say,
Contemplating in soberness the approach
Of an event so dire, by signs in earth
Or heaven made manifest, that I could share
That maniac's fond anxiety, and go   160
Upon like errand.   Oftentimes at least
Me hath such strong entrancement overcome,
When I have held a volume in my hand,
Poor earthly casket of immortal verse,
Shakespeare, or Milton, laborers divine !

Great and benign, indeed, must be the power
Of living nature, which could thus so long
Detain me from the best of other guides
And dearest helpers, left unthanked, unpraised,
Even in the time of lisping infancy ;   170
And later down, in prattling childhood even,
While I was travelling back among those days
How could I ever play an ingrate's part?

Once more should I have made those bowers resound,
By intermingling strains of thankfulness
With their own thoughtless melodies ; at least
It might have well beseemed me to repeat
Some simply fashioned tale, to tell again,
In slender accents of sweet verse, some tale
That did bewitch me then, and soothes me now.   180
O Friend ! O Poet ! brother of my soul,
Think not that I could pass along untouched
By these remembrances.   Yet wherefore speak?
Why call upon a few weak words to say
What is already written in the hearts
Of all that breathe? — what in the path of all
Drops daily from the tongue of every child,
Wherever man is found?   The trickling tear
Upon the cheek of listening Infancy
Proclaims it, and the insuperable look   190
That drinks as if it never could be full.

That portion of my story I shall leave
There registered : whatever else of power
Or pleasure sown, or fostered thus, may be
Peculiar to myself, let that remain
Where still it works, though hidden from all search
Among the depths of time.   Yet it is just
That here, in memory of all books which lay
Their sure foundations in the heart of man,
Whether by native prose, or numerous verse,   200
That in the name of all inspirèd souls —
From Homer the great Thunderer, from the voice
That roars along the bed of Jewish song,

And that more varied and elaborate,
Those trumpet-tones of harmony that shake
Our shores in England, — from those loftiest notes
Down to the low and wren-like warblings, made
For cottagers and spinners at the wheel,
And sun-burnt travellers resting their tired limbs,
Stretched under wayside hedge-rows, ballad tunes,   210
Food for the hungry ears of little ones,
And of old men who have survived their joys —
'Tis just that in behalf of these, the works,
And of the men that framed them, whether known
Or sleeping nameless in their scattered graves,
That I should here assert their rights, attest
Their honors, and should, once for all, pronounce
Their benediction ; speak of them as Powers
Forever to be hallowed ; only less,
For what we are and what we may become,   220
Than Nature's self, which is the breath of God,
Or His pure Word by miracle revealed.

    Rarely and with reluctance would I stoop
To transitory themes ; yet I rejoice,
And, by these thoughts admonished, will pour out
Thanks with uplifted heart, that I was reared
Safe from an evil which these days have laid
Upon the children of the land, a pest
That might have dried me up, body and soul.
This verse is dedicate to Nature's self,   230
And things that teach as Nature teaches : then,
Oh ! where had been the Man, the Poet where,
Where had we been, we two, beloved Friend !

If in the season of imperilous choice,
In lieu of wandering, as we did, through vales
Rich with indigenous produce, open ground
Of Fancy, happy pastures ranged at will,
We had been followed, hourly watched and noosed
Each in his several melancholy walk
Stringed like a poor man's heifer at its feed,   240
Led through the lanes in forlorn servitude ;
Or rather like a stallèd ox debarred
From touch of growing grass, that may not taste
A flower till it have yielded up its sweets
A prelibation to the mower's scythe.

Behold the parent hen amid her brood,
Though fledged and feathered, and well pleased to part
And straggle from her presence, still a brood,
And she herself from the maternal bond
Still undischarged ; yet doth she little more   250
Than move with them in tenderness and love,
A centre to the circle which they make ;
And now and then, alike from need of theirs
And call of her own natural appetites,
She scratches, ransacks up the earth for food,
Which they partake at pleasure.   Early died
My honored Mother, she who was the heart
And hinge of all our learnings and our loves :
She left us destitute, and, as we might,
Trooping together.   Little suits it me   260
To break upon the sabbath of her rest
With any thought that looks at others' blame ;
Nor would I praise her but in perfect love.

Hence am I checked : but let me boldly say,
In gratitude, and for the sake of truth,
Unheard by her, that she, not falsely taught,
Fetching her goodness rather from times past
Than shaping novelties for times to come,
Had no presumption, no such jealousy,
Nor did by habit of her thoughts mistrust,   270
Our nature, but had virtual faith, that He
Who fills the mother's breast with innocent milk
Doth also for our nobler part provide,
Under His great correction and control,
As innocent instincts, and as innocent food ;
Or draws for minds that are left free to trust
In the simplicities of opening life
Sweet honey out of spurned or dreaded weeds.
This was her creed, and therefore she was pure
From anxious fear of error or mishap,   280
And evil, overweeningly so called ;
Was not puffed up by false unnatural hopes,
Nor selfish with unnecessary cares,
Nor with impatience from the season asked
More than its timely produce ; rather loved
The hours for what they are, than from regard
Glanced on their promises in restless pride.
Such was she — not from faculties more strong
Than others have, but from the times, perhaps,
And spot in which she lived, and through a grace   290
Of modest meekness, simple-mindedness,
A heart that found benignity and hope,
Being itself benign.
                    My drift I fear

Is scarcely obvious : but, that common sense
May try this modern system by its fruits,
Leave let me take to place before her sight
A specimen portrayed with faithful hand.
Full early trained to worship seemliness,
This model of a child is never known
To mix in quarrels ; that were far beneath   300
Its dignity, with gifts he bubbles o'er
As generous as a fountain ; selfishness
May not come near him, nor the little throng
Of flitting pleasures tempt him from his path ;
The wandering beggars propagate his name,
Dumb creatures find him tender as a nun,
And natural or supernatural fear,
Unless it leap upon him in a dream,
Touches him not.   To enhance the wonder, see
How arch his notices, how nice his sense   310
Of the ridiculous ; not blind is he
To the broad follies of the licensed world,
Yet innocent himself withal, though shrewd.
And can read lectures upon innocence ;
A miracle of scientific lore,
Ships he can guide across the pathless sea,
And tell you all their cunning ; he can read
The inside of the earth, and spell the stars ;
He knows the policies of foreign lands,
Can string you names of districts, cities, towns,   320
The whole world over, tight as beads of dew
Upon a gossamer thread ; he sifts, he weighs,
All things are put to question ; he must live
Knowing that he grows wiser every day

Or else not live at all, and seeing too
Each little drop of wisdom as it falls
Into the dimpling cistern of his heart :
For this unnatural growth the trainer blame,
Pity the tree. — Poor human vanity,
Wert thou extinguished, little would be left   330
Which he could truly love ; but how escape?
For, ever as a thought of purer birth
Rises to lead him toward a better clime,
Some intermeddler still is on the watch
To drive him back, and pound him, like a stray,
Within the pinfold of his own conceit.
Meanwhile old grandame earth is grieved to find
The playthings, which her love designed for him,
Unthought of : in their woodland beds the flowers
Weep, and the river sides are all forlorn.   340
Oh ! give us once again the wishing cap
Of Fortunatus, and the invisible coat
Of Jack the Giant-killer, Robin Hood,
And Sabra in the forest with St. George !
The child, whose love is here, at least, doth reap
One precious gain, that he forgets himself.

These mighty workmen of our later age,
Who, with a broad highway, have overbridged
The forward chaos of futurity,
Tamed to their bidding ; they who have the skill   350
To manage books, and things, and make them act
On infant minds as surely as the sun
Deals with a flower ; the keepers of our time,
The guides and wardens of our faculties,

Sages who in their prescience would control
All accidents, and to the very road
Which they have fashioned would confine us down,
Like engines ; when will their presumption learn,
That in the unreasoning progress of the world
A wiser spirit is at work for us,   360
A better eye than theirs, most prodigal
Of blessings, and most studious of our good,
Even in what seem our most unfruitful hours ?

   There was a Boy : ye knew him well, ye cliffs
And islands of Winander ! — many a time
At evening, when the earliest stars began
To move along the edges of the hills,
Rising or setting, would he stand alone
Beneath the trees or by the glimmering lake,
And there, with fingers interwoven, both hands   370
Pressed closely palm to palm, and to his mouth
Uplifted, he, as through an instrument,
Blew mimic hootings to the silent owls,
That they might answer him ; and they would shout
Across the watery vale, and shout again,
Responsive to his call with quivering peals,
And long halloos and screams, and echoes loud,
Redoubled and redoubled, concourse wild
Of jocund din ; and, when a lengthened pause
Of silence came and baffled his best skill,   380
Then sometimes, in that silence while he hung
Listening, a gentle shock of mild surprise
Has carried far into his heart the voice
Of mountain torrents ; or the visible scene

Would enter unawares into his mind,
With all its solemn imagery, its rocks,
Its woods, and that uncertain heaven, received
Into the bosom of the steady lake.

This Boy was taken from his mates, and died
In childhood, ere he was full twelve years old.   390
Fair is the spot, most beautiful the vale,
Where he was born ; the grassy churchyard hangs
Upon a slope above the village school,
And through that churchyard when my way has led
On summer evenings, I believe that there
A long half hour together I have stood
Mute, looking at the grave in which he lies !
Even now appears before the mind's clear eye
That self-same village church ; I see her sit
(The thronèd Lady whom erewhile we hailed)   400
On her green hill, forgetful of this Boy
Who slumbers at her feet, — forgetful too,
Of all her silent neighborhood of graves,
And listening only to the gladsome sounds
That from the rural school ascending, play
Beneath her and about her.   May she long
Behold a race of young ones like to those
With whom I herded ! — (easily, indeed,
We might have fed upon a fatter soil
Of arts and letters — but be that forgiven) —   410
A race of real children ; not too wise,
Too learned, or too good ; but wanton, fresh,
And bandied up and down by love and hate ;
Not unresentful where self-justified ;

Fierce, moody, patient, venturous, modest, shy;
Mad at their sports like withered leaves in winds;
Though doing wrong and suffering, and full oft
Bending beneath our life's mysterious weight
Of pain, and doubt, and fear, yet yielding not
In happiness to the happiest upon earth.   420
Simplicity in habits, truth in speech,
Be these the daily strengtheners of their minds;
May books and Nature be their early joy!
And knowledge, rightly honored with that name —
Knowledge not purchased by the loss of power!

   Well do I call to mind the very week
When I was first intrusted to the care
Of that sweet Valley; when its paths, its shores,
And brooks were like a dream of novelty
To my half-infant thoughts; that very week,   430
While I was roving up and down alone,
Seeking I knew not what, I chanced to cross
One of those open fields, which, shaped like ears,
Make green peninsulas on Esthwaite's Lake:
Twilight was coming on, yet through the gloom
Appeared distinctly on the opposite shore
A heap of garments, as if left by one
Who might have there been bathing.   Long I watched,
But no one owned them; meanwhile the calm lake
Grew dark with all the shadows on its breast,   440
And, now and then, a fish up-leaping snapped
The breathless stillness.   The succeeding day,
Those unclaimed garments telling a plain tale
Drew to the spot an anxious crowd; some looked

In passive expectation from the shore,
While from a boat others hung o'er the deep,
Sounding with grappling irons and long poles.
At last, the dead man, 'mid that beauteous scene
Of trees and hills and water, bolt upright
Rose, with his ghastly face, a spectre shape   450
Of terror ; yet no soul-debasing fear,
Young as I was, a child not nine years old,
Possessed me, for my inner eye had seen
Such sights before, among the shining streams
Of faëry land, the forest of romance.
Their spirit hallowed the sad spectacle
With decoration of ideal grace ;
A dignity, a smoothness, like the works
Of Grecian art, and purest poesy.

A precious treasure had I long possessed,   460
A little yellow, canvas-covered book,
A slender abstract of the Arabian tales ;
And, from companions in a new abode,
When first I learnt that this dear prize of mine
Was but a block hewn from a mighty quarry —
That there were four large volumes, laden all
With kindred matter, 'twas to me, in truth,
A promise scarcely earthly.   Instantly,
With one not richer than myself, I made
A covenant that each should lay aside   470
The moneys he possessed, and hoard up more,
Till our joint savings had amassed enough
To make this book our own.   Through several months,
In spite of all temptation, we preserved

Religiously that vow ; but firmness failed,
Nor were we ever masters of our wish.

And when thereafter to my father's house
The holidays returned me, there to find
That golden store of books which I had left,
What joy was mine ! How often in the course   480
Of those glad respites, though a soft west wind
Ruffled the waters to the angler's wish,
For a whole day together, have I lain
Down by thy side, O Derwent ! murmuring **stream,**
On the hot stones, and in the glaring sun,
And there have read, devouring as I read,
Defrauding the day's glory, desperate !
Till with a sudden bound of smart reproach,
Such as an idler deals with in his shame,
I to the sport betook myself again.   490

A gracious spirit o'er this earth presides,
And o'er the heart of man ; invisibly
It comes, to works of unreproved delight,
And tendency benign, directing those
Who care not, know not, think not what they do.
The tales that charm away the wakeful night
In Araby, romances ; legends penned
For solace by dim light of monkish lamps ;
Fictions, for ladies of their love, devised
By youthful squires ; adventures endless, spun   500
By the dismantled warrior in old age,
Out of the bowels of those very schemes
In which his youth did first extravagate ;

These spread like day, and something in the shape
Of these will live till man shall be no more.
Dumb yearnings, hidden appetites, are ours,
And *they must* have their food.   Our childhood sits,
Our simple childhood, sits upon a throne
That hath more power than all the elements.
I guess not what this tells of Being past,   510
Nor what it augurs of the life to come ;
But so it is, and, in that dubious hour,
That twilight when we first begin to see
This dawning earth, to recognize, expect,
And, in the long probation that ensues,
The time of trial, ere we learn to live
In reconcilement with our stinted powers ;
To endure this state of meagre vassalage,
Unwilling to forego, confess, submit,
Uneasy and unsettled, yoke-fellows   520
To custom, mettlesome, and not yet tamed   .
And humbled down ; oh ! then we feel, we feel,
We know where we have friends.   Ye dreamers, then,
Forgers of daring tales ! we bless you then,
Impostors, drivellers, dotards, as the ape
Philosophy will call you : *then* we feel
With what and how great might ye are in league,
Who make our wish, our power, our thought a deed,
An empire, a possession, — ye whom time
And seasons serve ; all Faculties to whom   530
Earth crouches, the elements are potter's clay,
Space like a heaven filled up with northern lights,
Here, nowhere, there, and everywhere at once.

Relinquishing this lofty eminence
For ground, though humbler, not the less a tract
Of the same isthmus, which our spirits cross
In progress from their native continent
To earth and human life, the Song might dwell
On that delightful time of growing youth,
When craving for the marvellous gives way   540
To strengthening love for things that we have seen;
When sober truth and steady sympathies,
Offered to notice by less daring pens,
Take firmer hold of us, and words themselves
Move us with conscious pleasure.

                             I am sad
At thought of rapture now forever flown;
Almost to tears I sometimes could be sad
To think of, to read over, many a page,
Poems withal of name, which at that time
Did never fail to entrance me, and are now   550
Dead in my eyes, dead as a theatre
Fresh emptied of spectators.   Twice five years
Or less I might have seen, when first my mind
With conscious pleasure opened to the charm
Of words in tuneful order, found them sweet
For their own sakes, a passion, and a power;
And phrases pleased me chosen for delight,
For pomp, or love.   Oft in the public roads
Yet unfrequented, while the morning light
Was yellowing the hill tops, I went abroad   560
With a dear friend, and for the better part
Of two delightful hours we strolled along
By the still borders of the misty lake,

Repeating favorite verses with one voice,
Or conning more, as happy as the birds
That round us chaunted.   Well might we be glad,
Lifted above the ground by airy fancies,
More bright than madness or the dreams of wine ;
And, though full oft the objects of our love
Were false, and in their splendor overwrought,   570
Yet was there surely then no vulgar power
Working within us, — nothing less, in truth,
Than that most noble attribute of man,
Though yet untutored and inordinate,
That wish for something loftier, more adorned,
Than is the common aspect, daily garb,
Of human life.   What wonder, then, if sounds
Of exultation echoed through the groves !
For images, and sentiments, and words,
And everything encountered or pursued   580
In that delicious world of poesy,
Kept holiday, a never-ending show,
With music, incense, festival, and flowers !

   Here must we pause : this only let me add,
From heart experience, and in humblest sense
Of modesty, that he, who in his youth
A daily wanderer among woods and fields
With living Nature hath been intimate,
Not only in that raw unpractised time
Is stirred to ecstasy, as others are,   590
By glittering verse ; but further, doth receive,
In measure only dealt out to himself,
Knowledge and increase of enduring joy

From the great Nature that exists in works
Of mighty Poets.   Visionary power
Attends the motions of the viewless winds,
Embodied in the mystery of words :
There, darkness makes abode, and all the host
Of shadowy things work endless changes, — there,
As in a mansion like their proper home,   600
Even forms and substances are circumfused
By that transparent veil with light divine,
And, through the turnings intricate of verse,
Present themselves as objects recognized,
In flashes, and with glory not their own.

BOOK SIXTH.

CAMBRIDGE AND THE ALPS.

THE leaves were fading when to Esthwaite's banks
And the simplicities of cottage life
I bade farewell; and, one among the youth
Who, summoned by that season, reunite
As scattered birds troop to the fowler's lure,
Went back to Granta's cloisters, not so prompt
Or eager, though as gay and undepressed
In mind, as when I thence had taken flight
A few short months before.   I turned my face
Without repining from the coves and heights
Clothed in the sunshine of the withering fern;
Quitted, not loth, the mild magnificence
Of calmer lakes and louder streams; and you,
Frank-hearted maids of rocky Cumberland,
You and your not unwelcome days of mirth,
Relinquished, and your nights of revelry,
And in my own unlovely cell sate down
In lightsome mood — such privilege has youth
That cannot take long leave of pleasant thoughts.

The bonds of indolent society,
Relaxing in their hold, henceforth I lived

More to myself.   Two winters may be passed
Without a separate notice : many books
Were skimmed, devoured, or studiously perused,
But with no settled plan.   I was detached
Internally from academic cares ;
Yet independent study seemed a course
Of hardy disobedience toward friends
And kindred, proud rebellion and unkind.
This spurious virtue, rather let it bear   30
A name it now deserves, this cowardice,
Gave treacherous sanction to that over-love
Of freedom which encouraged me to turn
From regulations even of my own
As from restraints and bonds.   Yet who can tell—
Who knows what thus may have been gained, both then
And at a later season, or preserved ;
What love of nature, what original strength
Of contemplation, what intuitive truths
The deepest and the best, what keen research,   40
Unbiassed, unbewildered, and unawed ?

     The Poet's soul was with me at that time :
Sweet meditations, the still overflow
Of present happiness, while future years
Lacked not anticipations, tender dreams,
No few of which have since been realized ;
And some remain, hopes for my future life.
Four years and thirty, told this very week,
Have I been now a sojourner on earth,
By sorrow not unsmitten ; yet for me   50
Life's morning radiance hath not left the hills,

Her dew is on the flowers.   Those were the days
Which also first emboldened me to trust
With firmness, hitherto but slightly touched
By such a daring thought, that I might leave
Some monument behind me which pure hearts
Should reverence.   The instinctive humbleness,
Maintained even by the very name and thought
Of printed books and authorship, began
To melt away ; and further, the dread awe   60
Of mighty names was softened down and seemed
Approachable, admitting fellowship
Of modest sympathy.   Such aspect now,
Though not familiarly, my mind put on,
Content to observe, to achieve, and to enjoy.

    All winter long, whenever free to choose,
Did I by night frequent the College grove
And tributary walks ; the last, and oft
The only one, who had been lingering there
Through hours of silence, till the porter's bell,   70
A punctual follower on the stroke of nine,
Rang with its blunt unceremonious voice,
Inexorable summons !   Lofty elms,
Inviting shades or opportune recess,
Bestowed composure on a neighborhood
Unpeaceful in itself.   A single tree
With sinuous trunk, boughs exquisitely wreathed,
Grew there ; an ash which Winter for himself
Decked out with pride, and with outlandish grace :
Up from the ground, and almost to the top,   80
The trunk and every master branch were green

With clustering ivy, and the lightsome twigs
And outer spray profusely tipped with seeds
That hung in yellow tassels, while the air
Stirred them, not voiceless.   Often have I stood
Foot-bound uplooking at this lovely tree
Beneath a frosty moon.   The hemisphere
Of magic fiction, verse of mine perchance
May never tread ; but scarcely Spenser's self
Could have more tranquil visions in his youth,   90
Or could more bright appearances create
Of human forms with superhuman powers,
Than I beheld loitering on calm clear nights
Alone, beneath this fairy work of earth.

On the vague reading of a truant youth
'Twere idle to descant.   My inner judgment
Not seldom differed from my taste in books,
As if it appertained to another mind,
And yet the books which then I valued most
Are dearest to me *now ;* for, having scanned,   100
Not heedlessly, the laws, and watched the forms
Of Nature, in that knowledge I possessed
A standard, often usefully applied,
Even when unconsciously, to things removed
From a familiar sympathy. — In fine,
I was a better judge of thoughts than words,
Misled in estimating words, not only
By common inexperience of youth,
But by the trade in classic niceties,
The dangerous craft of culling term and phrase   110
From languages that want the living voice

To carry meaning to the natural heart;
To tell us what is passion, what is truth,
What reason, with simplicity and sense.

Yet may we not entirely overlook
The pleasure gathered from the rudiments
Of geometric science.   Though advanced
In these inquiries, with regret I speak,
No farther than the threshold, there I found
Both elevation and composed delight: 120
With Indian awe and wonder, ignorance pleased
With its own struggles, did I meditate
On the relation those abstractions bear
To Nature's laws, and by what process led,   ,
Those immaterial agents bowed their heads
Duly to serve the mind of earth-born man;
From star to star, from kindred sphere to sphere,
From system on to system without end.

More frequently from the same source I drew
A pleasure quiet and profound, a sense   130
Of permanent and universal sway,
And paramount belief: there, recognized
A type, for finite natures, of the one
Supreme Existence, the surpassing life
Which — to the boundaries of space and time,
Of melancholy space and doleful time,   ·
Superior and incapable of change,
Nor touched by welterings of passion — is,
And hath the name of, God.   Transcendent peace
And silence did await upon these thoughts   140
That were a frequent comfort to my youth.

'Tis told by one whom stormy waters threw,
With fellow-sufferers by the shipwreck spared,
Upon a desert coast, that having brought
To land a single volume, saved by chance,
A treatise of Geometry, he wont,
Although of food and clothing destitute,
And beyond common wretchedness depressed,
To part from company and take this book
(Then first a self-taught pupil in its truths)   150
To spots remote, and draw his diagrams
With a long staff upon the sand, and thus
Did oft beguile his sorrow, and almost
Forget his feeling : so (if like effect
From the same cause produced, 'mid outward things
So different, may rightly be compared),
So was it then with me, and so will be
With Poets ever.   Mighty is the charm
Of those abstractions to a mind beset
With images and haunted by herself,   160
And specially delightful unto me
Was that clear synthesis built up aloft
So gracefully ; even then when it appeared
Not more than a mere plaything, or a toy
To sense embodied : not the thing it is
In verity, an independent world,
Created out of pure intelligence.

Such dispositions then were mine unearned
By aught, I fear, of genuine desert —
Mine, through heaven's grace and inborn aptitudes. 170
And not to leave the story of that time

Imperfect, with these habits must be joined
Moods melancholy, fits of spleen, that loved
A pensive sky, sad days, and piping winds,
The twilight more than dawn, autumn than spring ;
A treasured and luxurious gloom of choice
And inclination mainly, and the mere
Redundancy of youth's contentedness.
— To time thus spent, add multitudes of hours
Pilfered away, by what the Bard who sang   180
Of the Enchanter Indolence hath called
" Good-natured lounging," and behold a map
Of my collegiate life — far less intense
Than duty called for, or, without regard
To duty, *might* have sprung up of itself
By change of accidents, or even, to speak
Without unkindness, in another place.
Yet why take refuge in that plea ? — the fault
This I repeat, was mine ; mine be the blame.

In summer, making quest for works of art,   190
Or scenes renowned for beauty, I explored
That streamlet whose blue current works its way
Beneath romantic Dovedale's spiry rocks ;
Pried into Yorkshire dales, or hidden tracts
Of my own native region, and was blest
Between these sundry wanderings with a joy
Above all joys, that seemed another morn
Risen on mid noon ; blest with the presence, Friend !
Of that sole Sister, her who hath been long
Dear to thee also, thy true friend and mine,   200
Now, after separation desolate,

Restored to me — such absence that she seemed
A gift then first bestowed.   The varied banks
Of Emont, hitherto unnamed in song,
And that monastic castle, 'mid tall trees,
Low standing by the margin of the stream,
A mansion visited (as fame reports)
By Sidney, where, in sight of our Helvellyn,
Or stormy Cross-fell, snatches he might pen
Of his Arcadia, by fraternal love   210
Inspired ; — that river and those mouldering towers
Have seen us side by side, when, having clomb
The darksome windings of a broken stair,
And crept along a ridge of fractured wall,
Not without trembling, we in safety looked
Forth, through some Gothic window's open space,
And gathered with one mind a rich reward
From the far-stretching landscape, by the light
Of morning beautified, or purple eve ;
Or, not less pleased, lay on some turret's head,   220
Catching from tufts of grass and hare-bell flowers
Their faintest whisper to the passing breeze,
Given out while mid-day heat oppressed the plains.

  Another maid there was, who also shed
A gladness o'er that season, then to me,
By her exulting outside look of youth
And placid under-countenance, first endeared ;
That other spirit, Coleridge ! who is now
So near to us, that meek confiding heart,
So reverenced by us both.   O'er paths and fields   230
In all that neighborhood, through narrow lanes

Of eglantine, and through the shady woods,
And o'er the Border Beacon, and the waste
Of naked pools, and common crags that lay
Exposed on the bare fell, were scattered love,
The spirit of pleasure, and youth's golden gleam.
O Friend! we had not seen thee at that time,
And yet a power is on me, and a strong
Confusion, and I seem to plant thee there.
Far art thou wandered now in search of health　　240
And milder breezes, — melancholy lot!
But thou art with us, with us in the past,
The present, with us in the times to come.
There is no grief, no sorrow, no despair,
No languor, no dejection, no dismay,
No absence scarcely can there be, for those
Who love as we do.　Speed thee well! divide
With us thy pleasure; thy returning strength,
Receive it daily as a joy of ours;
Share with us thy fresh spirits, whether gift　　250
Of gales Etesian or of tender thoughts.

　　I, too, have been a wanderer; but, alas!
How different the fate of different men.
Though mutually unknown, yea, nursed and reared
As if in several elements, we were framed
To bend at last to the same discipline,
Predestined, if two beings ever were,
To seek the same delights, and have one health,
One happiness.　Throughout this narrative,
Else sooner ended, I have borne in mind　　260
For whom it registers the birth, and marks the growth,

Of gentleness, simplicity, and truth,
And joyous loves, that hallow innocent days
Of peace and self-command. Of rivers, fields,
And groves I speak to thee, my Friend ! to thee,
Who, yet a liveried schoolboy, in the depths
Of the huge city, on the leaded roof
'Of that wide edifice, thy school and home,
Wert used to lie and gaze upon the clouds
Moving in heaven ; or, of that pleasure tired,   270
To shut thine eyes, and by internal light
See trees, and meadows, and thy native stream,
Far distant, thus beheld from year to year
Of a long exile. Nor could I forget,
In this late portion of my argument,
That scarcely, as my term of pupilage
Ceased, had I left those academic bowers
When thou wert thither guided. From the heart
Of London, and from cloisters there, thou camest,
And didst sit down in temperance and peace,   280
A rigorous student. What a stormy course
Then followed. Oh ! it is a pang that calls
For utterance, to think what easy change
Of circumstances might to thee have spared
A world of pain, ripened a thousand hopes,
Forever withered. Through this retrospect
Of my collegiate life I still have had,
Thy after-sojourn in the self-same place
Present before my eyes, have played with times
And accidents as children do with cards,   290
Or as a man, who, when his house is built,
A frame locked up in wood and stone, doth still,

As impotent fancy prompts, by his fireside,
Rebuild it to his liking.   I have thought
Of thee, thy learning, gorgeous eloquence,
And all the strength and plumage of thy youth,
Thy subtle speculations, toils abstruse
Among the schoolmen, and Platonic forms
Of wild ideal pageantry, shaped out
From things well-matched or ill, and words for things,
The self-created sustenance of a mind   301
Debarred from Nature's living images,
Compelled to be a life unto herself,
And unrelentingly possessed by thirst
Of greatness, love, and beauty.   Not alone,
Ah ! surely not in singleness of heart
Should I have seen the light of evening fade
From smooth Cam's silent waters : had we met,
Even at that early time, needs must I trust
In the belief that my maturer age,   310
My calmer habits, and more steady voice,
Would with an influence benign have soothed,
Or chased away, the airy wretchedness
That battened on thy youth.   But thou hast trod
A march of glory, which doth put to shame
These vain regrets ; health suffers in thee, else
Such grief for thee would be the weakest thought
That ever harbored in the breast of man.

A passing word erewhile did lightly touch
On wanderings of my own, that now embraced   320
With livelier hope a region wider far.

When the third summer freed us from restraint,
A youthful friend, he too a mountaineer,
Not slow to share my wishes, took his staff,
And sallying forth, we journeyed side by side,
Bound to the distant Alps.   A hardy slight
Did this unprecedented course imply
Of college studies and their set rewards ;
Nor had, in truth, the scheme been formed by me
Without uneasy forethought of the pain,   330
The censures, and ill-omening of those
To whom my worldly interests were dear.
But Nature then was sovereign in my mind,
And mighty forms, seizing a youthful fancy,
Had given a charter to irregular hopes.
In any age of uneventful calm
Among the nations, surely would my heart
Have been possessed by similar desire ;
But Europe at that time was thrilled with joy,
France standing on the top of golden hours,   340
And human nature seeming born again.

   Lightly equipped, and but a few brief looks
Cast on the white cliffs of our native shore
From the receding vessel's deck, we chanced
To land at Calais on the very eve
Of that great federal day, and there we saw,
In a mean city, and among a few,
How bright a face is worn when joy of one
Is joy for tens of millions.   Southward thence
We held our way, direct through hamlets, towns,   350
Gaudy with reliques of that festival,

Flowers left to wither on triumphal arcs,
And window-garlands.   On the public roads,
And, once, three days successively, through paths
By which our toilsome journey was abridged,
Among sequestered villages we walked
And found benevolence and blessedness
Spread like a fragrance everywhere, when spring
Hath left no corner of the land untouched ;
Where elms for many and many a league in files,   360
With their thin umbrage, on the stately roads
Of that great kingdom, rustled o'er our heads,
Forever near us as we paced along :
How sweet at such a time, with such delight
On every side, in prime of youthful strength,
To feed a Poet's tender melancholy
And fond conceit of sadness, with the sound
Of undulations varying as might please
The wind that swayed them ; once, and more than once,
Unhoused beneath the evening star we saw   370
Dances of liberty, and in late hours
Of darkness, dances in the open air
Deftly prolonged, though gray-haired lookers on
Might waste their breath in chiding.
                              Under hills —
The vine-clad hills and slopes of Burgundy,
Upon the bosom of the gentle Saone
We glided forward with the flowing stream.
Swift Rhone ! thou wert the *wings* on which we cut
A winding passage with majestic ease
Between thy lofty rocks.   Enchanting show   380
Those woods and farms, and orchards did present,

And single cottages and lurking towns,
Reach after reach, succession without end
Of deep and stately vales !   A lonely pair
Of strangers, till day closed, we sailed along
Clustered together with a merry crowd
Of those emancipated, a blithe host
Of travellers, chiefly delegates, returning
From the great spousals newly solemnized
At their chief city, in the sight of Heaven.   390
Like bees they swarmed, gaudy and gay as bees ;
Some vapored in the unruliness of joy,
And with their swords flourished as if to fight
The saucy air.   In this proud company
We landed — took with them our evening meal,
Guests welcome almost as the angels were
To Abraham of old.   The supper done,
With flowing cups elate and happy thoughts
We rose at signal given, and formed a ring
And, hand in hand, danced round and round the board ;
All hearts were open, every tongue was loud   401
With amity and glee ; we bore a name
Honored in France, the name of Englishmen,
And hospitably did they give us hail,
As their forerunners in a glorious course ;
And round and round the board we danced again.
With these blithe friends our voyage we renewed
At early dawn.   The monastery bells
Made a sweet jingling in our youthful ears ;
The rapid river flowing without noise,   410
And each uprising or receding spire
Spake with a sense of peace, at intervals

Touching the heart amid the boisterous crew
By whom we were encompassed.   Taking leave
Of this glad throng, foot-travellers side by side,
Measuring our steps in quiet, we pursued
Our journey, and ere twice the sun had set
Beheld the Convent of Chartreuse, and there
Rested within an awful *solitude.*
Yes ; for even then no other than a place   420
Of soul-affecting *solitude* appeared
That far-famed region, though our eyes had seen,
As toward the sacred mansion we advanced,
Arms flashing, and a military glare
Of riotous men commissioned to expel
The blameless inmates, and belike subvert
The frame of social being, which so long
Had bodied forth the ghostliness of things
In silence visible and perpetual calm.
— " Stay, stay your sacrilegious hands ! " — The voice
Was Nature's, uttered from her Alpine throne ;   431
I heard it then and seem to hear it now —   .
" Your impious work forbear : perish what may,
Let this one temple last, be this one spot
Of earth devoted to eternity ! "
She ceased to speak, but while St. Bruno's pines
Waved their dark tops, not silent as they waved,
And while below, along their several beds,
Murmured the sister streams of Life and Death,
Thus by conflicting passions pressed, my heart   440
Responded : " Honor to the patriot's zeal !
Glory and hope to new-born Liberty !
Hail to the mighty projects of the time !

Discerning sword that Justice wields, do thou
Go forth and prosper; and, ye purging fires,
Up to the loftiest towers of Pride ascend,
Fanned by the breath of angry Providence.
But oh! if Past and Future be the wings
On whose support harmoniously conjoined
Moves the great spirit of human knowledge, spare   450.
These courts of mystery, where a step advanced
Between the portals of the shadowy rocks
Leaves far behind Life's treacherous vanities,
For penitential tears and trembling hopes
Exchanged — to equalize in God's pure sight
Monarch and peasant; be the house redeemed
With its unworldly votaries, for the sake
Of conquest over sense, hourly achieved
Through faith and meditative reason, resting
Upon the word of heaven-imparted truth,   460
Calmly triumphant; and for humbler claim
Of that imaginative impulse sent
From these majestic floods, yon shining cliffs,
The untransmuted shapes of many worlds,
Cerulean ether's pure inhabitants,
These forests unapproachable by death,
That shall endure as long as man endures,
To think, to hope, to worship, and to feel,
To struggle, to be lost within himself
In trepidation, from the blank abyss   470
To look with bodily eyes, and be consoled."
Not seldom since that moment have I wished
That thou, O Friend! the trouble or the calm
Hadst shared, when, from profane regards apart,

In sympathetic reverence we trod
The floors of those dim cloisters, till that hour,
From their foundation, strangers to the presence
Of unrestricted and unthinking man.
Abroad how cheeringly the sunshine lay
Upon the open lawns !   Vallombre's groves   480
Entering, we fed the soul with darkness ; thence
Issued, and with uplifted eyes beheld,
In different quarters of the bending sky,
The cross of Jesus stand erect, as if
Hands of angelic powers had fixed it there,
Memorial reverenced by a thousand storms ;
Yet then, from the undiscriminating sweep
And rage of one State-whirlwind, insecure.

'Tis not my present purpose to retrace
That variegated journey step by step.   490
A march it was of military speed,
And Earth did change her images and forms
Before us, fast as clouds are changed in heaven
Day after day, up early and down late,
From hill to vale we dropped, from vale to hill
Mounted — from province on to province swept,
Keen hunters in a chase of fourteen weeks,
Eager as birds of prey, or as a ship
Upon the stretch, when winds are blowing fair :
Sweet coverts did we cross of pastoral life,   500
Enticing valleys, greeted them and left
Too soon, while yet the very flash and gleam
Of salutation were not passed away.
Oh ! sorrow for the youth who could have seen

Unchastened, unsubdued, unawed, unraised
To patriarchal dignity of mind,
And pure simplicity of wish and will,
Those sanctified abodes of peaceful man,
Pleased (though to hardship born, and compassed round
With danger, varying as the seasons change)   510
Pleased with his daily task, or, if not pleased,
Contented, from the moment that the dawn
(Ah ! surely not without attendant gleams
Of soul-illumination) calls him forth
To industry, by glistenings flung on rocks,
Whose evening shadows lead him to repose.

Well might a stranger look with bounding heart
Down on a green recess, the first I saw
Of those deep haunts, an aboriginal vale,
Quiet and lorded over and possessed   520
By naked huts, wood-built, and sown like tents
Or Indian cabins over the fresh lawns
And by the river side.
                            That very day
From a bare ridge we also first beheld
Unveiled the summit of Mont Blanc, and grieved
To have a soulless image on the eye
That had usurped upon a living thought
That never more could be.   The wondrous Vale
Of Chamouny stretched far below, and soon
With its dumb cataracts and streams of ice,   530
A motionless array of mighty waves,
Five rivers broad and vast, made rich amends,
And reconciled us to realities ;

There small birds warble from the leafy trees,
The eagle soars high in the element,
There doth the reaper bind the yellow sheaf,
The maiden spread the haycock in the sun,
While Winter, like a well-tamed lion walks,
Descending from the mountain to make sport
Among the cottages by beds of flowers.   540

Whate'er in this wide circuit we beheld,
Or heard, was fitted to our unripe state
Of intellect and heart.   With such a book
Before our eyes, we could not choose but read
Lessons of genuine brotherhood, the plain
And universal reason of mankind,
The truths of young and old.   Nor, side by side
Pacing, two social pilgrims, or alone
Each with his humor, could we fail to abound
In dreams and fictions, pensively composed :   550
Dejection taken up for pleasure's sake,
And gilded sympathies, the willow wreath,
And sober posies of funereal flowers,
Gathered among those solitudes sublime
From formal gardens of the lady Sorrow,
Did sweeten many a meditative hour.

Yet still in me with those soft luxuries
Mixed something of stern mood, an underthirst
Of vigor seldom utterly allayed :
And from that source how different a sadness   560
Would issue, let one incident make known.

When from the Vallais we had turned, and clomb
Along the Simplon's steep and rugged road,
Following a band of muleteers, we reached
A halting-place, where all together took
Their noon-tide meal.   Hastily rose our guide,
Leaving us at the board ; awhile we lingered,
Then paced the beaten downward way that led
Right to a rough stream's edge, and there broke off ;
The only track now visible was one   570
That from the torrent's further brink held forth
Conspicuous invitation to ascend
A lofty mountain.   After brief delay
Crossing the unbridged stream, that road we took,
And clomb with eagerness, till anxious fears
Intruded, for we failed to overtake
Our comrades gone before.   By fortunate chance,
While every moment added doubt to doubt,
A peasant met us, from whose mouth we learned
That to the spot which had perplexed us first,   580
We must descend, and there should find the road,
Which in the stony channel of the stream
Lay a few steps, and then along its banks :
And that our future course, all plain to sight,
Was downwards, with the current of that stream.
Loth to believe what we so grieved to hear,
For still we had hopes that pointed to the clouds,
We questioned him again, and yet again ;
But every word that from the peasant's lips
Came in reply, translated by our feelings,   590
Ended in this, — *that we had crossed the Alps.*

Imagination — here the Power so-called
Through sad incompetence of human speech,
That awful Power rose from the mind's abyss
Like an unfathered vapor that enwraps,
At once, some lonely traveller.   I was lost;
Halted without an effort to break through;
But to my conscious soul I now can say —
" I recognize thy glory;" in such strength
Of usurpation, when the light of sense   600
Goes out, but with a flash that has revealed
The invisible world, doth greatness make abode,
There harbors; whether we be young or old,
Our destiny, our being's heart and home,
Is with infinitude, and only there;
With hope it is, hope that can never die,
Effort, and expectation, and desire,
And something evermore about to be.
Under such banners militant, the soul
Seeks for no trophies, struggles for no spoils   610
That may attest her prowess, blest in thoughts
That are their own perfection and reward,
Strong in herself and in beatitude
That hides her, like the mighty flood of Nile
Poured from his fount of Abyssinian clouds
To fertilize the whole Egyptian plain.

The melancholy slackening that ensued
Upon those tidings by the peasant given
Was soon dislodged.   Downwards we hurried fast,
And, with the half-shaped road which we had missed,
Entered a narrow chasm.   The brook and road   621

Were fellow-travellers in this gloomy strait,
And with them did we journey several hours
At a slow pace. The immeasurable height
Of woods decaying, never to be decayed,
The stationary blasts of waterfalls,
And in the narrow rent at every turn
Winds thwarting winds, bewildered and forlorn,
The torrents shooting from the clear blue sky,
The rocks that muttered close upon our ears,   630
Black drizzling crags that spake by the wayside
As if a voice were in them, the sick sight
And giddy prospect of the raving stream,
The unfettered clouds and region of the Heavens,
Tumult and peace, the darkness and the light —
Were all like workings of one mind, the features
Of the same face, blossoms upon one tree ;
Characters of the great Apocalypse,
The types and symbols of Eternity,
Of first, and last, and midst, and without end.   640

    That night our lodging was a house that stood
Alone within the valley, at a point
Where, tumbling from aloft, a torrent swelled
The rapid stream whose margin we had trod ;
A dreary mansion, large beyond all need,
With high and spacious rooms, deafened and stunned
By noise of waters, making innocent sleep
Lie melancholy among weary bones.

    Uprisen betimes, our journey we renewed,
Led by the stream, ere noon-day magnified   650

Into a lordly river, broad and deep,
Dimpling along in silent majesty,
With mountains for its neighbors, and in view
Of distant mountains and their snowy tops,
And thus proceeding to Locarno's Lake,
Fit resting-place for such a visitant.
Locarno! spreading out in width like Heaven,
How dost thou cleave to the poetic heart,
Bask in the sunshine of the memory;
And Como! thou, a treasure whom the earth
Keeps to herself, confined as in a depth
Of Abyssinian privacy.   I spake
Of thee, thy chestnut woods, and garden plots
Of Indian corn tended by dark-eyed maids;
Thy lofty steeps, and pathways roofed with vines,
Winding from house to house, from town to town,
Sole link that binds them to each other; walks,
League after league, and cloistral avenues,
Where silence dwells if music be not there:
While yet a youth undisciplined in verse,
Through fond ambition of that hour I strove
To chant your praise; nor can approach you now
Ungreeted by a more melodious Song,
Where tones of Nature smoothed by learned Art
May flow in lasting current.   Like a breeze
Or sunbeam over your domain I passed
In motion without pause; but ye have left
Your beauty with me, a serene accord
Of forms and colors, passive, yet endowed
In their submissiveness with power as sweet
And gracious, almost might I dare to say,

As virtue is, or goodness ; sweet as love,
Or the remembrance of a generous deed,
Or mildest visitations of pure thought,
When God, the giver of all joy, is thanked
Religiously, in silent blessedness ;
Sweet as this last herself, for such it is.

With those delightful pathways we advanced,
For two days' space, in presence of the Lake,
That, stretching far among the Alps, assumed   690
A character more stern.   The second night,
From sleep awakened, and misled by sound
Of the church clock telling the hours with strokes
Whose import then we had not learned, we rose
By moonlight, doubting not that day was nigh,
And that meanwhile by no uncertain path,
Along the winding margin of the lake,
Led, as before, we should behold the scene
Hushed in profound repose.   We left the town
Of Gravedona with this hope ; but soon   700
Were lost, bewildered among woods immense,
And on a rock sate down, to wait for day.
An open place it was, and overlooked,
From high, the sullen water far beneath,
On which a dull red image of the moon
Lay bedded, changing oftentimes its form
Like an uneasy snake.   From hour to hour
We sate and sate, wondering, as if the night
Had been ensnared by witchcraft.   On the rock
At last we stretched our weary limbs for sleep,   710
But *could not* sleep, tormented by the stings

Of insects, which, with noise like that of noon,
Filled all the woods : the cry of unknown birds ;
The mountains more by blackness visible
And their own size, than any outward light ;
The breathless wilderness of clouds ; the clock
That told with unintelligible voice,
The widely parted hours ; the noise of streams,
And sometimes rustling motions nigh at hand,
That did not leave us free from personal fear ;   720
And, lastly, the withdrawing moon, that set
Before us, while she still was high in heaven ;—
These were our food ; and such a summer's night
Followed that pair of golden days that shed
On Como's Lake, and all that round it lay,
Their fairest, softest, happiest influence.

　　But here I must break off, and bid farewell
To days, each offering some new sight, or fraught
With some untried adventure, in a course
Prolonged till sprinklings of autumnal snow   730
Checked our unwearied steps.   Let this alone
Be mentioned as a parting word, that not
In hollow exultation, dealing out
Hyperboles of praise comparative ;
Not rich one moment to be poor forever ;
Not prostrate, overborne, as if the mind
Herself were nothing, a mere pensioner
On outward forms — did we in presence stand
Of that magnificent region.   On the front
Of this whole Song is written that my heart   740
Must, in such Temple, needs have offered up

A different worship.   Finally, whate'er
I saw, or heard, or felt, was but a stream
That flowed into a kindred stream ; a gale,
Confederate with the current of the soul,
To speed my voyage ; every sound or sight,
In its degree of power, administered
To grandeur or to tenderness, — to the one
Directly, but to tender thoughts by means
Less often instantaneous in effect ;   750
Led me to these by paths that, in the main,
Were more circuitous, but not less sure
Duly to reach the point marked out by Heaven.

Oh, most belovèd Friend ! a glorious time,
A happy time that was ; triumphant looks
Were then the common language of all eyes ;
As if awaked from sleep, the Nations hailed
Their great expectancy : the fife of war
Was then a spirit-stirring sound indeed,
A blackbird's whistle in a budding grove.   760
We left the Swiss exulting in the fate
Of their near neighbors ; and, when shortening fast
Our pilgrimage, nor distant far from home,
We crossed the Brabant armies on the fret
For battle in the cause of Liberty.
A stripling, scarcely of the household then
Of social life, I looked upon these things
As from a distance ; heard, and saw, and felt,
Was touched, but with no intimate concern ;
I seemed to move along them, as a bird   770
Moves through the air, or as a fish pursues

Its sport, or feeds in its proper element ;
I wanted not that joy, I did not need
Such help ; the ever-living universe,
Turn where I might, was opening out its glories,
And the independent spirit of pure youth
Called forth, at every season, new delights
Spread round my steps like sunshine o'er green fields.

BOOK SEVENTH.

RESIDENCE IN LONDON.

Six changeful years have vanished since I first
Poured out (saluted by that quickening breeze
Which met me issuing from the City's walls)
A glad preamble to this Verse : I sang
Aloud, with fervor irresistible
Of short-lived transport, like a torrent bursting,
From a black thunder-cloud, down Scafell's side
To rush and disappear.   But soon broke forth
(So willed the Muse) a less impetuous stream,
That flowed awhile with unabating strength,   10
Then stopped for years ; not audible again
Before last primrose-time.   Belovèd Friend !
The assurance which then cheered some heavy thoughts
On thy departure to a foreign land
Has failed ; too slowly moves the promised work,
Through the whole summer have I been at rest,
Partly from voluntary holiday,
And part through outward hindrance.   But I heard,
After the hour of sunset yester-even,
Sitting within doors between light and dark,   20
A choir of red-breasts gathered somewhere near

My threshold, — minstrels from the distant woods
Sent in on Winter's service, to announce,
With preparation artful and benign,
That the rough lord had left the surly North
On his accustomed journey.   The delight,
Due to his timely notice, unawares
Smote me, and, listening, I in whispers said,
"Ye heartsome Choristers, ye and I will be
Associates, and, unscared by blustering winds,   30
Will chant together."   Thereafter, as the shades
Of twilight deepened, going forth, I spied
A glow-worm underneath a dusky plume
Or canopy of yet unwithered fern,
Clear-shining, like a hermit's taper seen
Through a thick forest.   Silence touched me here
No less than sound had done before ; the child
Of Summer, lingering, shining, by herself,
The voiceless worm on the unfrequented hills,
Seemed sent on the same errand with the choir   40
Of Winter that had warbled at my door,
And the whole year breathed tenderness and love.

The last night's genial feeling overflowed
Upon this morning, and my favorite grove,
Tossing in sunshine its dark bough aloft,
As if to make the strong wind visible,
Wakes in me agitations like its own,
A spirit friendly to the Poet's task,
Which we will now resume with lively hope,
Nor checked by aught of tamer argument   50
That lies before us, needful to be told.

Returned from that excursion, soon I bade
Farewell forever to the sheltered seats
Of gownèd students, quitted hall and bower,
And every comfort of that privileged ground,
Well pleased to pitch a vagrant tent among
The unfenced regions of society.

    Yet, undetermined to what course of life
I should adhere, and seeming to possess
A little space of intermediate time   60
At full command, to London first I turned
In no disturbance of excessive hope,
By personal ambition unenslaved,
Frugal as there was need, and, though self-willed,
From dangerous passions free.   Three years had flown
Since I had felt in heart and soul the shock
Of the huge town's first presence, and had paced
Her endless streets, a transient visitant :
Now, fixed amid that concourse of mankind
Where Pleasure whirls about incessantly,   70
And life and labor seem but one, I filled
An idler's place ; an idler well content
To have a house (what matter for a home ?)
That owned him ; living cheerfully abroad
With unchecked fancy ever on the stir,
And all my young affections out of doors.

    There was a time when whatsoe'er is feigned
Of airy palaces, and gardens built
By Genii of romance : or hath in grave
Authentic history been set forth of Rome,   80

Alcairo, Babylon, or Persepolis;
Or given upon report by pilgrim friars,
Of golden cities ten months' journey deep
Among Tartarian wilds — fell short, far short,
Of what my fond simplicity believed
And thought of London — held me by a chain
Less strong of wonder and obscure delight.
Whether the bolt of childhood's Fancy shot
For me beyond its ordinary mark,
'Twere vain to ask; but in our flock of boys   90
Was One, a cripple from his birth, whom chance
Summoned from school to London; fortunate
And envied traveller! When the Boy returned,
After short absence, curiously I scanned
His mien and person, nor was free, in sooth,
From disappointment, not to find some change
In look and air, from that new region brought,
As if from Fairy-land. Much I questioned him;
And every word he uttered, on my ears
Fell flatter than a cagèd parrot's note,   100
That answers unexpectedly awry,
And mocks the prompter's listening. Marvellous things
Had vanity (quick Spirit that appears
Almost as deeply seated and as strong
In a Child's heart as fear itself) conceived
For my enjoyment. Would that I could now
Recall what then I pictured to myself,
Of mitred Prelates, Lords in ermine clad,
The King, and the King's Palace, and, not last,
Nor least, Heaven bless him! the renowned Lord Mayor:
Dreams not unlike to those which once begat   111

A change of purpose in young Whittington,
When he, a friendless and a drooping boy,
Sate on a stone, and heard the bells speak out
Articulate music. Above all, one thought
Baffled my understanding : how men lived
Even next-door neighbors, as we say, yet still
Strangers, not knowing each the other's name.

O, wondrous power of words, by simple faith
Licensed to take the meaning that we love ! 120
Vauxhall and Ranelagh ! I then had heard
Of your green groves, and wilderness of lamps
Dimming the stars, and fireworks magical,
And gorgeous ladies, under splendid domes,
Floating in dance, or warbling high in air
The songs of spirits ! Nor had Fancy fed
With less delight upon that other class
Of marvels, broad-day wonders permanent :
The River proudly bridged ; the dizzy top
And Whispering Gallery of St. Paul's ; the tombs 130
Of Westminster : the Giants of Guildhall ;
Bedlam, and those carved maniacs at the gates,
Perpetually recumbent ; Statues — man,
And the horse under him — in gilded pomp
Adorning flowery gardens, 'mid vast squares ;
The Monument, and that Chamber of the Tower
Where England's sovereigns sit in long array,
Their steeds bestriding, — every mimic shape
Cased in the gleaming mail the monarch wore,
Whether for gorgeous tournament addressed, 140
Or life or death upon the battle-field.

Those bold imaginations in due time
Had vanished, leaving others in their stead:
And now I looked upon the living scene;
Familiarly perused it; oftentimes,
In spite of strongest disappointment, pleased
Through courteous self-submission, as a tax
Paid to the object by prescriptive right.

   Rise up, thou monstrous ant-hill on the plain
Of a too busy world!   Before me flow,   150
Thou endless stream of men and moving things!
Thy every-day appearance, as it strikes —
With wonder heightened, or sublimed by awe —
On strangers, of all ages; the quick dance
Of colors, lights, and forms; the deafening din;
The comers and the goers face to face,
Face after face; the string of dazzling wares,
Shop after shop, with symbols, blazoned names,
And all the tradesman's honors overhead:
Here, fronts of houses, like a title-page,   160
With letters huge inscribed from top to toe,
Stationed above the door, like guardian saints;
There, allegoric shapes, female or male,
Or physiognomies of real men,
Land-warriors, kings, or admirals of the sea,
Boyle, Shakespeare, Newton, or the attractive head
Of some quack-doctor, famous in his day.

   Meanwhile the roar continues, till at length,
Escaped as from an enemy, we turn
Abruptly into some sequestered nook,   170

Still as a sheltered place when winds blow loud !
At leisure, thence, through tracts of thin resort,
And sights and sounds that come at intervals,
We take our way.   A raree-show is here,
With children gathered round ; another street
Presents a company of dancing dogs,
Or dromedary, with an antic pair
Of monkeys on his back ; a minstrel band
Of Savoyards ; or, single and alone,
An English ballad-singer.   Private courts,   180
Gloomy as coffins, and unsightly lanes
Thrilled by some female vendor's scream, belike
The very shrillest of all London cries,
May then entangle our impatient steps ;
Conducted through those labyrinths, unawares,
To privileged regions and inviolate,
Where from their airy lodge studious lawyers
Look out on waters, walks, and gardens green.

Thence back into the throng, until we reach,
Following the tide that slackens by degrees,   190
Some half-frequented scene, where wider streets
Bring straggling breezes of suburban air.
Here files of ballads dangle from dead walls ;
Advertisements, of giant-size, from high
Press forward, in all colors, on the sight ;
These bold in conscious merit, lower down ;
That, fronted with a most imposing word,
Is, peradventure, one in masquerade.
As on the broadening causeway we advance,
Behold, turned upwards, a face hard and strong   200

In lineaments, and red with over-toil.
'Tis one encountered here and everywhere ;
A travelling cripple, by the trunk cut short,
And stumping on his arms.   In sailor's garb
Another lies at length, beside a range
Of well-formed characters, with chalk inscribed
Upon the smooth flat stones : the Nurse is here,
The Bachelor, that loves to sun himself,
The military Idler, and the Dame,
That field-ward takes her walk with decent steps.   210

Now homeward through the thickening hubbub, where
See, among less distinguishable shapes,
The begging scavenger, with hat in hand ;
The Italian, as he thrids his way with care,
Steadying, far-seen, a frame of images
Upon his head ; with basket at his breast
The Jew ; the stately and slow-moving Turk,
With freight of slippers piled beneath his arm !

Enough ; — the mighty concourse I surveyed
With no unthinking mind, well pleased to note   220
Among the crowd all specimens of man,
Through all the colors which the sun bestows,
And every character of form and face :
The Swede, the Russian ; from the genial south,
The Frenchman and the Spaniard ; from remote
America, the Hunter-Indian ; Moors,
Malays, Lascars, the Tartar, the Chinese,
And Negro Ladies in white muslin gowns.

At leisure, then I viewed, from day to day,
The spectacles within doors, — birds and beasts   230
Of every nature, and strange plants convened
From every clime ; and, next, those sights that ape
The absolute presence of reality,
Expressing, as in mirror, sea and land,
And what earth is, and what she has to show.
I do not here allude to subtlest craft,
By means refined attaining purest ends,   .
But imitations, fondly made in plain
Confession of man's weakness and his loves.
Whether the Painter, whose ambitious skill   240
Submits to nothing less than taking in
A whole horizon's circuit, do with power,
Like that of angels or commissioned spirits,
Fix us upon some lofty pinnacle,
Or in a ship on waters, with a world
Of life, and life-like mockery beneath,
Above, behind, far stretching and before ;
Or more mechanic artist represent
By scale exact, in model, wood or clay,
From blended colors also borrowing help,   250
Some miniature of famous spots or things, —
St. Peter's Church ; or, more aspiring aim,
In microscopic vision, Rome herself ;
Or, haply, some choice rural haunt, — the Falls
Of Tivoli ; and, high upon that steep,
The Sibyl's mouldering Temple ! every tree,
Villa, or cottage, lurking among rocks
Throughout the landscape ; tuft, stone, scratch minute—
All that the traveller sees when he is there.

Add to these exhibitions, mute and still,   260
Others of wider scope, where living men,
Music, and shifting pantomimic scenes,
Diversified the allurement.   Need I fear
To mention by its name, as in degree,
Lowest of these and humblest in attempt,
Yet richly graced with honors of her own,
Half-rural Sadler's Wells?   Though at that time
Intolerant, as is the way of youth
Unless itself be pleased, here more than once
Taking my seat, I saw (nor blush to add,   270
With ample recompense)· giants and dwarfs,
Clowns, conjurers, posture-masters, harlequins,
Amid the uproar of the rabblement,
Perform their feats.   Nor was it mean delight
To watch crude Nature work in untaught minds;
To note the laws and progress of belief;
Though obstinate on this way, yet on that
How willingly we travel, and how far !
To have, for instance, brought upon the scene
The champion, Jack the Giant-killer :   Lo !   280
He dons his coat of darkness ; on the stage
Walks, and achieves his wonders, from the eye
Of living Mortal covert, " as the moon
Hid in her vacant interlunar cave."
Delusion bold ! and how can it be wrought?
The garb he wears is black as death, the word
"*Invisible*" flames forth upon his chest.

Here, too, were " forms and pressures of the time,"
Rough, bold, as Grecian comedy displayed

When Art was young ; dramas of living men,   290
And recent things yet warm with life ; a sea-fight,
Shipwreck, or some domestic incident
Divulged by Truth and magnified by Fame ;
Such as the daring brotherhood of late
Set forth, too serious theme for that light place —
I mean, O distant Friend ! a story drawn
From our own ground, — The Maid of Buttermere,
And how, unfaithful to a virtuous wife,
Deserted and deceived, the Spoiler came
And wooed the artless daughter of the hills,   300
And wedded her, in cruel mockery
Of love and marriage bonds.   These words to thee
Must needs bring back the moment when we first,
Ere the broad world rang with the maiden's name,
Beheld her serving at the cottage inn
Both stricken, as she entered or withdrew,
With admiration of her modest mien
And carriage, marked by unexampled grace.
We since that time not unfamiliarly
Have seen her, her discretion have observed,   310
Her just opinions, delicate reserve,
Her patience, and humility of mind
Unspoiled by commendation and the excess
Of public notice — an offensive light
To a meek spirit suffering inwardly.

From this memorial tribute to my theme
I was returning, when, with sundry forms
Commingled — shapes which met me in the way
That we must tread — thy image rose again,

Maiden of Buttermere !   She lives in peace   320
Upon the spot where she was born and reared ;
Without contamination doth she live
In quietness, without anxiety :
Beside the mountain chapel, sleeps in earth
Her new-born infant, fearless as a lamb
That, thither driven from some unsheltered place,
Rests underneath the little rock-like pile
When storms are raging.   Happy are they both —
Mother and child ! — These feelings, in themselves
Trite, do yet seem scarcely so when I think   330
On those ingenuous moments of our youth
Ere we have learnt by use to slight the crimes
And sorrows of the world.   Those simple days
Are now my theme : and, foremost of the scenes
Which yet survive in memory, appears
One, at whose centre sate a lovely Boy,
A sportive infant, who, for six months' space,
Not more, had been of age to deal about
Articulate prattle — Child as beautiful
As ever clung around a mother's neck,   340
Or father fondly gazed upon with pride.
There, too, conspicuous for stature tall
And large dark eyes, beside her infant stood
The mother ; but, upon her cheeks diffused,
False tints too well accorded with the glare
From play-house lustres thrown without reserve
On every object near.   The Boy had been
The pride and pleasure of all lookers-on
In whatsoever place, but seemed in this
A sort of alien scattered from the clouds.   350

Of lusty vigor, more than infantine
He was in limb, in chéek a summer rose
Just three parts blown — a cottage-child — if e'er,
By cottage-door on breezy mountain side,
Or in some sheltering vale, was seen a babe
By Nature's gifts so favored.   Upon a board
Decked with refreshments had this child been placed,
His little stage in the vast theatre,
And there he sate surrounded with a throng
Of chance spectators, chiefly dissolute men   360
And shameless women, treated and caressed ;
Ate, drank, and with the fruit and glasses played,
While oaths and laughter and indecent speech
Were rife about him as the songs of birds
Contending after showers.   The mother now
Is fading out of memory, but I see
The lovely Boy as I beheld him then
Among the wretched and the falsely gay,
Like one of those who walked with hair unsinged
Amid the fiery furnace.   Charms and spells   370
Muttered on black and spiteful instigation
Have stopped, as some believe, the kindliest growths.
Ah, with how different spirit might a prayer
Have been preferred, that this fair creature, checked
By special privilege of Nature's love,
Should in his childhood be detained forever !
But with its universal freight the tide
Hath rolled along, and this bright innocent,
Mary ! may now have lived till he could look
With envy on thy nameless babe that sleeps,   380
Beside the mountain chapel, undisturbed.

Four rapid years had scarcely then been told
Since, travelling southward from our pastoral hills,
I heard, and for the first time in my life,
The voice of woman utter blasphemy —
Saw woman as she is, to open shame
Abandoned, and the pride of public vice;
I shuddered, for a barrier seemed at once
Thrown in that from humanity divorced
Humanity, splitting the race of man
In twain, yet leaving the same outward form.
Distress of mind ensued upon the sight,
And ardent meditation.   Later years
Brought to such a spectacle a milder sadness,
Feelings of pure commiseration, grief
For the individual and the overthrow
Of her soul's beauty; farther I was then
But seldom led, or wished to go; in truth
The sorrow of the passion stopped me there.

But let me now, less moved, in order take
Our argument.   Enough is said to show
How casual incidents of real life,
Observed where pastime only had been sought,
Outweighed, or put to flight, the set events
And measured passions of the stage, albeit
By Siddons trod in the fulness of her power.
Yet was the theatre my dear delight;
The very gilding, lamps and painted scrolls,
And all the mean upholstery of the place,
Wanted not animation, when the tide
Of pleasure ebbed but to return as fast

With the ever-shifting figures of the scene,
Solemn or gay : whether some beauteous dame,
Advanced in radiance through a deep recess
Of thick entangled forest, like the moon
Opening the clouds ; or sovereign king, announced
With flourishing trumpet, came in full-blown state
Of the world's greatness, winding round with train
Of courtiers, banners, and a length of guards ;
Or captive led in abject weeds, and jingling   420
His slender manacles ; or romping girl,
Bounced, leapt, and pawed the air ; or mumbling sire,
A scare-crow pattern of old age dressed up
In all the tatters of infirmity
All loosely put together, hobbled in,
Stumping upon a cane with which he smites,
From time to time, the solid boards, and makes them
Prate somewhat loudly of the whereabout
Of one so overloaded with his years.
But what of this ! the laugh, the grin, grimace,   430
The antics striving to outstrip each other,
Were all received, the least of them not lost,
With an unmeasured welcome.   Through the night,
Between the show, and many-headed mass
Of the spectators, and each several nook
Filled with its fray or brawl, how eagerly
And with what flashes, as it were, the mind
Turned this way — that way ! sportive and alert
And watchful, as a kitten when at play,
While winds are eddying round her, among straws   440
And rustling leaves.   Enchanting age and sweet !
Romantic almost, looked at through a space,

How small, of intervening years ! For then,
Though surely no mean progress had been made
In meditations holy and sublime,
Yet something of a girlish child-like gloss
Of novelty survived for scenes like these ;
Enjoyment haply handed down from times
When at a country-playhouse, some rude barn
Tricked out for that proud use, if I perchance   450
Caught, on a summer evening through a chink
In the old wall, an unexpected glimpse
Of daylight, the bare thought of where I was
Gladdened me more than if I had been led
Into a dazzling cavern of romance,
Crowded with Genii busy among works
Not to be looked at by the common sun.

The matter that detains us now may seem
To many, neither dignified enough
Nor arduous, yet will not be scorned by them   460
Who, looking inward, have observed the ties
That bind the perishable hours of life
Each to the other, and the curious props
By which the world of memory and thought
Exists and is sustained. More lofty themes,
Such as at least do wear a prouder face,
Solicit our regard ; but when I think
Of these, I feel the imaginative power
Languish within me ; even then it slept,
When, pressed by tragic sufferings, the heart   470
Was more than full ; amid my sobs and tears
It slept, even in the pregnant season of youth.

For though I was most passionately moved
And yielded to all changes of the scene
With an obsequious promptness, yet the storm
Passed not beyond the suburbs of the mind;
Save when realities of act and mien,
The incarnation of the spirits that move
In harmony amid the Poet's world,
Rose to ideal grandeur, or called forth   480
By power of contrast, made me recognize,
As at a glance, the things which I had shaped,
And yet not shaped, had seen and scarcely seen,
When, having closed the mighty Shakespeare's **page**,
I mused, and thought, and felt, in solitude.

Pass we from entertainments, that are such
Professedly, to others titled higher,
Yet, in the estimate of youth at least,
More near akin to those than names imply, —
I mean the brawls of lawyers in their courts   490
Before the ermined judge, or that great stage
Where senators, tongue-favored men, perform,
Admired and envied.   Oh! the beating heart,
When one among the prime of these rose up,
One, of whose name from childhood we had heard
Familiarly, a household term, like those,
The Bedfords, Glosters, Salsburys, of old
Whom the fifth Harry talks of.   Silence! hush!
This is no trifler, no short-flighted wit,
No stammerer of a minute, painfully   500
Delivered.   No! the Orator hath yoked
The Hours, like young Aurora, to his car:

Thrice welcome Presence ! how can patience e'er
Grow weary of attending on a track
That kindles with such glory !   All are charmed,
Astonished ; like a hero in romance,
He winds away his never-ending horn ;
Words follow words, sense seems to follow sense ;
What memory and what logic ! till the strain
Transcendent, superhuman as it seemed,   510
Grows tedious even in a young man's ear.

Genius of Burke ! forgive the pen seduced
By specious wonders, and too slow to tell
Of what the ingenuous, what bewildered men,
Beginning to mistrust their boastful guides,
And wise men, willing to grow wiser, caught,
Rapt auditors ! from thy most eloquent tongue —
Now mute, forever mute in the cold grave.
I see him, — old, but vigorous in age, —
Stand like an oak whose stag-horn branches start   520
Out of its leafy brow, the more to awe
The younger brethren of the grove.   But some —
While he forewarns, denounces, launches forth,
Against all systems built on abstract rights,
Keen ridicule ; the majesty proclaims
Of Institutes and Laws, hallowed by time ;
Declares the vital power of social ties
Endeared by Custom ; and with high disdain,
Exploding upstart Theory, insists
Upon the allegiance to which men are born —   530
Some — say at once a froward multitude —
Murmur (for truth is hated, where not loved)

As the winds fret within the Æolian cave,
Galled by their monarch's chain.   The times were big
With ominous change, which, night by night, provoked
Keen struggles, and black clouds of passion raised ;
But memorable moments intervened,
When Wisdom, like the Goddess from Jove's brain,
Broke forth in armor of resplendent words,
Startling the Synod.   Could a youth, and one   540
In ancient story versed, whose breast had heaved
Under the weight of classic eloquence,
Sit, see, and hear, unthankful, uninspired?

    Nor did the Pulpit's oratory fail
To achieve its higher triumph.   Not unfelt
Were its admonishments, nor lightly heard
The awful truths delivered thence by tongues
Endowed by various power to search the soul ;
Yet ostentation, domineering, oft
Poured forth harangues, how sadly out of place ! — 550
There have I seen a comely bachelor,
Fresh from a toilette of two hours, ascend
His rostrum, with seraphic glance look up,
And, in a tone elaborately low
Beginning, lead his voice through many a maze
A minuet course ; and, winding up his mouth,
From time to time, into an orifice
Most delicate, a lurking eyelet, small,
And only not invisible, again
Open it out, diffusing thence a smile   560
Of rapt irradiation, exquisite.
Meanwhile the Evangelists, Isaiah, Job,

Moses, and he who penned, the other day,
The death of Abel, Shakespeare, and the Bard
Whose genius spangled o'er a gloomy theme
With fancies thick as his inspiring stars,
And Ossian (doubt not — 'tis the naked truth)
Summoned from streamy Morven — each and all
Would, in their turns, lend ornaments and flowers
To entwine the crook of eloquence that helped   570
This pretty Shepherd, pride of all the plains,
To rule and guide his captivated flock.

I glance but at a few conspicuous marks,
Leaving a thousand others, that, in hall,
Court, theatre, conventicle, or shop,
In public room or private, park or street,
Each fondly reared on his own pedestal,
Looked out for admiration.   Folly, vice,
Extravagance in gesture, mien, and dress,
And all the strife of singularity,   580
Lies to the ear, and lies to every sense —
Of these, and of the living shapes they wear,
There is no end.   Such candidates for regard,
Although well pleased to be where they were found,
I did not hunt after, nor greatly prize,
Nor made unto myself a secret boast
Of reading them with quick and curious eye ;
But, as a common produce, things that are
To-day, to-morrow will be, took of them
Such willing note as, on some errand bound   590
That asks not speed, a traveller might bestow

On sea-shells that bestrew the sandy beach,
Or daisies swarming through the fields of June.

But foolishness and madness in parade,
Though most at home in this their dear domain,
Are scattered everywhere, no rarities,
Even to the rudest novice of the Schools.
Me, rather, it employed, to note, and keep
In memory, those individual sights
Of courage, or integrity, or truth,   600
Or tenderness, which there, set off by foil,
Appeared more touching.   One will I select ;
A Father — for he bore that sacred name —
Him saw I, sitting in an open square,
Upon a corner-stone of that low wall,
Wherein were fixed the iron pales that fenced
A spacious grass-plot ; there, in silence, sate
This One Man, with a sickly babe outstretched
Upon his knee, whom he had thither brought
For sunshine, and to breathe the fresher air.   610
Of those who passed, and me who looked at him,
He took no heed ; but in his brawny arms
(The Artificer was to the elbow bare,
And from his work this moment had been stolen)
He held the child, and, bending over it,
As if he were afraid both of the sun
And of the air, which he had come to seek,
Eyed the poor babe with love unutterable.

As the black storm upon the mountain top
Sets off the sunbeam in the valley, so   620
That huge fermenting mass of human-kind

Serves as a solid back-ground, or relief,
To single forms and objects, whence they draw,
For feeling and contemplative regard,
More than inherent liveliness and power.
How oft, amid those overflowing streets,
Have I gone forward with the crowd, and said
Unto myself, " The face of every one
That passes by me is a mystery ! " ·
Thus have I looked, nor ceased to look, oppressed   630
By thoughts of what and whither, when and how,
Until the shapes before my eyes became
A second-sight procession, such as glides
Over still mountains, or appears in dreams ;
And once, far-travelled in such mood, beyond
The reach of common indication, lost
Amid the moving pageant, I was smitten
Abruptly, with the view (a sight not rare)
Of a blind Beggar, who, with upright face,
Stood, propped against a wall, upon his chest   640
Wearing a written paper, to explain
His story, whence he came, and who he was.
Caught by the spectacle my mind turned round
As with the might of waters ; and apt type
This label seemed of the utmost we can know,
Both of ourselves and of the universe ;
And, on the shape of that unmoving man
His steadfast face and sightless eyes, I gazed,
As if admonished from another world.

Though reared upon the base of outward things,   650
Structures like these the excited spirit mainly

Builds for herself; scenes different there are,
Full-formed, that take, with small internal help,
Possession of the faculties, — the peace
That comes with night : the deep solemnity
Of nature's intermediate hours of rest,
When the great tide of human life stands still :
The business of the day to come, unborn,
Of that gone by, locked up, as in the grave ;
The blended calmness of the heavens and earth,   660
Moonlight and stars, and empty streets, and sounds
Unfrequent as in deserts ; at late hours
Of winter evenings, when unwholesome rains
Are falling hard, with people yet astir,
The feeble salutation from the voice
Of some unhappy woman, now and then
Heard as we pass, when no one looks about,
Nothing is listened to.   But these, I fear,
Are falsely catalogued ; things that are, are not,
As the mind answers to them, or the heart   670
Is prompt, or slow, to feel.   What say you, then,
To times, when half the city shall break out
Full of one passion, vengeance, rage, or fear?
To executions, to a street on fire,
Mobs, riots, or rejoicings?   From these sights
Take one, — that ancient festival, the Fair,
Holden where martyrs suffered in past time,
And named of St. Bartholomew ; there, see
A work completed to our hands, that lays,
If any spectacle on earth can do,   680
The whole creative powers of man asleep ! —
For once, the Muse's help will we implore,

And she shall lodge us, wafted on her wings,
Above the press and danger of the crowd,
Upon some showman's platform.   What a shock   ..
For eyes and ears ! what anarchy and din,
Barbarian and infernal, — a phantasma,
Monstrous in color, motion, shape, sight, sound !
Below, the open space, through every nook
Of the wide area, twinkles, is alive   690
With heads ; the midway region, and above,
Is thronged with staring pictures and huge scrolls,
Dumb proclamations of the Prodigies ;
With chattering monkeys dangling from their poles,
And children whirling in their roundabouts ;
With those that stretch the neck and strain the eyes,
And crack the voice in rivalship, the crowd   ·
Inviting ; with buffoons against buffoons
Grimacing, writhing, screaming, — him who grinds
The hurdy-gurdy, at the fiddle weaves,   700
Rattles the salt-box, thumps the kettle-drum,
And him who at the trumpet puffs his cheeks,
The silver-collared Negro with his timbrel,
Equestrians, tumblers, women, girls, and boys,
Blue-breeched, pink-vested, with high towering plumes.—
All movables of wonder, from all parts,
Are here — Albinos, painted Indians, Dwarfs,
The Horse of knowledge, and the learned Pig,
The Stone-eater, the man that swallows fire,
Giants, ventriloquists, the Invisible Girl,   710
The Bust that speaks and moves its goggling eyes,
The Wax-work, clock-work, all the marvellous craft
Of modern Merlins, Wild Beasts, Puppet-shows

All out-o'-the-way, far-fetched, perverted things,
All freaks of nature, all Promethean thoughts
Of man, his dulness, madness, and their feats
All jumbled up together, to compose
A parliament of Monsters.   Tents and Booths
Meanwhile, as if the whole were one vast mill,
Are vomiting, receiving on all sides,   720
Men, Women, three-years' children, Babes in arms.

Oh, blank confusion ! true epitome
Of what the mighty City is herself,
To thousands upon thousands of her sons,
Living amid the same perpetual whirl
Of trivial objects, melted and reduced
To one identity, by differences
That have no law, no meaning, and no end —
Oppression, under which even highest minds
Must labor, whence the strongest are not free.   730
But though the picture weary out the eye,
By nature an unmanageable sight,
It is not wholly so to him who looks
In steadiness, who hath among least things
An under-sense of greatest ; sees the parts
As parts, but with a feeling of the whole.
This, of all acquisitions, first awaits
On sundry and most widely different modes
Of education, nor with least delight
On that through which I passed.   Attention springs, 740
And comprehensiveness and memory flow,
From early converse with the works of God
Among all regions ; chiefly where appear

Most obviously simplicity and power.
Think, how the everlasting streams and woods,
Stretched and still stretching far and wide, exalt
The roving Indian, on his desert sands :
What grandeur not unfelt, what pregnant show
Of beauty, meets the sun-burnt Arab's eye :
And, as the sea propels, from zone to zone,   750
Its currents ; magnifies its shoals of life
Beyond all compass ; spreads, and sends aloft
Armies of clouds, — even so, its powers and aspects
Shape for mankind, by principles as fixed,
The views and aspirations of the soul
To majesty. Like virtue have the forms
Perennial of the ancient hills ; nor less
The changeful language of their countenances
Quickens the slumbering mind, and aids the thoughts,
However multitudinous, to move   760
With order and relation. This, if still,
As hitherto, in freedom I may speak,
Not violating any just restraint,
As may be hoped, of real modesty, —
This did I feel, in London's vast domain.
The Spirit of Nature was upon me there ;
The soul of Beauty and enduring Life
Vouchsafed her inspiration, and diffused,
Through meagre lines and colors, and the press
Of self-destroying, transitory things,   770
Composure, and ennobling Harmony.

BOOK EIGHTH.

---◦◦◦---

RETROSPECT.—LOVE OF NATURE LEADING TO LOVE OF MAN.

WHAT sounds are those, Helvellyn, that are heard
Up to thy summit, through the depth of air
Ascending, as if distance had the power
To make the sounds more audible?   What crowd
Covers, or sprinkles o'er, yon village green?
Crowd seems it, solitary hill! to thee
Though but a little family of men,
Shepherds and tillers of the ground — betimes
Assembled with their children and their wives,
And here and there a stranger interspersed.   10
They hold a rustic fair — a festival,
Such as, on this side now, and now on that,
Repeated through his tributary vales,
Helvellyn, in the silence of his rest,
Sees annually, if clouds towards either ocean
Blown from their favorite resting-place, or mists
Dissolved, have left him an unshrouded head.
Delightful day it is for all who dwell
In this secluded glen, and eagerly
They give it welcome.   Long ere heat of noon,   20

From byre or field the kine were brought; the sheep
Are penned in cotes; the chaffering is begun.
The heifer lows, uneasy at the voice
Of a new master; bleat the flocks aloud.
Booths are there none; a stall or two is here;
A lame man or a blind, the one to beg,
The other to make music; hither, too,
From far, with basket, slung upon her arm,
Of hawker's wares — books, pictures, combs, and pins —
Some aged woman finds her way again,   30
Year after year, a punctual visitant!
There also stands a speech-maker by rote,
Pulling the strings of his boxed raree-show;
And in the lapse of many years may come
Prouder itinerant, mountebank, or he
Whose wonders in a covered wain lie hid.
But one there is, the loveliest of them all,
Some sweet lass of the valley, looking out
For gains, and who that sees her would not buy?
Fruits of her father's orchard are her wares,   40
And with the ruddy produce, she walks round
Among the crowd, half pleased with, half ashamed
Of her new office, blushing restlessly.
The children now are rich, for the old to-day
Are generous as the young, and, if content
With looking on, some ancient wedded pair
Sit in the shade together, while they gaze,
" A cheerful smile unbends the wrinkled brow,
The days departed start again to life,
And all the scenes of childhood reappear,   50
Faint, but more tranquil, like the changing sun

To him who slept at noon and wakes at eve."
Thus gayety and cheerfulness prevail,
Spreading from young to old, from old to young,
And no one seems to want his share. — Immense
Is the recess, the circumambient world
Magnificent, by which they are embraced.
They move about upon the soft green turf:
How little they, they and their doings, seem,
And all that they can further or obstruct !   60
Through utter weakness pitiably dear,
As tender infants are ; and yet how great !
For all things serve them ; them the morning light
Loves, as it glistens on the silent rocks ;
And them the silent rocks which now from high
Look down upon them ; the reposing clouds ;
The wild brooks prattling from invisible haunts ;
And old Helvellyn, conscious of the stir
Which animates this day their calm abode.

With deep devotion, Nature, did I feel,   70
In that enormous City's turbulent world
Of men and things, what benefit I owed
To thee, and those domains of rural peace,
Where to the sense of beauty first my heart
Was opened, tract more exquisitely fair
Than that famed paradise of ten thousand trees,
Or Gehol's matchless gardens, for delight
Of the Tartarian dynasty composed
(Beyond that mighty wall, not fabulous,
China's stupendous mound) by patient toil   80
Of myriads and boon nature's lavish help ;

There, in a clime from widest empire chosen,
Fulfilling (could enchantment have done more?)
A sumptuous dream of flowery lawns, with domes
Of pleasure sprinkled over, shady dells
For eastern monasteries, sunny mounts
With temples crested, bridges, gondolas,
Rocks, dens, and groves of foliage taught to melt
Into each other their obsequious hues,
Vanished and vanishing in subtle chase,   90
Too fine to be pursued; or standing forth
In no discordant opposition, strong
And gorgeous as the colors side by side
Bedded among rich plumes of tropic birds;
And mountains over all, embracing all;
And all the landscape, endlessly enriched
With waters running, falling, or asleep.

But lovelier far than this, the paradise
Where I was reared; in Nature's primitive gifts
Favored no less, and more to every sense   100
Delicious, seeing that the sun and sky,
The elements, and seasons as they change,
Do find a worthy fellow-laborer there —
Man free, man working for himself, with choice
Of time, and place and object; by his wants,
His comforts, native occupations, cares,
Cheerfully led to individual ends
Or social, and still followed by a train
Unwooed, unthought-of even — simplicity,
And beauty, and inevitable grace.   110

Yea, when a glimpse of those imperial bowers
Would to a child be transport over-great,
When but a half-hour's roam through such a place
Would leave behind a dance of images,
That shall break in upon his sleep for weeks;
Even then the common haunts of the green earth,
And ordinary interests of man,
Which they embosom, all without regard
As both may seem, are fastening on the heart
Insensibly, each with the other's help.   120
For me, when my affections first were led
From kindred, friends, and playmates, to partake
Love for the human creature's absolute self,
That noticeable kindliness of heart
Sprang out of fountains, there abounding most,
Where sovereign Nature dictated the tasks
And occupations which her beauty adorned,
And Shepherds were the men that pleased me first;
Not such as Saturn ruled 'mid Latian wilds,
With arts and laws so tempered that their lives   130
Left, even to us toiling in this late day,
A bright tradition of the golden age;
Not such as, 'mid Arcadian fastnesses
Sequestered, handed down among themselves
Felicity, in Grecian song renowned;
Nor such as — when an adverse fate had driven,
From house and home, the courtly band whose fortunes
Entered, with Shakespeare's genius, the wild woods
Of Arden — amid sunshine or in shade
Culled the best fruits of Time's uncounted hours,   140
Ere Phœbe sighed for the false Ganymede;

Or there where Perdita and Florizel
Together danced, Queen of the feast, and King;
Nor such as Spenser fabled.   True it is,
That I had heard (what he perhaps had seen)
Of maids at sunrise bringing in from far
Their May-bush, and along the streets in flocks
Parading with a song of taunting rhymes,
Aimed at the laggards slumbering within doors;
Had also heard, from those who yet remembered,   150
Tales of the May-pole dance, and wreaths that decked
Porch, door-way, or kirk-pillar; and of youths,
Each with his maid, before the sun was up,
By annual custom, issuing forth in troops,
To drink the waters of some sainted well
And hang it round with garlands.   Love survives;
But, for such purpose, flowers no longer grow:
The times, too sage, perhaps too proud, have dropped
These lighter graces; and the rural ways
And manners which my childhood looked upon   160
Were the unluxuriant produce of a life
Intent on little but substantial needs,
Yet rich in beauty, beauty that was felt.
But images of danger and distress,
Man suffering among awful Powers and Forms;
Of this I heard, and saw enough to make
Imagination restless; nor was free
Myself from frequent perils; nor were tales
Wanting, — the tragedies of former times,
Hazards and strange escapes, of which the rocks   170
Immutable and overflowing streams,
Where'er I roamed, were speaking monuments.

Smooth life had flock and shepherd in old time,
Long springs and tepid winters, on the banks
Of delicate Galesus ; and no less
Those scattered along Adria's myrtle shores :
Smooth life had herdsman, and his snow-white herd
To triumphs and to sacrificial rites
Devoted, on the inviolable stream
Of rich Clitumnus ; and the goat-herd lived   180
As calmly, underneath the pleasant brows
Of cool Lucretilis, where the pipe was heard
Of Pan, Invisible God, thrilling the rocks
With tutelary music, from all harm
The fold protecting.   I myself, mature
In manhood then, have seen a pastoral track
Like some of these, where Fancy might run wild,
Though under skies less generous, less serene ;
There, for her own delight had Nature framed
A pleasure-ground, diffused a fair expanse   190
Of level pasture, islanded with groves
And banked with woody risings ; but the Plain
Endless, here opening widely out, and there
Shut up in lesser lakes or beds of lawn
And intricate recesses, creek or bay
Sheltered within a shelter, where at large
The shepherd strays, a rolling hut his home.
Thither he comes with spring-time, there abides
All summer, and at sunrise ye may hear
His flageolet to liquid notes of love   200
Attuned, or sprightly fife resounding far.
Nook is there none, nor tract of that vast space
Where passage opens, but the same shall have

In turn its visitant, telling there his hours
In unlaborious pleasure, with no task
More toilsome than to carve a beechen bowl
For spring or fountain, which the traveller finds,
When through the region he pursues at will
His devious course.   A glimpse of such sweet life
I saw when, from the melancholy walls   210
Of Goslar, once imperial, I renewed
My daily walk along that wide champaign,
That, reaching to her gates, spreads east and west,
And northwards, from beneath the mountainous verge
Of the Hercynian forest.   Yet, hail to you
Moors, mountains, headlands, and ye hollow vales,
Ye long deep channels for the Atlantic's voice,
Powers of my native region !   Ye that seize   .
The heart with firmer grasp !   Your snows and streams
Ungovernable, and your terrifying winds,   220
That howl so dismally for him who treads
Companionless your awful solitudes !
There, 'tis the shepherd's task the winter long
To wait upon the storms : of their approach
Sagacious, into sheltering coves he drives
His flock, and thither from the homestead bears
A toilsome burden up the craggy ways,
And deals it out their regular nourishment   .
Strewn on the frozen snow.   And when the spring
Looks out, and all the pastures dance with lambs,   230
And when the flock, with warmer weather, climbs
Higher and higher, him his office leads
To watch their goings, whatsoever track
The wanderers choose.   For this he quits his home

At day-spring, and no sooner doth the sun
Begin to strike him with a fire-like heat,
Than he lies down upon some shining rock,
And breakfasts with his dog.   When they have stolen,
As is their wont, a pittance from strict time,
For rest not needed or exchange of love,   240
Then from his couch he starts ; and now his feet
Crush out a livelier fragrance from the flowers
Of lowly thyme, by Nature's skill enwrought
In the wild turf; the lingering dews of morn
Smoke round him, as from hill to hill he hies,
His staff protending like a hunter's spear,
Or by its aid leaping from crag to crag,
And o'er the brawling beds of unbridged streams.
Philosophy, methinks, at Fancy's call,
Might deign to follow him through what he does   250
Or sees in his day's march ; himself he feels,
In those vast regions where his service lies,
A freeman, wedded to his life of hope
And hazard, and hard labor interchanged
With that majestic indolence so dear
To native man.   A rambling school-boy, thus
I felt his presence in his own domain,
As of a lord and master, or a power,
Or genius, under Nature, under God,
Presiding ; and severest solitude   260
Had more commanding looks when he was there
When up the lonely brooks on rainy days
Angling I went, or trod the trackless hills
By mists bewildered, suddenly mine eyes
Have glanced upon him distant, a few steps,

In size a giant, stalking through thick fog,
His sheep like Greenland bears ; or, as he stepped
Beyond the boundary line of some hill shadow,
His form hath flashed upon me, glorified.
By the deep radiance of the setting sun ;   270
Or him have I descried in distant sky,
A solitary object and sublime.
Above all height ! like an aerial cross
Stationed alone upon a spiry rock
Of the Chartreuse, for worship.   Thus was man
Ennobled outwardly before my sight,
And thus my heart was early introduced
To an unconscious love and reverence
Of human nature ; hence the human form
To me became an index of delight,   280
Of grace and honor, power and worthiness.
Meanwhile this creature — spiritual almost
As those of books, but more exalted far ;
Far more of an imaginative form
Than the gay Corin of the groves, who lives
For his own fancies, or to dance by the hour,
In coronal, with Phyllis in the midst —
Was, for the purposes of kind, a man
With the most common ; husband, father ; learned,
Could teach, admonish ; suffered with the rest   290
From vice and folly, wretchedness and fear ;
Of this I little saw, cared less for it,
But something must have felt.
                              Call ye these appearances —
Which I beheld of shepherds in my youth,
This sanctity of Nature given to man —

A shadow, a delusion, ye who pore
On the dead letter, miss the spirit of things ;
Whose truth is not a motion or a shape
Instinct with vital functions, but a block
Or waxen image which yourselves have made,   300
And ye adore ! But blessed be the God
Of Nature and of Man that this was so ;
That men before my inexperienced eyes
Did first present themselves thus purified,
Removed, and to a distance that was fit :
And so we all of us in some degree
Are led to knowledge, wheresoever led,
And howsoever ; were it otherwise,
And we found evil fast as we find good
In our first years, or think that it is found,   310
How could the innocent heart bear up and live !
But doubly fortunate my lot ; not here
Alone, that something of a better life
Perhaps was round me than it is the privilege
Of most to move in, but that first I looked
At Man through objects that were great or fair ;
First communed with him by their help. And thus
Was founded a sure safeguard and defence
Against the weight of meanness, selfish cares,
Coarse manners, vulgar passions, that beat in   320
On all sides from the ordinary world
In which we traffic. Starting from this point
I had my face turned toward the truth, began
With an advantage furnished by that kind
Of prepossession, without which the soul
Receives no knowledge that can bring forth good,

No genuine insight ever comes to her.
From the restraint of over-watchful eyes
Preserved, I moved about, year after year,
Happy, and now most thankful that my walk   330
Was guarded from too early intercourse
With the deformities of crowded life,
And those ensuing laughters and contempts,
Self-pleasing, which, if we would wish to think
With a due reverence on earth's rightful lord,
Here placed to be the inheritor of heaven,
Will not permit us ; but pursue the mind,
That to devotion willingly would rise,
Into the temple and the temple's heart.

    Yet deem not, friend ! that human kind with me   340
Thus early took a place pre-eminent ;
Nature herself was, at this unripe time,
But secondary to my own pursuits
And animal activities, and all
Their trivial pleasure ; and when these had dropped
And gradually expired, and Nature, prized
For her own sake, became my joy, even then —
And upwards through late youth, until not less
Than two-and-twenty summers had been told —
Was Man in my affections and regards   350
Subordinate to her, her visible forms
And viewless agencies : a passion, she,
A rapture often, and immediate love
Ever at hand ; he, only a delight
Occasional, an accidental grace,
His hour being not yet come.   Far less had then

The inferior creatures, beast or bird, attuned
My spirit to that gentleness of love
(Though they had long been carefully observed),
Won from me those minute obeisances   360
Of tenderness, which I may number now
With my first blessings.   Nevertheless, on these
The light of beauty did not fall in vain,
Or grandeur circumfuse them to no end.

But when that first poetic faculty
Of plain Imagination and severe,
No longer a mute influence of the soul,
Ventured, at some rash Muse's earnest call,
To try her strength among harmonious words ;
And to book-notions and the rules of art   370
Did knowingly conform itself, there came
Among the simple shapes of human life
A wilfulness of fancy and conceit ;
And Nature and her objects beautified
These fictions, as in some sort, in their turn,
They burnished her.   From touch of this new power
Nothing was safe : the elder-tree that grew
Beside the well-known charnel-house had then
A dismal look : the yew-tree had its ghost,
That took his station there for ornament :   380
The dignities of plain occurrence then
Were tasteless, and truth's golden mean, a point
Where no sufficient pleasure could be found.
Then, if a widow, staggering with the blow
Of her distress, was known to have turned her steps
To the cold grave in which her husband slept,

One night, or haply more than one, through pain
Or half-insensate impotence of mind,
The fact was caught at greedily, and there
She must be visitant the whole year through,   390
Wetting the turf with never-ending tears.

Through quaint obliquities I might pursue
These cravings ; when the fox-glove, one by one,
Upwards through every stage of the tall stem,
Had shed beside the public way its bells,
And stood of all dismantled, save the last
Left at the tapering ladder's top, that seemed
To bend as doth a slender blade of grass
Tipped with a rain-drop, Fancy loved to seat,
Beneath the plant despoiled, but crested still   400
With this last relic, soon itself to fall,
Some vagrant mother, whose arch little ones,
All unconcerned by her dejected plight,
Laughed as with rival eagerness their hands
Gathered the purple cups that round them lay,
Strewing the turf's green slope.
                                        A diamond light
(Whene'er the summer sun, declining, smote
A smooth rock wet with constant springs) was seen
Sparkling from out a copse-clad bank that rose
Fronting our cottage.   Oft beside the hearth   410
Seated, with open door, often and long
Upon this restless lustre have I gazed,
That made my fancy restless as itself.
'Twas now for me a burnished silver shield
Suspended over a knight's tomb, who lay

Inglorious, buried in the dusky wood :
An entrance now into some magic cave
Or palace built by fairies of the rock ;
Nor could I have been bribed to disenchant
The spectacle, by visiting the spot.   420
Thus wilful Fancy, in no hurtful mood,
Engrafted far-fetched shapes on feelings bred
By pure Imagination : busy Power
She was, and with her ready pupil turned
Instinctively to human passions, then
Least understood.   Yet, 'mid the fervent swarm
Of these vagaries, with an eye so rich
As mine was through the bounty of a grand
And lovely region, I had forms distinct
To steady me : each airy thought revolved   430
Round a substantial centre, which at once
Incited it to motion, and controlled.
I did not pine like one in cities bred,
As was thy melancholy lot, dear Friend !
Great Spirit as thou art, in endless dreams
Of sickliness, disjoining, joining, things
Without the light of knowledge.   Where the harm
If, when the woodman languished with disease,
Induced by sleeping nightly on the ground
Within his sod-built cabin, Indian-wise,   440
I called the pangs of disappointed love,
And all the sad etcetera of the wrong,
To help him to his grave?   Meanwhile the man,
If not already from the wood retired
To die at home, was haply as I knew,
Withering by slow degrees, 'mid gentle airs,

Birds, running streams, and hills so beautiful
On golden evenings, while the charcoal pile
Breathed up its smoke, an image of his ghost
Or spirit that full soon must take her flight.
Nor shall we not be tending towards that point
Of sound humanity to which our Tale
Leads, though by sinuous ways, if here I show
How Fancy, in a season when she wove
Those slender cords, to guide the unconscious Boy
For the Man's sake, could feed at Nature's call
Some pensive musings, which might well beseem
Maturer years.

             A grove there is whose boughs
Stretch from the western marge of Thurstonmere,
With length of shade so thick that whoso glides
Along the line of low-roofed water, moves
As in a cloister.   Once — while, in that shade
Loitering, I watched the golden beams of light
Flung from the setting sun, as they reposed
In silent beauty on the naked ridge
Of a high eastern hill — thus flowed my thoughts
In a pure stream of words fresh from the heart:
Dear native Regions, wheresoe'er shall close
My mortal course, there will I think on you;
Dying, will cast on you a backward look;
Even as this setting sun (albeit the Vale
Is nowhere touched by one memorial gleam)
Doth with the fond remains of his last power
Still linger, and a farewell lustre sheds
On the dear mountain-tops where first he rose.

Enough of humble arguments ; recall,
My Song ! those high emotions which thy voice
Has heretofore made known ; that bursting forth
Of sympathy, inspiring and inspired,
When everywhere a vital pulse was felt,   480
And all the several frames of things, like stars,
Through every magnitude distinguishable,
Shone mutually indebted, or half lost
Each in the other's blaze, a galaxy
Of life and glory.   In the midst stood Man,
Outwardly, inwardly contemplated,
As, of all visible natures, crown, though born
Of dust, and kindred to the worm ; a Being,
Both in perception and discernment, first
In every capability of rapture,   490
Through the divine effect of power and love ;
As, more than anything we know, instinct
With godhead, and, by reason and by will,
Acknowledging dependency sublime.

Ere long, the lonely mountains left, I move,
Begirt, from day to day, with temporal shapes
Of vice and folly thrust upon my view,
Objects of sport, and ridicule, and scorn,
Manners and characters discriminate,
And little bustling passions that eclipse,   500
As well they might, the impersonated thought,
The idea, or abstraction of the kind.

An idler among academic bowers,
Such was my new condition, as at large

Has been set forth ; yet here the vulgar light
Of present, actual, superficial life,
Gleaming through coloring of other times,
Old usages and local privilege,
Was welcomed, softened, if not solemnized,
This notwithstanding, being brought more near   510
To vice and guilt, forerunning wretchedness,
I trembled, — thought, at times, of human life
With an indefinite terror and dismay,
Such as the storms and angry elements
Had bred in me ; but gloomier far, a dim
Analogy to uproar and misrule,
Disquiet, danger, and obscurity.

It might be told, (but wherefore speak of things
Common to all?) that, seeing, I was led
Gravely to ponder — judging between good   520
And evil, not as for the mind's delight,
But for her guidance — one who was to *act*,
As sometimes to the best of feeble means
I did, by human sympathy impelled :
And, through dislike and most offensive pain,
Was to the truth conducted ; of this faith
Never forsaken, that, by acting well,
And understanding, I should learn to love
The end of life, and everything we know.

Grave Teacher, stern Preceptress ! for at times   530
Thou canst put on an aspect most severe ;
London, to thee I willingly return.
Erewhile my verse played idly with the flowers

Enwrought upon thy mantle ; satisfied
With that amusement, and a simple look
Of child-like inquisition now and then
Cast upwards on thy countenance, to detect
Some inner meanings which might harbor there.
But how could I in mood so light indulge,
Keeping such fresh remembrance of the day   540
When, having thridded the long labyrinth
Of the suburban villages, I first
Entered thy vast dominions.   On the roof
Of an itinerant vehicle I sate,
With vulgar men about me, trivial forms
Of houses, pavement, streets, of men and things, —
Mean shapes on every side ; but, at the instant
When to myself it fairly might be said,
The threshold now is overpast, (how strange
That aught external to the living mind   550
Should have such mighty sway ! yet so it was),
A weight of ages did at once descend
Upon my heart ; no thought embodied, no
Distinct remembrances, but weight and power, —
Power growing under weight : alas ! I feel
That I am trifling : 'twas a moment's pause, —
All that took place within me came and went
As in a moment ; yet with Time it dwells,
And grateful memory, as a thing divine.

The curious traveller, who, from open day,   560
Hath passed with torches into some huge cave,
The Grotto of Antiparos, or the Den
In old time haunted by that Danish Witch,

Yordas : he looks around and sees the vault,
Widening on all sides ; sees, or thinks he sees,
Erelong, the massy roof above his head,
That instantly unsettles and recedes, —
Substance and shadow, light and darkness, all
Commingled, making up a canopy
Of shapes and forms and tendencies to shape   570
That shift and vanish, change and interchange
Like spectres, — ferment silent and sublime !
That after a short space works less and less,
Till, every effort, every motion gone,
The scene before him stands in perfect view
Exposed, and lifeless as a written book ! —
But let him pause awhile, and look again,
And a new quickening shall succeed, at first
Beginning timidly, then creeping fast,
Till the whole cave, so late a senseless mass,   580
Busies the eye with images and forms
Boldly assembled, — here is shadowed forth
From the projections, wrinkles, cavities,
A variegated landscape, — there the shape
Of some gigantic warrior clad in mail.
The ghostly semblance of a hooded monk,
Veiled nun, or pilgrim resting on his staff :
Strange congregation ! yet not slow to meet
Eyes that perceive through minds that can inspire.

Even in such sort had I at first been moved,   590
Nor otherwise continued to be moved,
As I explored the vast metropolis,
Fount of my country's destiny and the world's :

That great emporium, chronicle at once
And burial-place of passions, and their home
Imperial, their chief living residence.

With strong sensations teeming as it did
Of past and present, such a place must needs
Have pleased me, seeking knowledge at that time
Far less than craving power ; yet knowledge came, 600
Sought or unsought, and influxes of power
Came, of themselves, or at her call derived
In fits of kindliest apprehensiveness,
From all sides, when whate'er was in itself
Capacious found, or seemed to find, in me
A correspondent amplitude of mind ;
Such is the strength and glory of our youth !
The human nature unto which I felt
That I belonged, and reverenced with love,
Was not a punctual presence, but a spirit 610
Diffused through time and space, with aid derived
Of evidence from monuments, erect,
Prostrate, or leaning towards their common rest
In earth, the widely scattered wreck sublime
Of vanished nations, or more clearly drawn
From books and what they picture and record.

'Tis true, the history of our native land,
With those of Greece compared and popular Rome,
And in our high wrought modern narratives
Stript of their harmonizing soul, the life 620
Of manners and familiar incidents,
Had never much delighted me.   And less

Than other intellects had mine been used
To lean upon intrinsic circumstance
Of record or tradition ; but a sense
Of what in the Great City had been done
And suffered, and was doing, suffering, still,
Weighed with me, could support the test of thought ;
And, in despite of all that had gone by,
Or was departing never to return,   630
There I conversed with majesty and power
Like independent natures.   Hence the place
Was thronged with impregnations like the Wilds
In which my early feelings had been nursed —
Bare hills and valleys, full of caverns, rocks,
And audible seclusions, dashing lakes,
Echoes and waterfalls and pointed crags
That into music touch the passing wind.
Here then my young imagination found
No uncongenial element ; could here   640
Among new objects serve or give command,
Even as the heart's occasions might require,
To forward reason's else too-scrupulous march.
The effect was, still more elevated views
Of human nature.   Neither vice nor guilt,
Debasement undergone by body or mind,
Nor all the misery forced upon my sight,
Misery not lightly passed, but sometimes scanned
Most feelingly, could overthrow my trust
In what we *may* become ; induce belief   650
That I was ignorant, had been falsely taught,
A solitary, who with vain conceits
Had been inspired, and walked about in dreams.

From those sad scenes when meditation turned,
Lo ! everything that was indeed divine
Retained its purity inviolate,
Nay brighter shone, by this portentous gloom
Set off ; such opposition as aroused
The mind of Adam, yet in Paradise
Though fallen from bliss, when in the East he saw   660
Darkness ere day's mid course, and morning light
More orient in the western cloud, that drew
O'er the blue firmament a radiant white,
Descending slow with something heavenly fraught.

   Add also, that among the multitudes
Of that huge city, oftentimes was seen
Affectingly set forth, more than elsewhere
Is possible, the unity of man,
One spirit over ignorance and vice
Predominant, in good and evil hearts ;   670
One sense for moral judgments, as one eye
For the sun's light. The soul when smitten thus
By a sublime *idea* whencesoe'er
Vouchsafed for union or communion, feeds
On the pure bliss, and takes her rest with God.

   Thus from a very early age, O Friend !
My thoughts by slow gradations had been drawn
To human kind, and to the good and ill
Of human life, Nature had led me on ;
And oft amid the " busy hum " I seemed   680
To travel independent of her help,
As if I had forgotten her ; but no,

The world of human-kind outweighed not hers
In my habitual thoughts ; the scale of love,
Though filling daily, still was light, compared
With that in which *her* mighty objects lay.

BOOK NINTH.

—◦—

EVEN as a river — partly (it might seem)
Yielding to old remembrances, and swayed
In part by fear to shape a way direct,
That would engulph him soon in the ravenous sea —
Turns, and will measure back his course, far back,
Seeking the very regions which he crossed
In his first outset; so have we, my Friend,
Turned and returned with intricate delay.
Or as a traveller who has gained the brow
Of some aërial Down, while there he halts   10
For breathing-time, is tempted to review
The region left behind him; and, if aught
Deserving notice have escaped regard,
Or been regarded with too careless eye,
Strives, from that height, with one and yet one more
Last look, to make the best amends he may:
So have we lingered. Now we start afresh
With courage, and new hope risen on our toil.
Fair greetings to this shapeless eagerness,
Whene'er it comes! needful in work so long,   20
Thrice needful to the argument which now
Awaits us! Oh, how much unlike the past!

Free as a colt at pasture on the hill,
I ranged at large, through London's wide domain,
Month after month.   Obscurely did I live,
Not seeking frequent intercourse with men
By literature, or elegance, or rank,
Distinguished.   Scarcely was a year thus spent
Ere I forsook the crowded solitude,
With less regret for its luxurious pomp,   30
And all the nicely guarded shows of art,
Than for the humble book-stalls in the streets,
Exposed to eye and hand where'er I turned.

France lured me forth ; the realm that I had crossed
So lately, journeying towards the snow-clad Alps.
But now, relinquishing the scrip and staff,
And all enjoyment which the summer sun
Sheds round the steps of those who meet the day
With motion constant as his own, I went
Prepared to sojourn in a pleasant town,   40
Washed by the current of the stately Loire.

Through Paris lay my readiest course, and there
Sojourning a few days, I visited
In haste each spot of old or recent fame,
The latter chiefly ; from the field of Mars
Down to the suburbs of St. Antony,
And from Mont Martre southward to the Dome
Of Geneviève.   In both her clamorous Halls,
The National Synod and the Jacobins,
I saw the Revolutionary Power   50

Tossed like a ship at anchor, rocked by storms;
The Arcades I traversed in the Palace huge
Of Orleans; coasted round and round the line
Of Tavern, Brothel, Gaming-house, and Shop,
Great rendezvous of worst and best, the walk
Of all who had a purpose, or had not;
I stared and listened, with a stranger's ears,
To Hawkers and Haranguers, hubbub wild!
And hissing Factionists with ardent eyes,
In knots, or pairs, or single.   Not a look   60
Hope takes, or Doubt or Fear is forced to wear,
But seemed there present; and I scanned them all,
Watched every gesture uncontrollable,
Of anger, and vexation, and despite,
' All side by side, and struggling face to face,
With gayety and dissolute idleness.

    Where silent zephyrs sported with the dust
Of the Bastile I sat in the open sun
And from the rubbish gathered up a stone,
And pocketed the relic, in the guise   70
Of an enthusiast; yet, in honest truth,
I looked for something that I could not find,
Affecting more emotion than I felt;
For 'tis most certain that these various sights,
However potent their first shock, with me
Appeared to recompense the traveller's pains
Less than the painted Magdalene of Le Brun,
A beauty exquisitely wrought, with hair
Dishevelled, gleaming eyes, and rueful cheek
Pale and bedropped with overflowing tears.   80

But hence to my more permanent abode
I hasten; there, by novelties in speech,
Domestic manners, customs, gestures, looks,
And all the attire of ordinary life,
Attention was engrossed; and, thus amused,
I stood 'mid those concussions, unconcerned,
Tranquil almost, and careless as a flower
Glassed in a green-house, or a parlor shrub
That spreads its leaves in unmolested peace,
While every bush and tree, the country through,   90
Is shaking to the roots: indifference this
Which may seem strange; but I was unprepared
With needful knowledge, had abruptly passed
Into a theatre whose stage was filled
And busy with an action far advanced.
Like others, I had skimmed, and sometimes read
With care, the master pamphlets of the day;
Nor wanted such half-insight as grew wild
Upon that meagre soil, helped out by talk
And public news; but having never seen   100
A chronicle that might suffice to show
Whence the main organs of the public power
Had sprung, their transmigrations, when and how
Accomplished, giving thus unto events
A form and body; all things were to me
Loose and disjointed, and the affections left
Without a vital interest.   At that time,
Moreover, the first storm was overblown,
And the strong hand of outward violence
Locked up in quiet.   For myself, I fear   110
Now in connection with so great a theme

To speak (as I must be compelled to do)
Of one so unimportant ; night by night
Did I frequent the formal haunts of men,
Whom, in the city, privilege of birth
Sequestered from the rest, societies
Polished in arts, and in punctilio versed ;
Whence, and from deeper causes, all discourse
Of good and evil of the time was shunned
With scrupulous care : but these restrictions soon   120
Proved tedious, and I gradually withdrew
Into a noisier world, and thus ere long
Became a patriot ; and my heart was all
Given to the people, and my love was theirs.

    A band of military Officers,
Then stationed in the city, were the chief
Of my associates : some of these wore swords
That had been seasoned in the wars, and all
Were men well-born ; the chivalry of France.
In age and temper differing, they had yet   130
One spirit ruling in each heart ; alike
(Save only one, hereafter to be named)
Were bent upon undoing what was done :
This was their rest and only hope ; therewith
No fear had they of bad becoming worse,
For worst to them was come ; nor would have stirred,
Or deemed it worth a moment's thought to stir,
In anything, save only as the act
Looked thitherward.   One, reckoning by years,
Was in the prime of manhood, and erewhile   140
He had sate lord in many tender hearts ;

Though heedless of such honors now, and changed :
His temper was quite mastered by the times,
And they had blighted him, had eaten away
The beauty of his person, doing wrong
Alike to body and to mind : his port,
Which once had been erect and open, now
Was stooping and contracted, and a face,
Endowed by Nature with her fairest gifts
Of symmetry and light and bloom, expressed,   150
As much as any that was ever seen,
A ravage out of season, made by thoughts
Unhealthy and vexatious.   With the hour
That from the press of Paris duly brought
Its freight of public news, the fever came,
A punctual visitant, to shake this man,
Disarmed his voice and fanned his yellow cheek
Into a thousand colors ; while he read,
Or mused, his sword was haunted by his touch
Continually, like an uneasy place   160
In his own body.   'Twas in truth an hour
Of universal ferment ; mildest men
Were agitated ; and commotions, strife
Of passion and opinion, filled the walls
Of peaceful houses with unquiet sounds.
The soil of common life was, at that time,
Too hot to tread upon.   Oft said I then,
And not then only, " What a mockery this
Of history, the past and that to come !
Now do I feel how all men are deceived,   170
Reading of nations and their works, in faith,
Faith given to vanity and emptiness :

Oh ! laughter for the page that would reflect
To future times the face of what now is !"
The land all swarmed with passion, like a plain
Devoured by locusts, — Carra, Gorsas, — add
A hundred other names, forgotten now
Nor to be heard of more ; yet, they were powers,
Like earthquakes, shocks repeated day by day,
And felt through every nook of town and field.   180

    Such was the state of things.   Meanwhile the chief
Of my associates stood prepared for flight,
To augment the band of emigrants in arms
Upon the borders of the Rhine, and leagued
With foreign foes mustered for instant war.
This was their undisguised intent, and they
Were waiting with the whole of their desires
The moment to depart.

                An Englishman,
Born in a land whose very name appeared
To license some unruliness of mind ;   190
A stranger, with youth's further privilege,
And the indulgence that a half-learnt speech
Wins from the courteous ; I, who had been else
Shunned and not tolerated, freely lived
With these defenders of the Crown, and talked,
And heard their notions ; nor did they disdain
The wish to bring me over to their cause.

    But though untaught by thinking or by books
To reason well of polity or law,

And nice distinctions, then on every tongue,
Of natural rights and civil ; and to acts
Of nations and their passing interests,
(If with unworldly ends and aims compared)
Almost indifferent, even the historian's tale
Prizing but little otherwise than I prized
Tales of the poets, as it made the heart
Beat high, and filled the fancy with fair forms,
Old heroes and their sufferings and their deeds,
Yet in the regal sceptre, and the pomp
Of orders and degrees, I nothing found
Then, or had ever, even in crudest youth,
That dazzled me, but rather what I mourned
And ill could brook, beholding that the best
Ruled not, and feeling that they ought to rule.

For, born in a poor district, and which yet
Retaineth more of ancient homeliness
Than any other nook of English ground,
It was my fortune scarcely to have seen,
Through the whole tenor of my school-day time,
The face of one who, whether boy or man,
Was vested with attention or respect
Through claims of wealth or blood ; nor was it least
Of many benefits, in later years
Derived from academic institutes
And rules, that they held something up to view
Of a Republic, where all stood thus far
Upon equal ground ; that we were brothers all
In honor, as in one community,
Scholars and gentlemen ; where, furthermore,

Distinction open lay to all that came,   230
And wealth and titles were in less esteem
Than talents, worth, and prosperous industry.
Add unto this, subservience from the first
To presences of God's mysterious power
Made manifest in Nature's sovereignty,
And fellowship with venerable books,
To sanction the proud workings of the soul,
And mountain liberty.   It could not be
But that one tutored thus should look with awe
Upon the faculties of man, receive   240
Gladly the highest promises, and hail,
As best, the government of equal rights
And individual worth.   And hence, O Friend !
If at the first great outbreak I rejoiced
Less than might well befit my youth, the cause
In part lay here, that unto me the events
Seemed nothing out of nature's certain course,
A gift that was come rather late than soon.
No wonder, then, if advocates like these,
Inflamed by passion, blind with prejudice,   250
And stung with injury at this riper day,
Were impotent to make my hopes put on
The shape of theirs, my understanding bend
In honor to their honor : zeal, which yet
Had slumbered, now in opposition burst
Forth like a Polar summer : every word
They uttered was a dart, by counter-winds
Blown back upon themselves ; their reason seemed
Confusion-stricken by a higher power
Than human understanding, their discourse   260

Maimed, spiritless ; and in their weakness strong,
I triumphed.
                                Meantime, day by day, the roads
Were crowded with the bravest youth of France,
And all the promptest of her spirits, linked
In gallant soldiership, and posting on
To meet the war upon her frontier bounds.
Yet at this very moment do tears start
Into mine eyes : I do not say I weep, —
I wept not then, — but tears have dimmed my sight,
In memory of the farewells of that time,   270
Domestic severings, female fortitude
At dearest separation, patriot love
And self-devotion, and terrestrial hope,
Encouraged with a martyr's confidence ;
Even files of strangers merely seen but once,
And for a moment, men from far with sound
Of music, martial tunes, and banners spread,
Entering the city, here and there a face
Or person singled out among the rest,
Yet still a stranger and beloved as such ;   280
Even by these passing spectacles my heart
Was oftentimes uplifted, and they seemed
Arguments sent from Heaven to prove the cause
Good, pure, which no one could stand up against,
Who was not lost, abandoned, selfish, proud,
Mean, miserable, wilfully depraved,
Hater perverse of equity and truth.

    Among that band of Officers was one,
Already hinted at, of other mould —

A patriot, thence rejected by the rest,   290
And with an oriental loathing spurned,
As of a different cast.   A meeker man
Than this lived never, nor a more benign,
Meek though enthusiastic.   Injuries
Made *him* more gracious, and his nature then
Did breathe its sweetness out most sensibly,
As aromatic flowers on Alpine turf,
When foot hath crushed them.   He through the events
Of that great change wandered in perfect faith,
As through a book, an old romance, or tale   300
Of Fairy, or some dream of actions wrought
Behind the summer clouds.   By birth he ranked
With the most noble, but unto the poor
Among mankind he was in service bound,
As by some tie invisible, oaths professed
To a religious order.   Man he loved
As man ; and, to the mean and the obscure,
And all the homely in their homely works,
Transferred a courtesy which had no air
Of condescension ; but did rather seem   310
A passion and a gallantry, like that
Which he, a soldier, in his idler day
Had paid to woman : somewhat vain he was,
Or seemed so, yet it was not vanity,
But fondness, and a kind of radiant joy
Diffused around him, while he was intent
On words of love or freedom, or revolved
Complacently the progress of a cause
Whereof he was a part : yet this was meek
And placid, and took nothing from the man   320

That was delightful.   Oft in solitude
With him did I discourse about the end
Of civil government, and its wisest forms ;
Of ancient royalty, and chartered rights,
Custom and habit, novelty and change ;
Of self-respect, and virtue in the few
For patrimonial honor set apart,
And ignorance in the laboring multitude.
For he, to all intolerance indisposed,
Balanced these contemplations in his mind ;   330
And I, who at that time was scarcely dipped
Into the turmoil, bore a sounder judgment
Than later days allowed ; carried about me
With less alloy to its integrity,
The experience of past ages, as, through help
Of books and common life, it makes sure way
To youthful minds, by objects over near
Not pressed upon, nor dazzled or misled
By struggling with the crowd for present ends.

But though not deaf, nor obstinate to find   340
Error without excuse upon the side
Of them who strove against us, more delight
We took, and let this freely be confessed,
In painting to ourselves the miseries
Of royal courts, and that voluptuous life
Unfeeling, where the man who is of soul
The meanest thrives the most ; where dignity,
True personal dignity, abideth not ;
A light, a cruel, a vain world cut off
From the natural inlets of just sentiment,   350

From lowly sympathy and chastening truth ;
Where good and evil interchange their names,
And thirst for bloody spoils abroad is paired
With vice at home.   We added dearest themes —
Man and his noble nature, as it is
The gift which God has placed within his power,
His blind desires and steady faculties
Capable of clear truth, the one to break
Bondage, the other to build liberty
On firm foundations, making social life,   360
Through knowledge spreading and imperishable
As just in regulation and as pure
As individual in the wise and good.

We summed up the honorable deeds
Of ancient Story, thought of each bright spot,
That would be found in all recorded time,
Of truth preserved and error passed away :
Of single spirits that catch the flame from Heaven,
And how the multitudes of men will feed
And fan each other ; thought of sects, how keen   370
They are to put the appropriate nature on,
Triumphant over every obstacle
Of custom, language, country, love, or hate,
And what they do and suffer for their creed ;
How far they travel, and how long endure ;
How quickly mighty Nations have been formed,
From least beginnings ; how, together locked
By new opinions, scattered tribes have made
One body, spreading wide as clouds in heaven.
To aspirations then of our own minds   380

Did we appeal; and, finally, beheld
A living confirmation of the whole
Before us, in a people from the depth
Of shameful imbecility uprisen,
Fresh as the morning star.   Elate we looked
Upon their virtues; saw, in rudest men,
Self-sacrifice the firmest; generous love,
And continence of mind, and sense of right,
Uppermost in the midst of fiercest strife.

Oh, sweet it is, in academic groves,   390
Or such retirement, Friend! as we have known
In the green dales beside our Rotha's stream,
Greta, or Derwent, or some nameless rill,
To ruminate, with interchange of talk,
On rational liberty, and hope in man,
Justice and peace.   But far more sweet such toil —
Toil, say I, for it leads to thoughts abstruse —
If nature then be standing on the brink
Of some great trial, and we hear the voice
Of one devoted, — one whom circumstance   400
Hath called upon to embody his deep sense
In action, give it outwardly a shape,
And that of benediction, to the world
Then doubt is not, and truth is more than truth, —
A hope it is, and a desire; a creed
Of zeal, by an authority Divine
Sanctioned, of danger, difficulty, or death.
Such conversation, under Attic shades,
Did Dion hold with Plato; ripened thus
For a Deliverer's glorious task, — and such   410

He, on that ministry, already bound,
Held with Eudemus and Timonides,
Surrounded by adventurers in arms,
When those two vessels with their daring freight,
For the Sicilian Tyrant's overthrow,
Sailed from Zacynthus, philosophic war,
Led by Philosophers.   With harder fate,
Though like ambition, such was he, O Friend !
Of whom I speak.   So Beaupuis (let the name
Stand near the worthiest of Antiquity)   420
Fashioned his life ; and many a long discourse,
With like persuasion honored, we maintained :
He, on his part, accoutred for the worst,
He perished fighting, in supreme command,
Upon the borders of the unhappy Loire,
For liberty, against deluded men,
His fellow country-men ; and yet most blessed
In this, that he, for the fate of later times
Lived not to see, nor what we now behold,
Who have as ardent hearts as he had then.   430

Along that very Loire, with festal mirth
Resounding at all hours, and innocent yet
Of civil slaughter, was our frequent walk ;
Or in wide forests of continuous shade,
Lofty and over-arched, with open space
Beneath the trees, clear footing many a mile —
A solemn region.   Oft amid those haunts,
From earnest dialogues I slipped in thought,
And let remembrance steal to other times,
When, o'er those interwoven roots, moss-clad,   440

And smooth as marble or a waveless sea,
Some Hermit, from his cell forth-strayed, might pace
In sylvan meditation undisturbed ;
As on the pavement of a Gothic church
Walks a lone Monk, when service hath expired,
In peace and silence.   But if e'er was heard, —
Heard, though unseen, — a devious traveller,
Retiring or approaching from afar
With speed and echoes loud of trampling hoofs
From the hard floor reverberated, then   450
It was Angelica thundering through the woods
Upon her palfrey, or that gentle maid
Erminia, fugitive as fair as she.
Sometimes methought I saw a pair of knights
Joust underneath the trees, that as in storm
Rocked high above their heads ; anon, the din
Of boisterous merriment, and music's roar,
In sudden proclamation, burst from haunt
Of Satyrs in some viewless glade, with dance
Rejoicing o'er a female in the midst,   460
A mortal beauty, their unhappy thrall.
The width of those huge forests, unto me
A novel scene, did often in this way
Master my fancy while I wandered on
With that revered companion.   And sometimes —
When to a convent in a meadow green,
By a brook-side, we came, a roofless pile,
And not by reverential touch of Time
Dismantled, but by violence abrupt —
In spite of those heart-bracing colloquies,   470
In spite of real fervor, and of that

Less genuine and wrought up within myself —
I could not but bewail a wrong so harsh,
And for the Matin-bell to sound no more
Grieved, and the twilight taper, and the cross
High on the topmost pinnacle, a sign
(How welcome to the weary traveller's eyes !)
Of hospitality and peaceful rest.
And when the partner of those varied walks
Pointed upon occasion to the site   480
Of Romorentin, home of ancient kings,
To the imperial edifice of Blois,
Or to that rural castle, name now slipped
From my remembrance, where a lady lodged,
By the first Francis wooed, and bound to him
In chains of mutual passion, from the tower,
As a tradition of the country tells,
Practised to commune with her royal knight
By cressets and love-beacons, intercourse
'Twixt her high-seated residence and his   490
Far off at Chambord on the plain beneath ;
Even here, though less than with the peaceful house
Religious, 'mid those frequent monuments
Of Kings, their vices and their better deeds,
Imagination, potent to inflame
At times with virtuous wrath and noble scorn,
Did also often mitigate the force
Of civic prejudice, the bigotry,
So call it, of a youthful patriot's mind ;
And on these spots with many gleams I looked   500
Of chivalrous delight.   Yet not the less,
Hatred of absolute rule, where will of one

Is law for all, and of that barren pride
In them who, by immunities unjust,
Between the sovereign and the people stand,
His helper and not theirs, laid stronger hold
Daily upon me, mixed with pity too
And love ; for where hope is, there love will be
For the abject multitude.   And when we chanced
One day to meet a hunger-bitten girl,   510
Who crept along fitting her languid gait
Unto a heifer's motion, by a cord
Tied to her arm, and picking thus from the lane
Its sustenance, while the girl with pallid hands
Was busy knitting in a heartless mood
Of solitude, and at the sight my friend
In agitation said, " 'Tis against *that*
That we are fighting," I with him believed
That a benignant spirit was abroad
Which might not be withstood, that poverty   520
Abject as this would in a little time
Be found no more, that we should see the earth
Unthwarted in her wish to recompense
The meek, the lowly, patient child of toil,
All institutes forever blotted out
That legalized exclusion, empty pomp
Abolished, sensual state and cruel power,
Whether by edict of the one or few ;
And finally, as sum and crown of all,
Should see the people having a strong hand   530
In framing their own laws ; whence better days
To all mankind.   But these things set apart,
Was not this single confidence enough

To animate the mind that ever turned
A thought to human welfare? That henceforth
Captivity by mandate without law
Should cease ; and open accusation lead
To sentence in the hearing of the world,
And open punishment, if not the air
Be free to breathe in, and the heart of man   540
Dread nothing. From this height I shall not stoop
To humbler matter that detained us oft
In thought or conversation, public acts,
And public persons, and emotions wrought
Within the breast, as ever-varying winds
Of record or report swept over us ;
But I might here, instead, repeat a tale,
Told by my Patriot friend, of sad events
That prove to what low depth had struck the roots,
How widely spread the boughs of that old tree   550
Which, as a deadly mischief, and a foul
And black dishonor, France was weary of.

Oh, happy time of youthful lovers, (thus
The story might begin,) oh, balmy time,
In which a love-knot, on a lady's brow,
Is fairer than the fairest star in Heaven !
So might — and with that prelude *did* begin
The record ; and, in faithful verse, was given
The doleful sequel.
                        But our little bark
On a strong river boldly hath been launched ;   560
And from the driving current should we turn
To loiter wilfully within a creek,

Howe'er attractive, Fellow voyager !
Would'st thou chide?   Yet deem not my pains lost :
For Vaudracour and Julia (so were named
The ill-fated pair) in that plain tale will draw
Tears from the hearts of others, when their own
Shall beat no more.   Thou, also, there mayst read,
At leisure, how the enamoured youth was driven,
By public power abashed, to fatal crime,   570
Nature's rebellion against monstrous law ;
How between heart and heart, oppression thrust
Her mandates, severing whom true love had joined,
Harassing both ; until he sank and pressed
The couch his fate had made for him ; supine,
Save when the stings of viperous remorse,
Trying their strength, enforced him to start up,
Aghast and prayerless.   Into a deep wood
He fled, to shun the haunts of human kind ;
There dwelt, weakened in spirit more and more ;   580
Nor could the voice of Freedom, which through France
Full speedily resounded, public hope,
Or personal memory of his own worst wrongs,
Rouse him ; but, hidden in those gloomy shades,
His days he wasted, — an imbecile mind.

BOOK TENTH.

———◦✦◦———

IT was a beautiful and silent day
That overspread the countenance of earth,
Then fading with unusual quietness, —
A day as beautiful as e'er was given
To soothe regret, though deepening what it soothed,
When by the gliding Loire I paused, and cast
Upon his rich domains, vineyard and tilth,
Green meadow-ground, and many-colored woods,
Again, and yet again, a farewell look ;
Then from the quiet of that scene passed on,   10
Bound to the fierce Metropolis.   From his throne
The King had fallen, and that invading host —
Presumptuous cloud, on whose black front was written
The tender mercies of the dismal wind
That bore it — on the plains of Liberty
Had burst innocuous.   Say in bolder words,
They — who had come elate as eastern hunters
Banded beneath the Great Mogul, when he
Erewhile went forth from Agra or Lahore,
Rajahs and Omlahs in his train, intent   20
To drive their prey enclosed within a ring

Wide as a province, but the signal given,
Before the point of the life-threatening spear
Narrowing itself by moments — they, rash men,
Had seen the anticipated quarry turned
Into avengers, from whose wrath they fled
In terror.   Disappointment and dismay
Remained for all whose fancies had run wild
With evil expectations ; confidence
And perfect triumph for the better cause.   30

   The State, as if to stamp the final seal
On her security, and to the world
Show that she was, a high and fearless soul,
Exulting in defiance, or heart-stung
By sharp resentment, or belike to taunt
With spiteful gratitude the baffled League,
That had stirred up her slackening faculties
To a new transition, when the King was crushed,
Spared not the empty throne, and in proud haste
Assumed the body and venerable name   40
Of a Republic.   Lamentable crimes,
'Tis true, had gone before this hour, dire work
Of massacre, in which the senseless sword
Was prayed to as a judge ; but these were past,
Earth free from them forever, as was thought, —
Ephemeral monsters, to be seen but once !
Things that could only show themselves and die.

   Cheered with this hope, to Paris I returned,
And ranged, with ardor heretofore unfelt,
The spacious city, and in progress passed   50

The prison where the unhappy Monarch lay,
Associate with his children and his wife
In bondage ; and the palace, lately stormed
With roar of cannon by a furious host.
I crossed the square (an empty area then !)
Of the Carrousel, where so late had lain
The dead, upon the dying heaped, and gazed
On this and other spots, as doth a man
Upon a volume whose contents he knows
Are memorable, but from him locked up,   60
Being written in a tongue he cannot read,
So that he questions the mute leaves with pain,
And half upbraids their silence.   But that night
I felt most deeply in what world I was,
What ground I trod on, and what air I breathed.
High was my room and lonely, near the roof
Of a large mansion or hotel, a lodge
That would have pleased me in more quiet times ;
Nor was it wholly without pleasure then.
With unextinguished taper I kept watch,   70
Reading at intervals ; the fear gone by
Pressed on me almost like a fear to come.
I thought of those September massacres,
Divided from me by one little month,
Saw them and touched ; the rest was conjured up
From tragic fictions or true history,
Remembrances and dim admonishments.
The horse is taught his manage, and no star
Of wildest course but treads back his own steps ;
For the spent hurricane the air provides   80
As fierce a successor ; the tide retreats

But to return out of its hiding-place
In the great deep; all things have second birth;
The earthquake is not satisfied at once;
And in this way I wrought upon myself,
Until I seemed to hear a voice that cried,
To the whole city, "Sleep no more."   The trance
Fled with the voice to which it had given birth;
But vainly comments of a calmer mind
Promised soft peace and sweet forgetfulness.   90
The place, all hushed and silent as it was,
Appeared unfit for the repose of night,
Defenceless as a wood where tigers roam.

With early morning towards the Palace-walk
Of Orleans eagerly I turned; as yet
The streets were still; not so those long Arcades;
There, 'mid a peal of ill-matched sounds and cries,
That greeted me on entering, I could hear
Shrill voices from the hawkers in the throng,
Bawling, " Denunciation of the Crimes   100
Of Maximilian Robespierre ; " the hand,
Prompt as the voice, held forth a printed speech,
The same that had been recently pronounced,
When Robespierre, not ignorant for what mark
Some words of indirect reproof had been
Intended, rose in hardihood, and dared
The man who had an ill surmise of him
To bring his charge in openness; whereat,
When a dead pause ensued, and no one stirred
In silence of all present, from his seat   110
Louvet walked single through the avenue,

And took his station in the Tribune, saying,
" I, Robespierre, accuse thee ! "   Well is known
The inglorious issue of that charge, and how
He, who had launched the startling thunderbolt,
The one bold man, whose voice the attack had sounded,
Was left without a follower to discharge
His perilous duty, and retire lamenting
That Heaven's best aid is wasted upon men
Who to themselves are false.
　　　　　　　　But these are things　120
Of which I speak, only as they were storm
Or sunshine to my individual mind,
No further.　Let me then relate that now —
In some sort seeing with my proper eyes
That Liberty, and Life, and Death would soon
To the remotest corners of the land
Lie in the arbitrement of those who ruled
The capital City ; what was struggled for,
And by what combatants victory must be won ;
The indecision on their part whose aim　　130
Seemed best, and the straightforward path of those
Who in attack or in defence were strong
Through their impiety — my inmost soul
Was agitated ; yea, I could almost
Have prayed that throughout earth upon all men,
By patient exercise of reason made
Worthy of liberty, all spirits filled
With zeal expanding in Truth's holy light,
The gift of tongues might fall, and power arrive
From the four quarters of the winds to do　　140
For France, what without help she could not do,

A work of honor; think not that to this
I added, work of safety; from all doubt
Or trepidation for the end of things
Far was I, far as angels are from guilt.

Yet did I grieve, nor only grieved, but thought
Of opposition and of remedies :
An insignificant stranger and obscure,
And one, moreover, little graced with power
Of eloquence even in my native speech,   150
And all unfit for tumult or intrigue,
Yet would I at this time with willing heart
Have undertaken for a cause so great
Service however dangerous.   I revolved
How much the destiny of Man had still
Hung upon single persons; that there was,
Transcendent to all local patrimony,
One nature, as there is one sun in heaven;
That objects, even as they are great, thereby
Do come within the reach of humblest eyes;   160
That Man is only weak through his mistrust
And want of hope where evidence divine
Proclaims to him that hope should be most sure;
Nor did the inexperience of my youth
Preclude conviction that a spirit strong
In hope and trained to noble aspirations,
A spirit thoroughly faithful to itself,
Is for Society's unreasoning herd
A domineering instinct, serves at once
For way and guide, a fluent receptacle   170
That gathers up each petty straggling rill

And vein of water, glad to be rolled on
In safe obedience ; that a mind, whose rest
Is where it ought to be, in self-restraint,
In circumspection and simplicity,
Falls rarely in entire discomfiture
Below its aim, or meets with, from without,
A treachery that foils it or defeats ;
And, lastly, if the means on human will,
Frail human will, dependent should betray   180
Him who too boldly trusted them, I felt
That 'mid the loud distractions of the world
A sovereign voice subsists within the soul,
Arbiter undisturbed of right and wrong,
Of life and death, in majesty severe
Enjoining, as may best promote the aims
Of truth and justice, either sacrifice,
From whatsoever region of our cares
Or our infirm affections Nature pleads,
Earnest and blind, against the stern decree.   190

On the other side, I called to mind those truths
That are the common-places of the schools —
(A theme for boys, too hackneyed for their sires,)
Yet, with a revelation's liveliness,
In all their comprehensive bearings known
And visible to philosophers of old,
Men who, to business of the world untrained,
Lived in the shade ; and to Harmodius known
And his compeer, Aristogiton, known
To Brutus — that tyrannic power is weak,   200
Hath neither gratitude, nor faith, nor love,

Nor the support of good or evil men
To trust in ; that the godhead which is ours
Can never utterly be charmed or stilled ;
That nothing hath a natural right to last
But equity and reason ; that all else
Meets foes irreconcilable, and at best
Lives only by variety of disease.

Well might my wishes be intense, my thoughts
Strong and perturbed, not doubting at that time   210
But that the virtue of one paramount mind
Would have abashed those impious crests — have quelled
Outrage and bloody power, and — in despite
Of what the People long had been and were
Through ignorance and false teaching, sadder proof
Of immaturity, and in the teeth
Of desperate opposition from without —
Have cleared a passage for just government
And left a solid birthright to the State,
Redeemed, according to example given   220,
By ancient lawgivers.
                In this frame of mind,
Dragged by a chain of harsh necessity,
So seemed it, — now I thankfully acknowledge,
Forced by the gracious providence of Heaven —
To England I returned, else (though assured
That I both was and must be of small weight,
No better than a landsman on the deck
Of a ship struggling with a hideous storm)
Doubtless, I should have then made common cause
With some who perished ; haply perished too,   230

A poor mistaken and bewildered offering, —
Should to the breast of Nature have gone back,
With all my resolutions, all my hopes,
A Poet only to myself, to men
Useless, and even, beloved Friend ! a soul
To thee unknown !

        Twice had the trees let fall
Their leaves, as often Winter had put on
His hoary crown, since I had seen the surge
Beat against Albion's shore, since ear of mine
Had caught the accents of my native speech   240
Upon our native country's sacred ground.
A patriot of the world, how could I glide
Into communion with her sylvan shades,
Erewhile my tuneful haunt?   It pleased me more
To abide in the great City, where I found
The general air still busy with the stir
Of that first memorable onset made
By a strong levy of humanity
Upon the traffickers in Negro blood ;
Effort which, though defeated, had recalled   250
To notice old forgotten principles,
And through the nation spread a novel heat
Of virtuous feeling.   For myself, I own
That this particular strife had wanted power
To rivet my affections ; nor did now
Its unsuccessful issue much excite
My sorrow ; for I brought with me the faith
That, if France prospered, good men would not long
Pay fruitless worship to humanity,
And this most rotten branch of human shame,   260

Object, so seemed it, of superfluous pains,
Would fall together with its parent tree.
What, then, were my emotions, when in arms
Britain put forth her free-born strength in league,
Oh, pity and shame ! with those confederate Powers.
Not in my single self alone I found,
But in the minds of all ingenuous youth,
Change and subversion from that hour.   No shock
Given to my moral nature had I known
Down to that very moment ; neither lapse   270
Nor turn of sentiment that might be named
A revolution, save at this one time ;
All else was progress on the self-same path
On which, with a diversity of pace,
I had been travelling : this a stride at once
Into another region.   As a light
And pliant harebell, swinging in the breeze
On some gray rock — its birth-place — so had I
Wantoned, fast rooted on the ancient tower
Of my beloved country, wishing not   280
A happier fortune than to wither there :
Nor was I from that pleasant station torn
And tossed about in whirlwind.   I rejoiced,
Yea, afterwards — truth most painful to record ! —
Exulted, in the triumph of my soul.
When Englishmen by thousands were o'erthrown,
Left without glory on the field, or driven,
Brave hearts ! to shameful flight.   It was a grief, —
Grief call it not, 'twas anything but that, —
A conflict of sensations without name,   290
Of which *he* only, who may love the sight

Of a village steeple, as I do, can judge,
When, in the congregation bending all
To their great Father, prayers were offered up,
Or praises for our country's victories ;
And, 'mid the simple worshippers, perchance
I only, like an uninvited guest
Whom no one owned, sate silent ; shall I add,
Fed on the day of vengeance yet to come.

Oh ! much have they to account for, who could tear,
By violence, at one decisive rent,   301
From the best youth in England their dear pride,
Their joy, in England ; this, too, at a time
In which worst losses easily might wean
The best of names, when patriotic love   .
Did of itself in modesty give way,
Like the Precursor when the Deity
Is come Whose harbinger he was ; a time
In which apostasy from ancient faith
Seemed but conversion to a higher creed ;   310
Withal a season dangerous and wild,
A time when sage Experience would have snatched
Flowers out of any hedge-row to compose
A chaplet in contempt of his gray locks.

When the proud fleet that bears the red-cross flag
In that unworthy service was prepared
To mingle, I beheld the vessels lie,
A brood of gallant creatures, on the deep ;
I saw them in their rest, a sojourner

Through a whole month of calm and glassy days   320
In that delightful island which protects
Their place of convocation ; there I heard,
Each evening, pacing by the still sea-shore,
A monitory sound that never failed, —
The sunset cannon.   While the orb went down
In the tranquillity of nature, came
That voice, ill requiem ! seldom heard by me
Without a spirit overcast by dark
Imaginations, sense of woes to come,
Sorrow for human kind, and pain of heart.   330

In France, the men who, for their desperate ends,
Had plucked up mercy by the roots, were glad
Of this new enemy.   Tyrants, strong before
In wicked pleas, were strong as demons now ;
And thus, on every side beset with foes,
The goaded land waxed mad ; the crimes of few
Spread into madness of the many ; blasts
From hell became sanctified like airs from heaven.
The sternness of the just, the faith of those
Who doubted not that Providence had times   340
Of vengeful retribution, theirs who throned
The human Understanding paramount,
And made of that their God, the hopes of men
Who were content to barter short-lived pangs
For a paradise of ages, the blind rage
Of insolent tempers, the light vanity
Of intermeddlers, steady purposes
Of the suspicious, slips of the indiscreet,
And all the accidents of life were pressed

Into one service, busy with one work.   350
The Senate stood aghast, her prudence quenched,
Her wisdom stifled, and her justice scared,
Her frenzy only active to extol
Past outrages, and shape the way for new,
Which no one dared to oppose or mitigate.

Domestic carnage now filled the whole year
With feast-days ; old men from the chimney-nook,
The maiden from the bosom of her love,
The mother from the cradle of her babe,
The warrior from the field — all perished, all —   360
Friends, enemies, of all parties, ages, ranks,
Head after head, and never heads enough
For those that bade them fall.   They found their joy,
They made it proudly, eager as a child
(If like desires of innocent little ones
May with such heinous appetites be compared),
Pleased in some open field to exercise
A toy that mimics with revolving wings
The motion of a wind-mill : though the air
Do of itself blow fresh, and make the vanes   370
Spin in his eyesight, *that* contents him not,
But, with the plaything at arm's length, he sets
His front against the blast, and runs amain,
That it may whirl the faster.
                                    Amid the depth
Of those enormities, even thinking minds
Forgot, at seasons, whence they had their being ;
Forgot that such a sound was ever heard
As Liberty upon earth : yet all beneath

Her innocent authority was wrought,
Nor could have been, without her blessed name.   380
The illustrious wife of Roland, in the hour
Of her composure, felt that agony,
And gave it vent in her last words.   O Friend !
It was a lamentable time for man,
Whether a hope had e'er been his or not ;
A woful time for them whose hopes survived
The shock ; most woful for those few who still
Were flattered, and had trust in human kind :
They had the deepest feeling of the grief.
Meanwhile the Invaders fared as they deserved :   390
The Herculean Commonwealth had put forth her arms,
And throttled with an infant godhead's might
The snakes about her cradle ; that was well,
And as it should be ; yet no cure for them
Whose souls were sick with pain of what would be
Hereafter brought in charge against mankind.
Most melancholy at that time, O Friend !
Were my day-thoughts, — my nights were miserable ;
Through months, through years, long after the last beat
Of those atrocities, the hour of sleep   400
To me came rarely charged with natural gifts,
Such ghastly visions had I of despair
And tyranny, and implements of death ;
And innocent victims sinking under fear,
And momentary hope, and worn-out prayer,
Each in his separate cell, or penned in crowds
For sacrifice, and struggling with fond mirth
And levity in dungeons, where the dust
Was laid with tears.   Then suddenly the scene

Changed, and the unbroken dream entangled me   410
In long orations, which I strove to plead
Before unjust tribunals, — with a voice
Laboring, a brain confounded, and a sense,˙
Death-like, of treacherous desertion, felt
In the last place of refuge — my own soul.

When I began in youth's delightful prime
To yield myself to Nature, when that strong
And holy passion overcame me first,
Nor day nor night, evening or morn, was free
From its oppression. But, O Power Supreme !   420
Without whose call this world would cease to breathe,
Who from the fountain of Thy grace dost fill
The veins that branch through every frame of life,
Making man what he is, creature divine,
In single or in social eminence,
Above the rest raised infinite ascents
When reason that enables him to be
Is not sequestered — what a change is here !
How different ritual for this after-worship,
What countenance to promote this second love !   430
The first was service paid to things which lie
Guarded within the bosom of Thy will.
Therefore to serve was high beatitude ;
Tumult was therefore gladness, and the fear
Ennobling, venerable ; sleep secure,
And waking thoughts more rich than happiest dreams.

But as the ancient Prophets, borne aloft
In vision, yet constrained by natural laws

With them to take a troubled human heart,
Wanted not consolations, nor a creed   440
Of reconcilement, then when they denounced,
On towns and cities, wallowing in the abyss
Of their offences, punishment to come ;
Or saw, like other men, with bodily eyes,
Before them, in some desolated place,
The wrath consummate and the threat fulfilled.
So, with devout humility be it said,
So did a portion of that spirit fall
On me uplifted from the vantage-ground
Of pity and sorrow to a state of being   450
That through the time's exceeding fierceness saw
Glimpses of retribution, terrible,
And in the order of sublime behests ;
But, even if that were not, amid the awe
Of unintelligible chastisement,
Not only acquiescences of faith
Survived, but daring sympathies with power,
Motions not treacherous or profane, else why
Within the folds of no ungentle breast
Their dread vibration to this hour prolonged?   460
Wild blasts of music thus could find their way
Into the midst of turbulent events ;
So that worst tempests might be listened to.
Then was the truth received into my heart,
That, under heaviest sorrow earth can bring,
If from the affliction somewhere do not grow
Honor which could not else have been, a faith,
An elevation, and a sanctity,
If new strength be not given nor old restored,

The blame is ours, not Nature's.   When a taunt   470
Was taken up by scoffers in their pride,
Saying, " Behold the harvest that we reap
From popular government and equality,"
I clearly saw that neither these nor aught
Of wild belief engrafted on their names
By false philosophy had caused the woe,
But a terrible reservoir of guilt
And ignorance filled up from age to age,
That could no longer hold its loathsome charge,
But burst and spread in deluge through the land.   480

   And as the desert hath green spots, the sea
Small islands scattered amid stormy waves,
So *that* disastrous period did not want
Bright sprinklings of all human excellence,
To which the silver wands of saints in Heaven
Might point with rapturous joy.   Yet not the less,
For those examples, in no age surpassed,
Of fortitude and energy and love,
And human nature faithful to herself
Under worst trials, was I driven to think   490
Of the glad times when first I traversed France
A youthful pilgrim ; above all reviewed
That eventide, when under windows bright
With happy faces and with garlands hung,
And through a rainbow-arch that spanned the street,
Triumphal pomp for liberty confirmed,
I paced, a dear companion at my side,
The town of Arras, whence with promise high
Issued, on delegation to sustain

Humanity and right, *that* Robespierre,　　　500
He who thereafter, and in how short time !
Wielded the sceptre of the Atheist crew.
When the calamity spread far and wide —
And this same city, that did then appear
To outrun the rest in exultation, groaned
Under the vengeance of her cruel son,
As Lear reproached the winds — I could almost
Have quarrelled with that blameless spectacle
For lingering yet an image in my mind
To mock me under such a strange reverse.　　　510

　　O Friend ! few happier moments have been mine
Than that which told the downfall of this Tribe
So dreaded, so abhorred.　The day deserves
A separate record.　Over the smooth sands
Of Leven's ample estuary lay
My journey, and beneath a genial sun,
With distant prospect among gleams of sky
And clouds, and intermingling mountain tops,
In one inseparable glory clad,
Creatures of one ethereal substance met　　　520
In consistory, like a diadem
Or crown of burning seraphs as they sit
In the empyrean.　Underneath that pomp
Celestial, lay unseen the pastoral vales
Among whose happy fields I had grown up
From childhood.　On the fulgent spectacle,
That neither passed away nor changed, I gazed
Enrapt ; but brightest things are wont to draw
Sad opposites out of the inner heart,

As even their pensive influence drew from mine.　530
How could it otherwise? for not in vain
That very morning had I turned aside
To seek the ground where, 'mid a throng of graves,
An honored teacher of my youth was laid,
And on the stone were graven by his desire
Lines from the churchyard elegy of Gray.
This faithful guide, speaking from his death-bed,
Added no farewell to his parting counsel,
But said to me, "My head will soon lie low;"
And when I saw the turf that covered him,　540
After the lapse of full eight years, those words,
With sound of voice and countenance of the Man,
Came back upon me, so that some few tears
Fell from me in my own despite. But now
I thought, still traversing that widespread plain,
With tender pleasure of the verses graven
Upon this tombstone, whispering to myself.
He loved the Poets, and, if now alive,
Would have loved me, as one not destitute
Of promise, nor belying the kind hope　550
That he had formed, when I, at his command,
Began to spin, with toil, my earliest songs.

As I advanced, all that I saw or felt
Was gentleness and peace. Upon a small
And rocky island near, a fragment stood
(Itself like a sea rock), the low remains
(With shells encrusted, dark with briny weeds)
Of a dilapidated structure, once
A Romish chapel, where the vested priest

Said matins at the hour that suited those 560
Who crossed the sands with ebb of morning tide.
Not far from that still ruin all the plain
Lay spotted with a variegated crowd
Of vehicles and travellers, horse and foot,
Wading beneath the conduct of their guide
In loose procession through the shallow stream
Of inland waters ; the great sea meanwhile
Heaved at safe distance, far retired.   I paused,
Longing for skill to paint a scene so bright
And cheerful, but the foremost of the band 570
As he approached, no salutation given
In the familiar language of the day,
Cried, " Robespierre is dead ! " — nor was a doubt,
After strict question, left within my mind
That he and his supporters all were fallen.

Great was my transport, deep my gratitude
To everlasting Justice, by this fiat
Made manifest.   " Come now, ye golden times,"
Said I forth-pouring on those open šands
A hymn of triumph : " as the morning comes 580
From out the bosom of the night, come ye :
Thus far our trust is verified ; behold !
They who with clumsy desperation, brought
A river of Blood, and preached that nothing else
Could cleanse the Augean stable by the might
Of their own helper have been swept away ;
Their madness stands declared and visible ;
Elsewhere will safety now be sought, and earth
March firmly towards righteousness and peace." —

Then schemes I framed more calmly, when and how   590
The madding factions might be tranquillized,
And how through hardships manifold and long
The glorious renovation would proceed.
Thus interrupted by uneasy bursts
Of exultation, I pursued my way
Along that very shore which I had skimmed
In former days, when — spurring from the Vale
Of Nightshade and St. Mary's mouldering fane,
And the stone abbot, after circuit made
In wantonness of heart, a joyous band   600
Of school-boys hastening to their distant home
Along the margin of the moonlight sea —
We beat with thundering hoofs the level sand.

BOOK ELEVENTH.

———•◦•———

FRANCE. — Concluded.

FROM that time forward, Authority in France
 • Put on a milder face ; Terror had ceased,
Yet everything was wanting that might give
Courage to them who looked for good by light
Of rational Experience, for the shoots
And hopeful blossoms of a second spring ;
Yet, in me, confidence was unimpaired ;
The Senate's language, and the public acts
And measures of the Government, though both
Weak, and of heartless omen, had not power   10
To daunt me ; in the People was my trust :
And in the virtues which mine eyes had seen,
I knew that wound external could not take
Life from the young Republic ; that new foes
Would only follow, in the path of shame,
Their brethren, and her triumphs be in the end
Great, universal, irresistible.
This intuition led me to confound
One victory with another, higher far, —
Triumphs of unambitious peace at home,   20
And noiseless fortitude.   Beholding still

Resistance strong as heretofore, I thought
That what was in degree the same was likewise
The same in quality, — that, as the worse
Of the two spirits then at strife remained
Untired, the better, surely, would preserve
The heart that first had roused him.   Youth maintains,
In all conditions of society,
Communion more direct and intimate
With Nature, — hence, ofttimes, with reason too —   30
Than age or manhood, even.   To Nature, then,
Power had reverted, habit, custom, law,
Had left an interregnum's open space,
For *her* to move about in, uncontrolled.
Hence could I see how Babel-like their task,
Who, by the recent deluge stupefied,
With their whole souls went culling from the day
Its petty promises, to build a tower
For their own safety ; laughed with my compeers
At gravest heads, by enmity to France   40
Distempered, till they found, in every blast
Forced from the street-disturbing newsman's horn,
For her great cause record or prophecy
Of utter ruin.   How might we believe
That wisdom could, in any shape, come near
Men clinging to delusions so insane?
And thus, experience proving that no few
Of our opinions had been just, we took
Like credit to ourselves where less was due,
And thought that other notions were as sound,   50
Yea, could not but be right, because we saw
That foolish men opposed them.

                                    To a strain
More animated I might here give way,
And tell, since juvenile errors are my theme,
What in those days, through Britain, was performed
To turn *all* judgments out of their right course ;
But this is passion over-near ourselves,
Reality too close and too intense,
And intermixed with something, in my mind,
Of scorn and condemnation personal,   60
That would profane the sanctity of verse.
Our Shepherds, this say, merely, at that time
Acted, or seemed at least to act, like men
Thirsting to make the guardian crook of law
A tool of murder ; they who ruled the State,
Though with such awful proof before their eyes
That he, who would sow death, reaps death, or worse,
And can reap nothing better, child-like longed
To imitate, not wise enough to avoid ;
Or left (by mere timidity betrayed)   70
The plain straight road, for one no better chosen
Than if their wish had been to undermine
Justice, and make an end of Liberty.

    But from these bitter truths I must return
To my own history.   It hath been told
That I was led to take an eager part
In arguments of civil polity,
Abruptly, and indeed before my time :
I had approached, like other youths, the shield
Of human nature from the golden side,   80
And would have fought, even to the death, to attest

The quality of the metal which I saw.
What there is best in individual man,
Of wise in passion, and sublime in power,
Benevolent in small societies,
And great in large ones, I had oft revolved,
Felt deeply, but not thoroughly understood
By reason : nay, far from it ; they were yet,
As cause was given me afterwards to learn,
Not proof against the injuries of the day ;   90
Lodged only at the sanctuary's door,
Not safe within its bosom.   Thus prepared,
And with such general insight into evil,
And of the bounds which sever it from good,
As books and common intercourse with life
Must needs have given — to the inexperienced mind,
When the world travels in a beaten road,
Guide faithful as is needed — I began
To meditate with ardor on the rule
And management of nations ; what it is   100
And ought to be ; and strove to learn how far
Their power or weakness, wealth or poverty,
Their happiness or misery, depends
Upon their laws, and fashion of the State.

O pleasant exercise of hope and joy !
For mighty were the auxiliars which then stood
Upon our side, us who were strong in love !
Bliss was it in that dawn to be alive,
But to be young was very Heaven !   O times,
In which the meagre, stale, forbidding ways   110
Of custom, law, and statute, took at once

The attraction of a country in romance !
When Reason seemed the most to assert her rights
When most intent on making of herself
A prime enchantress — to assist the work,
Which then was going forward in her name !
Not favored spots alone, but the whole Earth,
The beauty wore of promise — that which sets
(As at some moments might not be unfelt
Among the bowers of Paradise itself)   120
The budding rose above the rose full blown
What temper at the prospect did not wake
To happiness unthought of?   The inert
Were roused, and lively natures rapt away !
They who had fed their childhood upon dreams,
The play-fellows of fancy, who had made
All powers of swiftness, subtilty, and strength
Their ministers, — who in lordly wise had stirred
Among the grandest objects of the sense,
And dealt with whatsoever they found there   130
As if they had within some lurking right
To wield it ; — they, too, who of gentle mood
Had watched all gentle motions, and to these
Had fitted their own thoughts, schemers more mild,
And in the region of their peaceful selves ; —
Now was it that *both* found, the meek and lofty
Did both find helpers to their hearts' desire,
And stuff at hand, plastic as they could wish, —
Were called upon to exercise their skill,
Not in Utopia, — subterranean fields, —   140
Or some secreted island, Heaven knows where !
But in the very world, which is the world

Of all of us, — the place where, in the end,
We find our happiness, or not at all !

Why should I not confess that Earth was then
To me what an inheritance, new-fallen,
Seems, when the first time visited, to one
Who thither comes to find in it his home !
He walks about and looks upon the spot
With cordial transport, moulds it and remoulds,   150
And is half pleased with things that are amiss,
'Twill be such joy to see them disappear.

An active partisan, I thus convoked
From every object pleasant circumstance
To suit my ends ; I moved among mankind
With genial feelings still predominant ;
When erring, erring on the better part,
And in the kinder spirit ; placable,
Indulgent, as not uninformed that men
See as they have been taught — Antiquity   160
Gives rights to error ; and aware, no less,
That throwing off oppression must be work
As well of License as of Liberty ;
And above all — for this was more than all —
Not caring if the wind did now and then
Blow keen upon an eminence that gave
Prospect so large into futurity ;
In brief, a child of Nature, as at first,
Diffusing only those affections wider
That from the cradle had grown up with me,   170
And losing, in no other way than light
Is lost in light, the weak in the more strong.

In the main outline, such it might be said
Was my condition, till with open war
Britain opposed the liberties of France.
This threw me first out of the pale of love;
Soured and corrupted, upwards to the source,
My sentiments; was not, as hitherto,
A swallowing up of lesser things in great,
But change of them into their contraries;   180
And thus a way was opened for mistakes
And false conclusions, in degree as gross,
In kind more dangerous.   What had been a pride
Was now a shame; my likings and my loves
Ran in new channels, leaving old ones dry:
And hence a blow that, in maturer age,
Would but have touched the judgment, struck more deep
Into sensations near the heart: meantime,
As from the first, wild theories were afloat,
To whose pretensions, sedulously urged,   190
I had but lent a careless ear, assured
That time was ready to set all things right,
And that the multitude, so long oppressed,
Would be oppressed no more.
                                        But when events
Brought less encouragement, and unto these
The immediate proof of principles no more
Could be entrusted, while the events themselves,
Worn out in greatness, stripped of novelty,
Less occupied the mind, and sentiments
Could through my understanding's natural growth   200
No longer keep their ground, by faith maintained
Of inward consciousness, and hope that laid

Her hand upon her object — evidence
Safer, of universal application, such
As could not be impeached, was sought elsewhere.

But now, become oppressors in their turn,
Frenchmen had changed a war of self-defence
For one of conquest, losing sight of all
Which they had struggled for : up mounted now,
Openly in the eye of earth and heaven,   ·   210
The scale of liberty.   I read her doom,
With anger vexed, with disappointment sore,
But not dismayed, nor taking to the shame
Of a false prophet.   While resentment rose
Striving to hide, what naught could heal the wounds
Of mortified presumption, I adhered
More firmly to old tenets, and, to prove
Their temper, strained them more ; and thus, in heat
Of contest, did opinions every day
Grow into consequence, till round my mind   220
They clung, as if they were its life, nay more,
The very being of the immortal soul.

This was the time, when, all things tending fast
To depravation, speculative schemes —
That promised to abstract the hopes of Man
Out of his feelings, to be fixed thenceforth
Forever in a purer element —
Found ready welcome.   Tempting region *that*
For zeal to enter and refresh herself,
Where passions had the privilege to work,   230
And never hear the sound of their own names.

But, speaking more in charity, the dream
Flattered the young, pleased with extremes, nor least
With that which makes our Reason's naked self
The object of its fervor.   What delight !
How gloriòus ! in self-knowledge and self-rule,
To look through all the frailties of the world,
And, with a resolute mastery shaking off
Infirmities of nature, time, and place,
Build social upon personal Liberty,   240
Which, to the blind restraints of general laws
Superior, magisterially adopts
One guide, the light of circumstances, flashed
Upon an independent intellect.
Thus expectation rose again ; thus hope,
From her first ground expelled, grew proud once more.
Oft, as my thoughts were turned to human kind,
I scorned indifference ; but, inflamed with thirst
Of a secure intelligence, and sick
Of other longing, I pursued what seemed   250
A more exalted nature ; wished that Man
Should start out of his earthly, worm-like state,
And spread abroad the wings of Liberty,
Lord of himself, in undisturbed delight —
A noble aspiration ! *yet* I feel
(Sustained by worthier as by wiser thoughts)
The aspiration, nor shall ever cease
To feel it ; — but return we to our course.

Enough, 'tis true — could such a plea excuse
Those aberrations — had the clamorous friends   260
Of ancient Institutions said and donc

To bring disgrace upon their very names ;
Disgrace, of which, custom and written law,
And sundry moral sentiments as props
Or emanations of those institutes,
Too justly bore a part.   A veil had been
Uplifted ; why deceive ourselves? in sooth
'Twas even so ; and sorrow for the man
Who either had not eyes wherewith to see,
Or, seeing, had forgotten !   A strong shock   270
Was given to old opinions ; all men's minds
Had felt its power, and mine was both let loose,
Let loose and goaded.   After what hath been
Already said of patriotic love,
Suffice it here to add, that, somewhat stern
In temperament, withal a happy man,
And therefore bold to look on painful things,
Free likewise of the world, and thence more bold,
I summoned my best skill, and toiled, intent
To anatomize the frame of social life,   280
Yea, the whole body of society
Searched to its heart.   Share with me, Friend ! the wish
That some dramatic tale, endued with shapes
Livelier, and flinging out less guarded words
Than suit the work we fashion, might set forth
What then I learned, or think I learned, of truth,
And the errors into which I fell, betrayed
By present objects, and by reasonings false
From their beginnings, inasmuch as drawn
Out of a heart that had been turned aside   290
From Nature's way by outward accidents,
And which was thus confounded, more and more

Misguided and misguiding. So I fared,
Dragging all precepts, judgments, maxims, creeds,
Like culprits to the bar; calling the mind,
Suspiciously, to establish in plain day
Her titles and her honors; now believing,
Now disbelieving; endlessly perplexed
With impulse, motive, right and wrong, the ground
Of obligation, what the rule and whence   300
The sanction; till, demanding formal *proof*,
And seeking it in every thing, I lost
All feeling of conviction, and, in fine,
Sick, wearied out with contrarieties,
Yielded up moral questions in despair.

   This was the crisis of that strong disease,
This the soul's last and lowest ebb; I drooped.
Deeming our blessèd reason of least use
Where wanted most: "The lordly attributes
Of will and choice," I bitterly exclaimed,   310
" What are they but a mockery of a Being
Who hath in no concerns of his a test
Of good and evil; knows not what to fear
Or hope for, what to covet or to shun :
And who, if those could be discerned, would yet
Be little profited, would see, and ask   .
Where is the obligation to enforce?
And, to acknowledged law rebellious, still,
As selfish passion urged, would act amiss;
The dupe of folly, or the slave of crime."   320

   Depressed, bewildered thus, I did not walk,
With scoffers, seeking light and gay revenge

From indiscriminate laughter, nor sate down
In reconcilement with an utter waste
Of intellect; such sloth I could not brook,
(Too well I loved, in that my spring of life,
Pains-taking thoughts, and truth, their dear reward)
But turned to abstract science, and there sought
Work for the reasoning faculty enthroned
Where the disturbances of space and time   330
Whether in matters various, properties
Inherent, or from human will and power
Derived — find no admission.   Then it was —
Thanks to the bounteous Giver of all good ! —
That the beloved Sister in whose sight
Those days were passed, now speaking in a voice
Of sudden admonition — like a brook
That did but *cross* a lonely road, and now
Is seen, heard, felt, and caught at every turn,
Companion never lost through many a league —   340
Maintained for me a saving intercourse
With my true self; for, though bedimmed and changed
Much, as it seemed, I was no further changed
Than as a clouded and a waning moon :
She whispered still that brightness would return,
She, in the midst of all, preserved me still
A Poet, made me seek beneath that name,
And that alone, my office upon earth ;
And, lastly, as hereafter will be shown,
If willing audience fail not, Nature's self,   350
By all varieties of human love
Assisted, led me back through opening day
To whose sweet counsels between head and heart

Whence grew that genuine knowledge, fraught with peace,
Which, through the later sinkings of this cause,
Hath still upheld me, and upholds me now
In the catastrophe (for so they dream,
And nothing less), when, finally to close
And seal up all the gains of France, a Pope
Is summoned in, to crown an Emperor —   360
This last opprobrium, when we see a people,
That once looked up in faith, as if to Heaven
For manna, take a lesson from the dog
Returning to his vomit; when the sun
That rose in splendor, was alive, and moved ·
In exultation with a living pomp
Of clouds — his glory's natural retinue —
Hath dropped all functions by the gods bestowed,
And, turned into a gewgaw, a machine,
Sets like an Opera phantom.
                        Thus, O Friend !   370
Through times of honor and through times of shame
Descending, have I faithfully retraced
The perturbations of a youthful mind
Under a long-lived storm of great events —
A story destined for thy ear, who now,
Among the fallen of nations, dost abide
Where Etna, over hill and valley, casts
His shadow stretching towards Syracuse,
The city of Timoleon !   Righteous Heaven !
How are the mighty prostrated !   They first,   380
They first of all that breathe, should have awaked
When the great voice was heard from out the tombs
Of ancient heroes.   If I suffered grief

For ill-requited France, by many deemed
A trifler only in her proudest day ;
Have been distressed to think of what she once
Promised, now is ; a far more sober cause
Thine eyes must see of sorrow in a land,
To the reanimating influence lost
Of memory, to virtue lost and hope,   390
Though with the wreck of loftier years bestrewn.

But indignation works where hope is not,
And thou, O Friend ! wilt be refreshed.   There is
One great society alone on earth :
The noble Living and the noble Dead.

Thine be such converse strong and sanative,
A ladder for thy spirit to reascend
To health-and joy and pure contentedness ;
To me the grief confined, that thou art gone
From this last spot of earth, where freedom now   400
Stands single in her only sanctuary ;
A lonely wanderer art gone, by pain
Compelled and sickness, at this latter day,
This sorrowful reverse for all mankind.
I feel for thee, must utter what I feel :
The sympathies, erewhile in part discharged,
Gather afresh, and will have vent again :
My own delights do scarcely seem to me
My own delights ; the lordly Alps themselves,
Those rosy peaks from which the Morning looks   410
Abroad on many nations, are no more
For me that image of pure gladsomeness

Which they were wont to be.   Through kindred scenes,
For purpose, at a time, how different?
Thou tak'st thy way, carrying the heart and soul
That Nature gives to Poets, now by thought
Matured, and in the summer of their strength.
Oh ! wrap him in your shades, ye giant woods,
On Etna's side ; and thou, O flowery field
Of Enna ! is there not some nook of thine,   42c
From the first play-time of the infant world
Kept sacred to restorative delight,
When from afar invoked by anxious love?

    Child of the mountains, among shepherds reared,
Ere yet familiar with the classic page,
I learnt to dream of Sicily ; and lo,
The gloom, that, but a moment past, was deepened
At thy command, at her command gives way ;
A pleasant promise, wafted from her shores,
Comes o'er my heart : in fancy I behold   43c
Her seas yet smiling, her once happy vales ;
Nor can thy tongue give utterance to a name
Of note belonging to that honored isle,
Philosopher or Bard, Empedocles,
Or Archimedes, pure abstracted soul !
That doth not yield a solace to my grief :
And, O Theocritus, so far have some
Prevailed among the powers of heaven and earth,
By their endowments, good or great, that they
Have had, as thou reportest, miracles   440
Wrought for them in old time : yea, not unmoved,
When thinking on my own beloved friend,

I hear thee tell how bees with honey fed
Divine Comates by his impious lord
Within a chest imprisoned ; how they came
Laden from blooming grove or flowery field,
And feed him there, alive, month after month,
Because the goatherd, blessed man ! had lips
Wet with the Muses' nectar.
      Thus I soothe
The pensive moments by his calm fireside   450
And find a thousand bounteous images
To cheer the thoughts of those I love, and mine.
Our prayers have been accepted ; thou wilt stand
On Etna's summit, above earth and sea,
Triumphant, winning from the invaded heavens
Thoughts without bound, magnificent designs,
Worthy of poets who attuned their harps
In wood or echoing cave, for discipline
Of heroes ; or, in reverence to the gods,
'Mid temples, served by sapient priests, and choirs   460
Of virgins crowned with roses.   Not in vain
Those temples, where they in their ruins yet
Survive for inspiration, shall attract
Thy solitary steps : and on the brink
Thou wilt recline of pastoral Arethuse ;
Or, if that fountain be in truth no more,
Then near some other spring — which by the name
Thou gratulatest, willingly deceived —
I see thee linger a glad votary,
And not a captive pining for his home.   470

BOOK TWELFTH.

——◦◦——

IMAGINATION AND TASTE, HOW IMPAIRED AND RESTORED.

LONG time have human ignorance and guilt ·
Detained us, on what spectacles of woe
Compelled to look, and inwardly impress
With sorrow, disappointment, vexing thoughts,
Confusion of the judgment, zeal decayed,
And, lastly, utter loss of hope itself
And things to hope for !   Not with these began
Our song, and not with these our song must end. —
Ye motions of delight, that haunt the sides
Of the green hills ; ye breezes and soft airs,   10
Whose subtle intercourse with breathing flowers,
Feelingly watched, might teach Man's haughty race
How without injury to take, to give
Without offence ; ye who, as if to show
The wondrous influence of power gently used,
Bend the complying heads of lordly pines,
And, with a touch, shift the stupendous clouds
Through the whole compass of the sky ; ye brooks,
Muttering along the stones, a busy noise

By day, a quiet sound in silent night ;   20
Ye waves, that out of the great deep steal forth
In a calm hour to kiss the pebbly shore,
Not mute, and then retire, fearing no storm ;
And you, ye groves, whose ministry it is
To interpose the covert of your shades,
Even as a sleep, between the heart of man
And outward troubles, between man himself,
Not seldom, and his own uneasy heart :
Oh, that I had a music and a voice
Harmonious as your own, that I might tell   30
What ye have done for me.   The morning shines,
Nor heedeth Man's perverseness ; Spring returns, —
I saw the Spring return, and could rejoice,
In common with the children of love,
Piping on boughs, or sporting on fresh fields,
Or boldly seeking pleasure nearer heaven
On wings that navigate cerulean skies.
So neither were complacency, nor peace,
Nor tender yearnings, wanting for my good
Through these distracted times ; in Nature still   40
Glorying, I found a counterpoise in her,
Which when the spirit of evil reached its height
Maintained for me a secret happiness.

  This narrative, my Friend ! hath chiefly told
Of intellectual power, fostering love,
Dispensing truth, and, over men and things,
Where reason yet might hesitate, diffusing
Prophetic sympathies of genial faith :
So was I favored — such my happy lot —

Until that natural graciousness of mind
Gave way to overpressure from the times
And their disastrous issues.   What availed,
When spells forbade the voyager to land,
That fragrant notice of a pleasant shore
Wafted, at intervals, from many a bower
Of blissful gratitude and fearless love?
Dare I avow that wish was mine to see,
And hope that future times *would* surely see,
The man to come, parted, as by a gulph,
From him who had been; that I could no more
Trust the elevation which had made me one
With the great family that still survives
To illuminate the abyss of ages past,
Sage warrior, patriot, hero; for it seemed
That their best virtues were not free from taint
Of something false and weak, that could not stand
The open eye of Reason.   Then I said,
" Go to the Poets, they will speak to thee
More perfectly of purer creatures; — yet
If reason be nobility in man,
Can aught be more ignoble than the man
Whom they delight in, blinded as he is
By prejudice, the miserable slave
Of low ambition or distempered love?"

In such strange passion, if I may once more
Review the past, I warred against myself —
A bigot to a new idolatry —
Like a cowled monk who hath forsworn the world,
Zealously labored to cut off my heart

From all the sources of her former strength ;   80
And as, by simple waving of a wand,
The wizard instantaneously dissolves
Palace or grove, even so could I unsoul
As readily by syllogistic words
Those mysteries of being which have made,
And shall continue evermore to make,
Of the whole human race one brotherhood.

  What wonder, then, if, to a mind so far
Perverted, even the visible Universe
Fell under the dominion of a taste   90
Less spiritual with microscopic view
Was scanned, as I had scanned the moral world?

  O Soul of Nature ! excellent and fair !
That didst rejoice with me, with whom I, too,
Rejoiced through early youth, before the winds
And roaring waters, and in lights and shades
That marched and countermarched about the hills
In glorious apparition, Powers on whom
I daily waited, now all eye and now
All ear ; but never long without the heart   100
Employed, and man's unfolding intellect :
O Soul of Nature ! that, by laws divine
Sustained and governed, still dost overflow
With an impassioned life, what feeble ones
Walk on this earth ! how feeble have I been
When thou wert in thy strength ! Nor this through stroke
Of human suffering, such as justifies
Remissness and inaptitude of mind,

But through presumption; even in pleasure pleased
Unworthily, disliking here, and there   110
Liking; by rules of mimic art transferred
To things above all art; but more, — for this,
Although a strong infection of the age,
Was never much my habit — giving way
To a comparison of scene with scene,
Bent overmuch on superficial things,
Pampering myself with meagre novelties
Of color and proportion; to the moods
Of time and season, to the moral power,
The affections and the spirit of the place,   120
Insensible.   Nor only did the love
Of sitting thus in judgment interrupt
My deeper feelings, but another cause,
More subtle and less easily explained,
That almost seems inherent in the creature,
A twofold frame of body and of mind.
I speak in recollection of a time
When the bodily eye, in every stage of life
The most despotic of our senses, gained
Such strength in *me* as often held my mind   130
In absolute dominion.   Gladly here,
Entering upon abstruser argument,
Could I endeavor to unfold the means
Which Nature studiously employs to thwart
This tyranny, summons all the senses each
To counteract the other, and themselves,
And makes them all, and the objects with which all
Are conversant, subservient in their turn
To the great ends of Liberty and Power.

But leave we this ; enough that my delights   140
(Such as they were) were sought insatiably.
Vivid the transport, vivid though not profound ;
I roamed from hill to hill, from rock to rock,
Still craving combinations of new forms,
New pleasure, wider empire for the sight,
Proud of her own endowments, and rejoiced
To lay the inner faculties asleep.
Amid the turns and counterturns, the strife
And various trials of our complex being,
As we grow up, such thraldom of that sense   150
Seems hard to shun.   And yet I knew a maid,
A young enthusiast, who escaped these bonds ;
Her eye was not the mistress of her heart ;
Far less did rules prescribed by passive taste,
Or barren intermeddling subtleties,
Perplex her mind ; but, wise as women are
When genial circumstance hath favored them,
She welcomed what was given, and craved no more ;
Whate'er the scene presented to her view
That was the best, to that she was attuned   160
By her benign simplicity of life,
And through a perfect happiness of soul,
Whose variegated feelings were in this
Sisters, that they were each some new delight.
Birds in the bower, and lambs in the green field,
Could they have known her, would have loved ;
     methought
Her very presence such a sweetness breathed,
That flowers, and trees, and even the silent hills,
And everything she looked on, should have had

An intimation how she bore herself   170
Towards them and to all creatures.   God delights
In such a being; for, her common thoughts
Are piety, her life is gratitude.

    Even like this maid, before I was called forth
From the retirement of my native hills,
I loved whate'er I saw : nor lightly loved,
But most intensely; never dreamt of aught
More grand, more fair, more exquisitely framed
Than those few nooks to which my happy feet
Were limited.   I had not at that time   180
Lived long enough, nor in the least survived
The first diviner influence of this world,
As it appears to unaccustomed eyes,
Worshipping them among the depth of things,
As piety ordained; could I submit
To measured admiration, or to aught
That should preclude humility and love?
I felt, observed, and pondered ; did not judge, _
Yea, never thought of judging ; with the gift
Of all this glory filled and satisfied.   190
And afterwards, when through the gorgeous Alps
Roaming, I carried with me the same heart :
In truth, the degredation — howsoe'er
Induced, effect, in whatsoe'er degree,
Of custom that prepares a partial scale
In which the little oft outweighs the great ;
Or any other cause that hath been named ;
Or lastly, aggravated by the times
And their impassioned sounds, which well might make

The milder minstrelsies of rural scenes 200
Inaudible — was transient ; I had known
Too forcibly, too early in my life,
Visitings of imaginative power
For this to last : I shook the habit off
Entirely and forever, and again
In Nature's presence stood, as now I stand,
A sensitive being, a *creative* soul.

There are in our existence spots of time,
That with distinct pre-eminence retain
A renovating virtue, whence, depressed 210
By false opinion and contentious thought,
Or aught of heavier or more deadly weight,
In trivial occupations, and the round
Of ordinary intercourse, our minds
Are nourished and invisibly repaired ;
A virtue, by which pleasure is enhanced,
That penetrates, enables us to mount,
When high, more high, and lifts us up when fallen.
This efficacious spirit chiefly lurks
Among those passages of life that give 220
Profoundest knowledge to what point, and how,
The mind is lord and master — outward sense
The obedient servant of her will. Such moments
Are scattered everywhere, taking their date
From our first childhood. I remember well,
That once, while yet my inexperienced hand
Could scarcely hold a bridle, with proud hopes
I mounted, and we journeyed towards the hills :
An ancient servant of my father's house

Was with me, my encourager and guide :   230
We had not travelled long, ere some mischance
Disjoined me from my comrade ; and, through fear
Dismounting, down the rough and stony moor
I led my horse, and, stumbling on, at length
Came to a bottom, where in former times
A murderer had been hung in iron chains.
The gibbet-mast had mouldered down, the bones
And iron case were gone ; but on the turf,
Hard by, soon after that fell deed was wrought,
Some unknown hand had carved the murderer's name.
The monumental letters were inscribed   241
In times long past ; but still, from year to year,
By superstition of the neighborhood,
The grass is cleared away, and to this hour
The characters are fresh and visible ;
A casual glance had shown them, and I fled,
Faltering and faint, and ignorant of the road :
Then, reascending to the bare common, saw
A naked pool that lay beneath the hills,
The beacon on the summit, and, more near,   250
A girl, who bore a pitcher on her head,
And seemed with difficult steps to force her way
Against the blowing wind.   It was, in truth,
An ordinary sight ; but I should need
Colors and words that are unknown to man,
To paint the visionary dreariness
Which, while I looked all round for my lost guide,
Invested moorland waste, and naked pool,
The beacon crowning the lone eminence,
The female and her garments vexed and tossed   260

By the strong wind.   When, in the blessed hours
Of early love, the loved one at my side,
I roamed, in daily presence of this scene,
Upon the naked pool and dreary crags,
And on the melancholy beacon, fell
A spirit of pleasure and youth's golden gleam ;
And think ye not with radiance more sublime
For these remembrances, and for the power
They had left behind ?   So feeling comes in aid
Of feeling, and diversity of strength   270
Attends us, if but once we have been strong.
Oh ! mystery of man, from what a depth
Proceed thy honors.   I am lost, but see
In simple childhood something of the base
On which thy greatness stands ; but this I feel,
That from thyself it comes, that thou must give,
Else never canst receive.   The days gone by
Return upon me almost from the dawn
Of life : the hiding-places of man's power
Open ; I would approach them, but they close.   280
I see by glimpses now ; when age comes on,
May scarcely see at all ; and I would give,
While yet we may, as far as words can give,
Substance and life to what I feel, enshrining,
Such is my hope, the spirit of the Past
For future restoration. — Yet another
Of these memorials : —
                    One Christmas-time,
On the glad eve of its dear holidays,
Feverish, and tired, and restless, I went forth
Into the fields, impatient for the sight   290

Of those led palfreys that should bear us home ;
My brothers and myself.   There rose a crag,
That, from the meeting-point of two highways
Ascending, overlooked them both, far stretched ;
Thither, uncertain on which road to fix
My expectation, thither I repaired,
Scout-like, and gained the summit ; 'twas a day
Tempestuous, dark, and wild, and on the grass
I sate half sheltered by a naked wall ;
Upon my right hand couched a single sheep,   300
Upon my left a blasted hawthorn stood ;
With those companions at my side, I watched,
Straining my eyes intensely, as the mist
Gave intermitting prospect of the copse
And plain beneath.   Ere we to school returned, —
That dreary time, — ere we had been ten days
Sojourners in my father's house, he died,
And I and my three brothers, orphans then,
Followed his body to the grave.   The event,
With all the sorrow that it brought, appeared   310
A chastisement ; and when I called to mind
That day so lately past, when from the crag
I looked in such anxiety of hope ;
With trite reflections of morality,
Yet in the deepest passion, I bowed low
To God, Who thus corrected my desires ;
And, afterwards, the wind and sleety rain,
And all the business of the elements,
The single sheep, and the one blasted tree,
And the bleak music from that old stone wall,   320
The noise of wood and water, and the mist

That on the line of each of those two roads
Advanced in such indisputable shapes ;
All these were kindred spectacles and sounds
To which I oft repaired, and thence would drink,
As at a fountain ; and on winter nights,
Down to this very time, when storm and rain
Beat on my roof, or, haply, at noon-day,
While in a grove I walk, whose lofty trees,
Laden with summer's thickest foliage, rock   330
In a strong wind, some working of the spirit,
Some inward agitations thence are brought,
Whate'er their office, whether to beguile
Thoughts over busy in the course they took,
Or animate an hour of vacant ease.

BOOK THIRTEENTH.

IMAGINATION AND TASTE, HOW IMPAIRED AND
RESTORED. — Concluded.

FROM Nature doth emotion come, and moods
Of calmness equally are Nature's gift :
This is her glory ; these two attributes
Are sister horns that constitute her strength.
Hence Genius, born to thrive by interchange
Of peace and excitation, finds in her
His best and purest friend ; from her receives
That energy by which he seeks the truth,
From her that happy stillness of the mind
Which fits him to receive it when unsought.   10

   Such benefit the humblest intellects
Partake of, each in their degree ; 'tis mine
To speak, what I myself have known and felt ;
Smooth task ! for words find easy way, inspired
By gratitude, and confidence in truth.
Long time in search of knowledge did I range
The field of human life, in heart and mind
Benighted ; but, the dawn beginning now
To reappear, 'twas proved that not in vain

I had been taught to reverence a Power   20
That is the visible quality and shape
And image of right reason ; that matures
Her processes by steadfast laws ; gives birth
To no impatient or fallacious hopes,
No heat of passion or excessive zeal,
No vain conceits : provokes to no quick turns
Of self-applauding intellect ; but trains
To meekness, and exalts by humble faith ;
Holds up before the mind intoxicate
With present objects, and the busy dance   30
Of things that pass away, a temperate show
Of objects that endure ; and by this course
Disposes her, when over-fondly set
On throwing off incumbrances, to seek
In man, and in the frame of social life,
Whate'er there is desirable and good
Of kindred permanence, unchanged in form
And function, or, through strict vicissitude
Of life and death, revolving.   Above all
Were re-established now those watchful thoughts   40
Which, seeing little worthy or sublime
In what the Historian's pen so much delights
To blazon — power and energy detached
From moral purpose — early tutored me
To look with feelings of fraternal love
Upon the unassuming things that hold
A silent station in this beauteous world.

  Thus moderated, thus composed, I found
Once more in Man an object of delight,

Of pure imagination, and of love;   50
And, as the horizon of my mind enlarged,
Again I took the intellectual eye
For my instructor, studious more to see
Great truths, than touch and handle little ones.
Knowledge was given accordingly; my trust
Became more firm in feelings that had stood
The test of such a trial; clearer far
My sense of excellence — of right and wrong:
The promise of the present time retired
Into its true proportion; sanguine schemes,   60
Ambitious projects, pleased me less; I sought
For present good in life's familiar face,
And built thereon my hopes of good to come.

      With settling judgments now of what would last
And what would disappear; prepared to find
Presumption, folly, madness, in the men
Who thrust themselves upon the passive world
As Rulers of the world; to see in these,
Even when the public welfare is their aim,
Plans without thought, or built on theories   70
Vague and unsound; and having brought the books
Of modern statists to their proper test,
Life, human life, with all its sacred claims
Of sex and age, and heaven-descended rights,
Mortal, of those beyond the reach of death;
And having thus discerned how dire a thing
Is worshipped in that idol proudly named
"The Wealth of Nations," *where* alone that wealth
Is lodged, and how increased; and having gained

A more judicious knowledge of the worth   80
And dignity of individual man,
No composition of the brain, but man
Of whom we read, the man whom we behold
With our own eyes — I could not but inquire —
Not with less interest than heretofore,
But greater, though in spirit more subdued —
Why is this glorious creature to be found
One only in ten thousand?   What one is,
Why may not millions be?   What bars are thrown
By Nature in the way of such a hope?   90
Our animal appetites and daily wants,
Are these obstructions insurmountable?
If not, then others vanish into air.
"Inspect the basis of the social pile :
Inquire," said I, " how much of mental power
And genuine virtue they possess who live
By bodily toil, labor exceeding far
Their due proportion, under all the weight
Of that injustice, which upon ourselves
Ourselves entail."   Such estimate to frame   100
I chiefly looked (what need to look beyond?)
Among the natural abodes of men,
Fields with their rural works ; recalled to mind
My earliest notices ; with these compared
The observations made in later youth,
And to that day continued. — For the time
Had never been when throes of mighty Nations
And the world's tumult unto me could yield,
How far soe'er transported and possessed,
Full measure of content ; but still I craved   110

An intermingling of distinct regards
And truths of individual sympathy
Nearer ourselves.   Such often might be gleaned
From the great City, else it must have proved
To me a heart-depressing wilderness;
But much was wanting: therefore did I turn
To you, ye pathways, and ye lonely roads;
Sought you enriched with everything I prized,
With human kindnesses and simple joys.

    Oh! next to one dear state of bliss, vouchsafed   120
Alas! to few in this untoward world,
The bliss of walking daily in life's prime
Through field or forest with the maid we love,
While yet our hearts are young, while yet we breathe
Nothing but happiness, in some low nook,
Deep vale, or anywhere, the home of both,
From which it would be misery to stir:
Oh! next to such enjoyment of our youth,
In my esteem, next to such dear delight,
Was that of wandering on from day to day   130
Where I could meditate in peace, and cull
Knowledge that step by step might lead me on
To wisdom; or, as lightsome as a bird
Wafted upon the wind from distant lands,
Sing notes of greeting to strange fields or groves,
Which lacked not voice to welcome me in turn:
And, when that pleasant toil had ceased to please,
Converse with men, where if we meet a face
We almost meet a friend, on naked heaths

With long long ways before, by cottage bench, 140
Or well-spring where the weary traveller rests.

Who doth not love to follow with his eye
The windings of a public way? the sight,
Familiar object as it is, hath wrought
On my imagination since the morn
Of childhood, when a disappearing line
One daily present to my eyes, that crossed
The naked summit of a far-off hill
Beyond the limits that my feet had trod,
Was like an invitation into space 150
Boundless, or guide into eternity.
Yes, something of the grandeur which invests
The mariner who sails the roaring sea
Through storm and darkness, early in my mind
Surrounded, too, the wanderers of the earth;
Grandeur as much, and loveliness far more.
Awed have I been by strolling Bedlamites;
From many other uncouth vagrants (passed
In fear) have walked with quicker step; but why
Take note of this? When I began to enquire, 160
To watch and question those I met, and speak
Without reserve to them, the lonely roads
Were open schools in which I daily read
With most delight the passions of mankind,
Whether by words, looks, sighs, or tears, revealed;
There saw into the depth of human souls,
Souls that appear to have no depth at all
To careless eyes. And — now convinced at heart
How little those formalities, to which

With overweening trust alone we give   170
The name of Education, have to do
With real feeling and just sense ; how vain
A correspondence with the talking world
Proves to the most ; and called to make good search
If man's estate, by doom of Nature yoked
With toil, be therefore yoked with ignorance ;
If virtue be indeed so hard to rear,
And intellectual strength so rare a boon —
I prized such walks still more, for there I found
Hope to my hope, and to my pleasure peace   180
And steadiness, and healing and repose
To every angry passion. There I heard,
From mouths of men obscure and lowly, truths
Replete with honor ; sounds in unison
With loftiest promises of good and fair.

    There are who think that strong affection, love
Known by whatever name, is falsely deemed
A gift, — to use a term which they would use, —
Of vulgar nature ; that its growth requires
Retirement, leisure, language purified   190
By manners studied and elaborate ;
That whoso feels such passion in its strength
Must live within the very light and air
Of courteous usages refined by art.
True is it, where oppression worse than death
Salutes the being at his birth, where grace
Of culture hath been utterly unknown,
And poverty and labor in excess
From day to day pre-occupy the ground

Of the affections, and to Nature's self   200
Oppose a deeper nature; there, indeed,
Love cannot be; nor does it thrive with ease
Among the close and overcrowded haunts
Of cities, where the human heart is sick,
And the eye feeds it not, and cannot feed.
— Yes, in those wanderings deeply did I feel
How we mislead each other; above all,
How books mislead us, seeking their reward
From judgments of the wealthy Few, who see
By artificial lights; how they debase   210
The Many for the pleasure of those Few;
Effeminately level down the truth
To certain general notions, for the sake
Of being understood at once, or else
Through want of better knowledge in the heads
That framed them; flattering self-conceit with words,
That, while they most ambitiously set forth
Extrinsic differences, the outward marks
Whereby society has parted man
From man, neglect the universal heart.   220

Here, calling up to mind what then I saw,
A youthful traveller, and see daily now
In the familiar circuit of my home,
Here might I pause, and bend in reverence
To Nature, and the power of human minds,
To men as they are men within themselves.
How oft high service is performed within,
When all the external man is rude in show, —
Not like a temple rich with pomp and gold,

But a mere mountain chapel, that protects
Its simple worshippers from sun and shower.
Of these, said I, shall be my song; of these,
If future years mature me for the task,
Will I record the praises, making verse
Deal boldly with substantial things; in truth
And sanctity of passion, speak of these,
That justice may be done, obeisance paid
Where it is due : thus happy shall I teach,
Inspire; through unadulterated ears
Pour rapture, tenderness, and hope, — my theme
No other than the very heart of man,
As found among the best of those who live,
Not unexalted by religious faith,
Nor uninformed by books, good books, though few,
In Nature's presence : thence may I select
Sorrow, that is not sorrow, but delight;
And miserable love, that is not pain
To hear of, for the glory that redounds
Therefrom to human kind, and what we are.
Be mine to follow with no timid step
Where knowledge leads me : it shall be my pride
That I have dared to tread this holy ground,
Speaking no dream, but things oracular;
Matter not lightly to be heard by those
Who to the letter of the outward promise
Do read the invisible soul; by men adroit
In speech, and for communion with the world
Accomplished; minds whose faculties are then
Most active when they are most eloquent,
And elevated most when most admired.

Men may be found of other mould than these,
Who are their own upholders, to themselves
Encouragement, ard energy, and will,
Expressing liveliest thoughts in lively words
As native passion dictates. Others, too,
There are among the walks of homely life
Still higher, men for contemplation framed,
Shy, and unpractised in the strife of phrase ;
Meek men, whose very souls perhaps would sink
Beneath them, summoned to such intercourse :   270
Theirs is the language of the heavens, the power,
The thought, the image, and the silent joy ;
Words are but under-agents in their souls :
When they are grasping with their greatest strength,
They do not breathe among them : this I speak
In gratitude to God, who feeds our hearts
For his own service ; knoweth, loveth us,
When we are unregarded by the world.

    Also, about this time did I receive
Convictions still more strong than heretofore,   280
Not only that the inner frame is good,
And graciously composed, but that, no less,
Nature for all conditions wants not power
To consecrate, if we have eyes to see,
The outside of her creatures, and to breathe
Grandeur upon the very humblest face
Of human life. I felt that the array
Of act and circumstance, and visible form,
Is mainly to the pleasure of the mind
What passion makes them ; that meanwhile the forms 290

Of Nature have a passion in themselves,
That intermingles with those works of man
To which she summons him ; although the works
Be mean, have nothing lofty of their own ;
And that the Genius of the Poet hence
May boldly take his way among mankind
Wherever Nature leads, that he hath stood
By Nature's side among the men of old,
And so shall stand forever.   Dearest Friend !
If thou partake the animating faith   300
That poets, even as Prophets, each with each
Connected in a mighty scheme of truth,
Have each his own peculiar faculty,
Heaven's gift, a sense that fits him to perceive
Objects unseen before, thou wilt not blame
The humblest of this band who dares to hope
That unto him hath also been vouchsafed
An insight that in some sort he possesses,
A privilege whereby a work of his,
Proceeding from a source of untaught things,   310
Creative and enduring, may become
A power like one of Nature's.   To a hope
Not less ambitious once among the wilds
Of Sarum's Plain, my youthful spirit was raised ;
There, as I ranged at will the pastoral downs
Trackless and smooth, or paced the bare white roads
Lengthening in solitude their dreary line,
Time with his retinue of ages fled
Backwards, nor checked his flight until I saw
Our dim ancestral Past in vision clear ;   320
Saw multitudes of men, and, here and there,

A single Briton clothed in wolf-skin vest,
With shield and stone-axe, stride across the wold;
The voice of spears was heard, the rattling spear
Shaken by arms of mighty bone, in strength,
Long mouldered, of barbaric majesty.
I called on Darkness — but before the word
Was uttered, midnight darkness seemed to take
All objects from my sight; and lo! again
The Desert visible by dismal flames;   330
It is the sacrificial altar, fed
With living men — how deep the groans! the voice
Of those that crowd the giant wicker thrills
The monumental hillocks, and the pomp
Is for both worlds, the living and the dead.
At other moments —(for through that wide waste
Three summer days I roamed) where'er the Plain
Was figured o'er with circles, lines, or mounds,
That yet survive, a work, as some divine,
Shaped by the Druids, so to represent   340
Their knowledge of the heavens, and image forth
The constellations — gently was I charmed
Into a waking dream, a reverie
That, with believing eyes, where'er I turned,
Beheld long-bearded teachers, with white wands
Uplifted, pointing to the starry sky,
Alternately, and plain below, while breath
Of music swayed their motions, and the waste
Rejoiced with them and me in those sweet sounds.

   This for the past, and things that may be viewed 350
Or fancied in the obscurity of years

From monumental hints : and thou, O Friend !
Pleased with some unpremeditated strains
That served those wanderings to beguile, hast said
That then and there my mind had exercised
Upon the vulgar forms of present things,
The actual world of our familiar days,
Yet higher power ; had caught from them a tone,
An image, and a character, by books
Not hitherto reflected.   Call we this   360
A partial judgment — and yet why? for *then*
We were as strangers ; and I may not speak
Thus wrongfully of verse, however rude,
Which on thy young imagination, trained
In the great City, broke like light from far.
Moreover, each man's Mind is to herself
Witness and judge ; and I remember well
That in life's every-day appearances
I seemed about this time to gain clear sight
Of a new world — a world, too, that was fit   370
To be transmitted, and to other eyes
Made visible ; as ruled by those fixed laws
Whence spiritual dignity originates,
Which do both give it being and maintain
A balance, an ennobling interchange
Of action from without and from within ;
The excellence, pure function, and best power
Both of the object seen, and eye that sees.

BOOK FOURTEENTH.

CONCLUSION.

In one of those excursions (may they ne'er
Fade from remembrance !) through the Northern tracts
Of Cambria ranging with a youthful friend,
I left Bethgelert's huts at couching-time,
And westward took my way, to see the sun
Rise, from the top of Snowdon.   To the door
Of a rude cottage at the mountain's base
We came, and roused the shepherd who attends
The adventurous stranger's steps, a trusty guide ;
Then, cheered by short refreshment, sallied forth.   10

 It was a close, warm, breezeless summer night,
Wan, dull, and glaring, with a dripping fog
Low-hung and thick that covered all the sky ;
But, undiscouraged, we began to climb
The mountain-side.   The mist soon girt us round,
And, after ordinary travellers' talk
With our conductor, pensively we sank
Each into commerce with his private thoughts :
Thus did we breast the ascent, and by myself
Was nothing either seen or heard that checked   20

Those musings or diverted, save that once
The shepherd's lurcher, who, among the crags,
Had to his joy unearthed a hedgehog, teased
His coiled-up prey with barkings turbulent.
This small adventure, for even such it seemed
In that wild place and at the dead of night,
Being over and forgotten, on we wound
In silence as before.   With forehead bent
Earthward, as if in opposition set
Against an enemy, I panted up   30
With eager pace and no less eager thoughts.
Thus might we wear a midnight hour away,
Ascending at loose distance each from each,
And I, as chanced, the foremost of the band;
When at my feet the ground appeared to brighten
And with a step or two seemed brighter still;
Nor was time given to ask or learn the cause,
For instantly a light upon the turf
Fell like a flash, and lo ! as I looked up,
The Moon hung naked in a firmament   40
Of azure without cloud, and at my feet
Rested a silent sea of hoary mist.
A hundred hills their dusky backs upheaved
All over this still ocean ; and beyond,
Far, far beyond, the solid vapors stretched,
In headlands, tongues, and promontory shapes,
Into the main Atlantic, that appeared
To dwindle, and give up his majesty,
Usurped upon far as the sight could reach.
Not so the ethereal vault ; encroachment none   50
Was there, nor loss ; only the inferior stars

Had disappeared, or shed a fainter light
In the clear presence of the full-orbed Moon,
Who, from her sovereign elevation, gazed
Upon the billowy ocean, as it lay
All meek and silent, save that through a rift —
Not distant from the shore whereon we stood,
A fixed, abysmal, gloomy, breathing-place —
Mounted the roar of waters, torrents, streams
Innumerable, roaring with one voice !   60
Heard over earth and sea, and, in that hour,
For so it seemed, felt by the starry heavens.

When into air partially dissolved
That vision, given to spirits of the night,
And three chance human wanderers, in calm thought
Reflected, it appeared to me the type
Of a majestic intellect, its acts
And its possessions, what it has and craves,
What in itself it is, and would become.
There I beheld the emblem of a mind   70
That feeds upon infinity, that broods
Over the dark abyss, intent to hear
Its voices issuing forth to silent light
In one continuous stream ; a mind sustained
By recognitions of transcendent power,
In sense conducting to ideal form,
In soul of more than mortal privilege.
One function, above all, of such a mind
Had Nature shadowed there, by putting forth,
'Mid circumstances awful and sublime,   80
That mutual domination which she loves

To exert upon the face of outward things,
So moulded, joined, abstracted, so endowed
With interchangeable supremacy,
That men, least sensitive, see, hear, perceive,
And cannot choose but feel.   The power, which all
Acknowledge when thus moved, which Nature thus
To bodily sense exhibits, is the express
Resemblance of that glorious faculty
That higher minds bear with them as their own.   90
This is the very spirit in which they deal
With the whole compass of the universe :
They from their native selves can send abroad
Kindred mutations ; for themselves create
A like existence ; and, whene'er it dawns
Created for them, catch it, or are caught
By its inevitable mastery,
Like angels stopped upon the wing by sound
Of harmony from Heaven's remotest spheres.
Them the enduring and the transient both   100
Serve to exalt ; they build up greatest things
From least suggestions ; ever on the watch,
Willing to work and to be wrought upon,
They need not extraordinary calls
To rouse them ; in a world of life they live,
By sensible impressions not enthralled,
But by their quickening impulse made more prompt
To hold fit converse with the spiritual world,
And with the generations of mankind
Spread over time, past, present, and to come,   110
Age after age, till Time shall be no more.
Such minds are truly from the Deity,

For they are Powers ; and hence the highest bliss
That flesh can know is theirs — the consciousness
Of Whom they are, habitually infused
Through every image and through every thought,
And all affections by communion raised
From earth to heaven, from human to divine ;
Hence endless occupation for the Soul,
Whether discursive or intuitive ;   120
Hence cheerfulness for acts of daily life,
Emotions which best foresight need not fear,
Most worthy then of trust when most intense.
Hence, amid ills that vex and wrongs that crush
Our hearts — if here the words of Holy Writ
May with fit reverence be applied — that peace
Which passeth understanding, that repose
In moral judgments which from this pure source
Must come, or will by man be sought in vain.

Oh ! who is he that hath his whole life long   130
Preserved, enlarged, this freedom in himself?
For this alone is genuine liberty :
Where is the favored being who hath held
That course unchecked, unerring, and untired,
In one perpetual progress smooth and bright?—
A humbler destiny have we retraced,
And told of lapse and hesitating choice,
And backward wanderings along thorny ways :
Yet — compassed round by mountain solitudes,
Within whose solemn temple I received   140
My earliest visitations, careless then
Of what was given me ; and which now I range,

A meditative, oft a suffering man—
Do I declare—in accents which, from truth
Deriving cheerful confidence, shall blend
Their modulation with these vocal streams—
That, whatsoever falls my better mind,
Revolving with the accidents of life,
May have sustained, that, howsoe'er misled,
Never did I, in quest of right and wrong,   150
Tamper with conscience from a private aim;
Nor was in any public hope the dupe
Of selfish passions; nor did ever yield
Wilfully to mean cares or low pursuits,
But shrunk with apprehensive jealousy
From every combination which might aid
The tendency, too potent in itself,
Of use and custom to bow down the soul
Under a growing weight of vulgar sense,
And substitute a universe of death   160
For that which moves with light and life informed,
Actual, divine, and true.   To fear and love,
To love as prime and chief, for there fear ends,
Be this ascribed; to early intercourse,
In presence of sublime or beautiful forms,
With the adverse principles of pain and joy—
Evil, as one is rashly named by men
Who know not what they speak.   By love subsists
All lasting grandeur, by pervading love,
That gone, we are as dust.—Behold the fields   170
In balmy spring-time full of rising flowers
And joyous creatures; see that pair, the lamb
And the lamb's mother, and their tender ways

Shall touch thee to the heart ; thou callest this love,
And not inaptly so, for love it is,
Far as it carries thee.   In some green bower
Rest, and be not alone, but have thou there
The One who is thy choice of all the world :
There linger, listening, gazing, with delight
Impassioned, but delight how pitiable !   180
Unless this love by a still higher love
Be hallowed, love that breathes not without awe,
Love that adores, but on the knees of prayer,
By heaven inspired ; that frees from chains the soul,
Lifted, in union with the purest, best,
Of earth-born passions, on the wings of praise
Bearing a tribute to the Almighty's Throne.

   This spiritual Love acts not nor can exist
Without Imagination, which, in truth,
Is but another name for absolute power   190
And clearest insight, amplitude of mind,
And Reason in her most exalted mood.
This faculty hath been the feeding source
Of our long labor : we have traced the stream
From the blind cavern whence is faintly heard
Its natal murmur ; followed it to light
And open day ; accompanied its course
Among the ways of Nature, for a time
Lost sight of it bewildered and engulphed ;
Then given it greeting as it rose once more   200
In strength, reflecting from its placid breast
The works of man, and face of human life ;
And lastly, from its progress have we drawn

Faith in life endless, the sustaining thought
Of human Being, Eternity, and God.

Imagination having been our theme,
So also hath that intellectual Love,
For they are each in each, and cannot stand
Dividually. — Here must thou be, O man !
Power to thyself; no helper hast thou here ;
Here keepest thou in singleness thy state :
No other can divide with thee this work :
No secondary hand can intervene
To fashion this ability ; 'tis thine,
The prime and vital principle is thine
In the recesses of thy nature, far
From any reach of outward fellowship,
Else is not thine at all.   But joy to him,
Oh, joy to him who here hath sown, hath laid
Here, the foundation of his future years !
For all that friendship, all that love can do,
All that a darling countenance can look
Or dear voice utter, to complete the man,
Perfect him, made imperfect in himself,
All shall be his : and he whose soul hath risen
Up to the height of feeling intellect
Shall want no humbler tenderness ; his heart
Be tender as a nursing mother's heart ;
Of female softness shall his life be full,
Of humble cares and delicate desires,
Mild interests and gentle sympathies.

Child of my parents !   Sister of my soul !
Thanks in sincerest verse have been elsewhere

Poured out for all the early tenderness
Which I from thee imbibed : and 'tis most true
That later seasons owed to thee no less ;
For, spite of thy sweet influence and the touch
Of kindred hands that opened out the springs
Of genial thought. in childhood, and in spite
Of all that unassisted I had marked   240
In life or nature of those charms minute
That win their way into the heart by stealth,
Still, to the very going out of youth,
I too exclusively esteemed *that* love,
And sought *that* beauty, which, as Milton sings,
Hath terror in it. Thou didst soften down
This over-sternness ; but for thee, dear Friend !
My soul, too reckless of mild grace, had stood
In her original self too confident,
Retained too long a countenance severe ;   250
A rock with torrents roaring, with the clouds
Familiar, and a favorite of the stars :
But thou didst plant its crevices with flowers,
Hang it with shrubs that twinkle in the breeze,
And teach the little birds to build their nests
And warble in its chambers.   At a time
When Nature, destined to remain so long
Foremost in my affections, had fallen back
Into a second place, pleased to become
A handmaid to a nobler than herself,   260
When every day brought with it some new sense
Of exquisite regard for common things,
And all the earth was budding with these gifts
Of more refined humanity, thy breath,

Dear Sister ! was a kind of gentler spring
That went before my steps.   Thereafter came
One whom with thee friendship had early paired ;
She came, no more a phantom to adorn
A moment, but an inmate of the heart,
And yet a spirit, there for me enshrined   270
To penetrate the lofty and the low ;
Even as one essence of pervading light
Shines, in the brightness of ten thousand stars,
And the meek worm that feeds her lonely lamp
Couched in the dewy grass.
                   With such a theme,
Coleridge ! with this my argument, of thee
Shall I be silent?   O capacious Soul !
Placed on this earth to love and understand,
And from thy presence shed the light of love,
Shall I be mute, ere thou be spoken of ?   280
Thy kindred influence to my heart of hearts
Did also find its way.   Thus fear relaxed
Her over-weening grasp ; thus thoughts and things
In the self-haunting spirit learned to take
More rational proportions ; mystery,
The incumbent mystery of sense and soul,
Of life and death, time and eternity, ·
Admitted more habitually a mild
Interposition — a serene delight
In closelier gathering cares, such as become   290
A human creature, howsoe'er endowed,
Poet, or destined for a humbler name ;
And so the deep and enthusiastic joy,
The rapture of the hallelujah sent

From all that breathes and is, was chastened, stemmed
And balanced by pathetic truth, by trust
In hopeful reason, leaning on the stay
Of Providence ; and in reverence for duty,
Here, if need be, struggling with storms, and there
Strewing in peace life's humblest ground with herbs,　300
At every season green, sweet at all hours.

　And now, O Friend ! this history is brought
To its appointed close : the discipline
And consummation of a Poet's mind,
In everything that stood most prominent,
Have faithfully been pictured : we have reached
The time (our guiding object from the first)
When we may, not presumptuously, I hope,
Suppose my powers so far confirmed, and such
My knowledge, as to make me capable　310
Of building up a Work that shall endure.
Yet much hath been omitted, as need was ;
Of books how much ! and even of the other wealth
That is collected among woods and fields,
Far more : for nature's secondary grace
Hath hitherto been barely touched upon,
The charm more superficial that attends
Her works, as they present to Fancy's choice
Apt illustrations of the moral world,
Caught at a glance, or traced with curious pains.　320

　Finally, and above all, O Friend ! (I speak
With due regret) how much is overlooked
In human nature and her subtle ways,

As studied first in our own hearts, and then
In life among the passions of mankind
Varying their composition and their hue,
Where'er we move, under the diverse shapes
That individual character presents
To an attentive eye.   For progress meet,
Along this intricate and difficult path,   330
Whate'er was wanting, something had I gained,
As one of many schoolfellows compelled
In hardy independence to stand up
Amid conflicting interests, and the shock
Of various tempers ; to endure and note
What was not understood, though known to be ;
Among the mysteries of love and hate,
Honor and shame, looking to right and left,
Unchecked by innocence too delicate,
And moral notions too intolerant,   340
Sympathies too contracted.   Hence, when called
To take a station among men, the step
Was easier, the transition more secure,
More profitable also ; for the mind
Learns from such timely exercise to keep
In wholesome separation the two natures,
The one that feels, the other that observes.

Yet one word more of personal concern ; —
Since I withdrew unwillingly from France,
I led an undomestic wanderer's life,   350
In London chiefly harbored, whence I roamed,
Tarrying at will in many a pleasant spot
Of rural England's cultivated vales

Or Cambrian solitudes.   A youth — (he bore
The name of Calvert — it shall live, if words
Of mine can give it life,) in firm belief
That by endowments not from me withheld
Good might be furthered — in his last decay
By a bequest sufficient for my needs
Enabled me to pause for choice, and walk   360
At large and unrestrained, nor damped too soon
By mortal cares.   Himself no Poet, yet
Far less a common follower of the world,
He deemed that my pursuits and labors lay
Apart from all that leads to wealth, or even
A necessary maintenance insures,
Without some hazard to the finer sense :
He cleared a passage for me, and the stream
Flowed in the bent of Nature.
                                            Having now
Told what best merits mention, further pains   370
Our present purpose seems not to require,
And I have other tasks.   Recall to mind
The mood in which this labor was begun,
O Friend !   The termination of my course
Is nearer now, much nearer ; yet even then,
In that distraction and intense desire,
I said unto the life which I had lived,
Where art thou?   Hear I not a voice from thee,
Which 'tis reproach to hear?   Anon I rose
As if on wings, and saw beneath me stretched   380
Vast prospect of the world which I had been
And was ; and hence this Song, which like a lark
I have protracted, in the unwearied heavens

Singing, and often with more plantive voice
To earth attempered and her deep-drawn sighs,
Yet centring all in love, and in the end
All gratulant, if rightly understood.

   Whether to me shall be allotted life,
And, with life, power to accomplish aught of worth,
That will be deemed no insufficient plea   390
For having given the story of myself,
Is all uncertain : but, beloved Friend !
When, looking back, thou seest, in clearer view
Than any liveliest sight of yesterday,
That summer, under whose indulgent skies
Upon smooth Quantock's airy ridge we roved
Unchecked, or loitered 'mid her sylvan combs,
Thou in bewitching words, with happy heart,
Didst chaunt the vision of that Ancient Man,
The bright-eyed Mariner, and rueful woes   400
Didst utter of the Lady Christabel ;
And I, associate with such labor, steeped
In soft forgetfulness the livelong hours,
Murmuring of him who, joyous hap, was found,
After the perils of his moonlight ride,
Near the loud waterfall ; or her who sate
In misery near the miserable Thorn ;
When thou dost to that summer turn thy thoughts,
And hast before thee all which then we were,
To thee, in memory of that happiness,   410
It will be known, by thee at least, my Friend !
Felt, that the history of a Poet's mind

Is labor not unworthy of regard :
To thee the work shall justify itself.

The last and later portions of this gift
Have been prepared, not with the buoyant spirits
That were our daily portion when we first
Together wantoned in wild Poesy,
But, under pressure of a private grief,
Keen and enduring, which the mind and heart,⠀⠀⠀420
That in this meditative history
Have been laid open, needs must make me feel
More deeply, yet enable me to bear
More firmly ;- and a comfort now hath risen
From hope that thou art near, and wilt be soon
Restored to us in renovated health ;
When, after the first mingling of our tears,
'Mong other consolations we may draw
Some pleasure from the offering of my love.

Oh ! yet a few short years of useful life,⠀⠀⠀430
And all will be complete, thy race be run,
Thy monument of glory will be raised ;
Then, though (too weak to tread the ways of truth)
This age fall back to old idolatry,
Though men return to servitude as fast
As the tide ebbs, to ignominy and shame
By nations sink together, we shall still
Find solace — knowing what we have learnt to know,
Rich in true happiness if allowed to be
Faithful alike in forwarding a day⠀⠀⠀440
Of firmer trust, joint laborers in the work

(Should Providence such grace to us vouchsafe)
Of their deliverance surely yet to come.
Prophets of Nature, we to them will speak
A lasting inspiration, sanctified
By reason, blest by faith : what we have loved,
Others will love, and we will teach them how ;
Instruct them how the mind of man becomes
A thousand times more beautiful than the earth
On which he dwells, above this frame of things   450
(Which, 'mid all revolution in the hopes
And fears of men, doth still remain unchanged)
In beauty exalted, as it is itself
Of quality and fabric more divine.

CHRONOLOGICAL AND ITINERARY.

1770. Birth.
1778. At Hawkshead School.
1787. At Cambridge.
1790. Tour through Italy, France, and Switzerland.
1791. Graduation; Visits London, Wales, and France.
1792. Return to London.
1793. At Isle of Wight.
1794. At Penrith with Calvert.
1795. Settled at Racedown.
1797. Removed to Alfoxden.
1798. At Goslar in Germany.
1799. Leaves Goslar, begins Prelude; At Sockburn; Settled at Dove Cottage, Grasmere.
1802. Marriage.
1803. Tour in Scotland.
1805. Death of his brother, Captain Wordsworth.
1808. Removes to Allan Bank, Grasmere, where he writes the Excursion.
1811. Removes to the Parsonage, Grasmere.
1813. Removes to Rydal Mount.
1814. Second visit to Scotland.
1820. Visits the Continent.
1831. Visits Sir Walter Scott.
1839. Oxford Degree.
1842. Appointed Poet Laureate.
1850. Death.

NOTES.

BOOK FIRST.

PREFATORY NOTE. — In July, 1797, Coleridge visited Wordsworth, for the first time, at Racedown in Dorsetshire, where he and his sister had set up their home two years before. The two poets were mutually pleased with each other, and they desired to be nearer in order to have frequent intercourse, and a month later the Wordsworths removed to Alfoxden near Nether Stowey, Somersetshire, where Coleridge resided.

The poets rambled over the Quantock Hills and held high communion. During one of these excursions, feeling the need of money, they planned a joint production for the *New Monthly Magazine*. They set about the work in earnest, and selected as a subject the "Ancient Mariner," founded upon a dream of one of Coleridge's friends. Coleridge supplied most of the incidents and almost all the lines. Wordsworth contributed the incident of the killing of the albatross and some of the lines. They soon found that their methods did not harmonize, and the "Mariner" was left to Coleridge, while Wordsworth wrote upon the common incidents of everyday life. When the "Mariner" was finished Wordsworth had so many pieces ready that they concluded to publish a joint volume, and this they did under the title "Lyrical Ballads," with the "Rime of the Ancient Marinere" heading the volume. Cottle, the publisher, gave Wordsworth £30 for his poems, and made a separate bargain with Coleridge for the "Mariner." With the proceeds of their work in their pockets they concluded to visit Germany and study the language, and in September, 1798, they went to Hamburg where they met Klopstock, the "German Milton." At Hamburg Coleridge left the Wordsworths and went to

Göttingen, dived into metaphysics, and the world got no more "Ancient Mariners." Wordsworth and his sister wintered in Goslar, an old imperial town in Hanover.

Lines 1–10. In the spring of 1799 the Wordsworths, after a cold dreary winter at Goslar, returned to England; as they left the city and felt the spring breeze fan their cheeks Wordsworth poured forth the gladsome strain with which the Prelude opens. This was in his thirtieth year. The Prelude was completed in 1805.

47. *Friend:* Samuel Taylor Coleridge.

62. *Place:* At Sockburn-on-Tees, county Durham, where, on returning to England, they visited their kindred, the Hutchinsons.

72. *Vale:* Grasmere.

74. *Cottage:* While at Sockburn, Wordsworth, with his brother John and Coleridge, made a pedestrian tour of the Lake district, and it was on this occasion that they saw the cottage which is here mentioned. It had once been a public house, with a sign of "The Dove and Olive Bough," and is now known as Dove Cottage. It stands on the right of the road entering Grasmere from Rydal; it fronts the lake, while in the rear is a garden and orchard leading to the wooded mountains above it. Here still bloom the primroses and daffodils planted by the poet, and here he wrote many of his poems. See De Quincey's *Recollections of the Lakes.*

84. *Rustled:* The sense of hearing was remarkably acute in Wordsworth, and its workings are prominent in his poetry.

106. *Journey:* Wordsworth and his sister left Sockburn on the 19th of December, 1799, and walking over the frozen ground, turning aside to see the icy waterfalls and the changing aspects of cloud and sunshine, they consumed three days in the journey. At night they lodged in the cottages, and Wordsworth gave voice to the thoughts of the day. A great part of "Heartleap Well" was composed on one of these evenings, from a tradition he heard that day from a shepherd. They reached their cottage on the 21st.

108–20. *The life:* This seemed to many of the poet's friends a mad project. With only a hundred pounds a year they were turning their backs upon the world, with dalesmen for their neighbors and verse-making for their business. Here was produced the most of that poetry which has made Wordsworth immortal.

187–90. *Mithridates* of Pontus, after having been vanquished by Pompey, fled into Armenia, B.C. 131. See Morley's *English Writers,* Ch. V.

191. *Sertorius :* A Roman general who, being proscribed by Sulla, fled into Spain and thence to Mauritania.

192. *Fortunate Isles :* In the Straits of Gibraltar Sertorius met some sailors, who told him of the islands in the Atlantic supposed to be the Canaries.

202. *Heroes,* who were reported to have been seen by an old pilot of the seas, who landed at Lisbon in the early part of the fifteenth century. They claimed to have descended from a band of Christians who fled from Spain when it was conquered by the Moslems.

206–10. *Frenchman :* Dominique de Gourgues, who in 1567 sailed from Bordeaux with a force, to avenge the massacre of French colonists in Florida by the Spaniards under Menendez.

212. Gustavus I. of Sweden who, during the conflict with Denmark, was obliged to flee for his life, and disguised in rags worked as a miner and woodcutter in Dalecarlia. When the time came he aroused the peasants and defeated the Danes, and was offered the crown.

215.
> " At Wallace's name what Scottish blood
> But boils up in a spring-tide flood." — BURNS.

270–75. Wordsworth was born at Cockermouth in the north country of England and in sight of the Scottish hills. The town is situated at the junction of two rivers, the Cocker and the Derwent. He was sprung from the old North-Humbrian stock.

283. *Towers:* Cockermouth Castle, standing on an eminence not far from the manor-house in which Wordsworth was born, was built by the first lord of Allerdale in the reign of William I. as a border defence. It was taken by Douglas in the border foray (1387), and was the prison of Mary Queen of Scots (1568). It was dismantled by the Parliamentarians. It is one of the finest castle ruins in England. See sonnet, "Spirit of Cockermouth Castle."

286. *Terrace-walk :* At the garden, in the rear of the manor-house, is the terrace upon which the poet had his childish sports. The house and its surroundings are unaltered since the poet's father lived there, and the present owner is glad to show strangers the house and grounds.

288–300. At this early age he took delight in his own thoughts and his own company, and was touched with "those visions of the hills" which produced in him the feeling of reverence and awe in the presence of Nature. The necessary sequence of this life at Cockermouth is the incident described so magnificently in 357 and the following lines, where he sings of how his mind was affected by that imaginative loneliness of spirit in which he was so overawed by the mysterious and the terrible in Nature.

304. *Vale:* At Hawkshead, a small market-town in the vale of Esthwaite, the most picturesque district of Lancashire. This old town presents us more of interest as connected with Wordsworth than Grasmere even, as it has suffered less from modern "improvements," and for this reason is less frequented by the hasty tourist who allows only a few days in which to "do" the Lakes. There is no more delightful spot in the district for recreative enjoyment; whether we wander by the lakeside, or loiter on the fellside, whether we ascend the summit of Wetherlam where the ravens build, or rest in the vale where "woodcocks sange," Nature, by its color and forms, moods and movements, is both a delight and a revelation.

> A quaint old town is Hawkshead, and the ancient look it bears,
> Its church, its school, its dwellings, its streets, its lanes, its squares,
> All are irregularities, all angles, twists, and crooks,
> Penthouses and gables over archways, weints, and nooks.

307. *Birthdays:* Wordsworth, at the age of nine, entered the Hawkshead school, where he led the life that did so much to fit him for a poet. "High pressure was unknown in that school. Nature and freedom had full swing." — PROFESSOR SHAIRP.

311. *The heights:* The hills leading up to the moor between Hawkshead and Coniston. See *Through the Wordsworth Country*, Knight and Goodwin.

326. *Vale:* Yewdale. A beautiful pastoral vale near Hawkshead.

335. *Crag:* Ravens' Crag in Yewdale. There are no naked crags in Esthwaite. — KNIGHT.

357. See note, lines 288–300.

359. *Cove:* By the side of Esthwaite lake. One going from Hawkshead by the east shore of the lake can realize this spot.

370. *Craggy ridge:* The mountain (Ironkeld) from High Arnside to Tom Heights.

378. *Huge peak:* To what mountain this refers it is difficult to say, for it might be Nab Scar, if he rowed from the west bank of the lake, or, if he started from the east side, Pike o' Stickle.

400–10. This educational power of Nature never ceased; day and night, summer and winter, its silent influence stole into his soul, and brought him near to Nature and near to God.

425–63. A picture more vivid, more true to fact, more instinct with fine imagination and delicate feeling, was never drawn. Coleridge cites it in proof of his fourth characteristic excellency of Wordsworth's work. See Preface.

490. Becks amongst the hills of Yewdale.

499. *Cottages:* Wordsworth lived for nine years with one Anne Tyson for whose simple character he had a profound regard. The house still remains unaltered. It is a stone dwelling of two storys; the basement floor is of Coniston slate. The door is interesting as having upon it the old "latch" mentioned in Book Second.

543. The concluding line of this exquisitely drawn picture might seem to some an exaggeration, but the dalesmen tell us that the sound of the ice breaking up in this valley is just as here described. It is partly owing to the fact that the lake is surrounded by mountains, causing the sound to reverberate.

586. The school life was just what you would expect of a vigorous country youth. In all his sports there was nothing to distinguish him from other boys, except that in the midst of the scramble for the raven's nest or the run of "hare and hounds," feelings came to him from Nature herself; the invisible, quiet Life of the world spake to him rememberable things.

BOOK SECOND.

5–10. Never did boy spend a healthier, purer, or happier school-time. His love for Nature was no different from that of other boys.

It was a time full of giddy bliss and joy of being, yet he was gaining

Truths that wake to perish never.

26. In after life, when sorrow and pain come upon us, it will help us rise above them if we recollect the joy and force of youth. The possibility of turning the lamentable waste of excessive sorrow into a source of strength is a central idea in Wordsworth's philosophy.

32. The remembrance of the brightness and gladness of his youth seemed to arouse another consciousness.

39. Notwithstanding the presence of the "Assembly room" in the "square" at Hawkshead, it is easy for the visitor to picture there the centre of the school-boy's sports.

56. *Windermere:* The largest of the English lakes, and not far from Hawkshead.

58–65. The three islands are easily identified: Belle Isle, Lily of the Valley Island, and Lady Holme. Upon Lady Holme there was, in the time of Henry VIII., a chapel dedicated to St. Mary.

77. The stillness of the place quieted their emulation and jealousy. This influence of Nature upon Wordsworth was what developed his peculiarity as a man and a poet.

102. At Conishead Priory. There are many remains of the Druid worship in the Lake country, as it was the home of the Brigantes, the least civilized tribe of Britain. See sonnet, *Long Meg and her Daughters.* The Circle at Keswick is composed of forty-eight upright stones.

103. Furness Abbey, the largest abbey in England with the exception of Fountain's Abbey, contained sixty-five acres; it was founded by Stephen in 1127. The old name of Furness was Bekansghyll — Glen of Deadly Nightshade — from an herb Bekan which grew there. It was dedicated to the Blessed Trinity and St. Mary. In these grounds, under the shadow of the old walls, now is seen a hotel for summer tourists!

137. Cartmell Sands, where Windermere, through the Leven, enters the sea.

140. White Lion Inn at Bowness. The location is easily identified at the present time.

159. An exact description of the scene from Bowness Church where the old tavern stood.

168. Robert Greenwood, afterwards Senior Fellow of Trinity College, Cambridge.

171. These silent influences "instilled drop by drop" into his being, were moulding his future.

185. *Mountain:* Wetherlam or Coniston Old Man.

193–94. This is an accurate description of the rising of the moon over the southern shore of Esthwaite, with Gunners How at the left.

197. Esthwaite, —

> Where deep and low the hamlets lie
> Beneath their little patch of sky
> And little plot of stars. — *Peter Bell.*

201–3. The first step in Wordsworth's education, when the influences of Nature were unconsciously received, was now closing, and the second, when the influences were consciously sought, was opening.

280. The props of his early impressions were his boyish sports, and when he turned away from them, still the impression remained. He had begun to realize all that he had been learning unconsciously.

302–10. In these scenes of sublimity and calm he was consecrated to be the poet-priest of Nature.

333. *Friend:* The Rev. John Flemming, of Rayrigg, Windermere.

339. *Latch:* Still on the door of the old cottage.

343. *Eminence:* One of the heights northeast of Hawkshead.

347. The light which came to him here became the "Master-light of all his seeing." See *Ode on Intimations of Immortality.*

368–9. He now began to feel the influence of his own soul on Nature; he began to be a poet.

401–9. Nature now began to put on the appearance of personality, with whom he could commune. It is a wonderful picture of a youthful life in communion with the Being of the world.

413. *Towards the Uncreated:* "The looking thitherward through Nature and his own moral being, so as to have both based on one Divine order" is what Dr. Hudson considered Wordsworth's "Master Vision."

421. In the following lines we have both a prayer and an anthem, the "Gloria in Excelsis" He was now in his seventeenth year. The history of his boyhood is completed in the adoration and love of God.

Looking back upon these years he recognizes that the faithful, temperate, and quiet character of his life has been due to the early association with the beautiful and the sublime things in the outward world. This is the philosophy of the great " Ode." There is here the same atmosphere which permeates the Psalms : " I will lift up mine eyes unto the mountains." Also St. Paul : "In Him we live and move and have our being." Dean Stanley illustrated the blessings of the *pure in heart* from the writings of Wordsworth.

452. Coleridge was a charity boy at Christ's Hospital, London. It was founded on the site of Grey Friars Monastery, by Edward VI. It is commonly called "The Blue Coat School," as the dress of the boys is a blue coat, a yellow petticoat, a red girdle about the waist, yellow stockings, a clergyman's band round the neck, and a closely fitting black cap. The classes are called "Grecians" and "Deputy-Grecians." Coleridge belonged to the former. Every Easter Monday the boys visit the Royal Exchange, and every Easter Tuesday the Lord Mayor, at the Mansion House.

454-60. Wordsworth's ideas of society and the state had been received contemptuously by those who did not give themselves the trouble to understand them.

466. Coleridge had gone to the Mediterranean in search of health.

BOOK THIRD.

1-6. Through the liberality of two uncles, the education of Wordsworth was prolonged beyond his school-days. Lord Lonsdale, whose agent the poet's father was, had forcibly borrowed from him £500 and refused to repay it. This left the fortunes of the Wordsworths at a low ebb, and the uncles discerning the talents of the brothers (William and Christopher) enabled them to obtain a Cambridge education. Wordsworth, in October, 1787, entered St. Johns College, Cambridge. His education at the hands of Nature was to cease for a time. It was a great change from the retirement of the Grammar School at Hawkshead. Cambridge represents to the approaching student no such picturesque array of steeples, towers, and domes as her sister Oxford; but her special boast is King's College Chapel, with its lofty pinnacles, fretted roof of stone, and huge windows of stained glass. The University consists of seventeen colleges. Trinity is the largest in the number of its buildings and students, and St. Johns, founded by the mother of Henry VII. is next. In the Dining Hall of St. Johns may be seen the portrait of Wordsworth painted at the request of the Master and Fellows.

7. Wordsworth went from York to Cambridge by the road which enters the city from Girton. — KNIGHT.

8. The Academical costume of a University man, or gownsman, is a closely fitting cap with a covered board forming the crown, from the centre of which hangs a tassel; a gown of black reaching nearly to the ankles; knee-breeches, and silk stockings. These are worn all of the time except from 12 M. to 4 P.M., when the student is at his exercise.

13, 14. How many a country boy has had a similar experience as he entered the college town for the first time!

15. Near Magdalene College are the ruins of a camp or fortress used to defend the Fen-land (Cambridge) against William I.

16. Named from the college, which it connects with those on the other side of the Cam.

17. The Hoop Inn still exists.

26. The newcomer at Cambridge is inducted into his rooms by a *gyp*, or college servant, who attends upon a number of students; he takes the former tenant's furniture at a valuation by the college upholsterer. But he has to supply one deficiency, — a tea-set, decanters, etc.

32. The gowns of the various colleges were different from each other, and also from those worn by the officers.

43. "These *wine parties* are the most common entertainments, being the cheapest and most convenient." — BRISTED, *Five Years in an English University.*

47, 48. All of the colleges are constructed in quadrangles, or *courts.* Although Wordsworth's room is not pointed out to us by the officials, we know that it is one of two answering to this description. The entrances to the rooms are dark and low, a contrast to the comfortable rooms themselves. The quaint appurtenances, such as bookcases of scholastic sort sunk into the walls; little nooks of studies large enough to hold a man in an arm-chair; garrets which the old priests used for oratories, but which now hold the Cantab's wine.

61. All of the details here are exact. The statue of Newton is full-size. In his right hand he holds a roll which rests upon the forefinger of the left hand; his face is raised as if looking off into the upper sphere.

64–75. "The little interests of the place were not great enough for one accustomed to the solemn and awful interests of Nature." — REV. S. BROOKE. Medallists and wranglers could be had for the asking, but a Wordsworth could not afford to delay in such small matters as striving for University prizes or for a high place upon the Tripos. A Chinese system which produced "stall-fed" memories was not his ideal of education.

90–143. He was living a double life at Cambridge: one with the students; another with himself. Even in the Fen-country he turned to Nature instinctively and lived in her presence. He was thus saved from becoming artificial.

144–54. Sometimes he betrayed his inner life, but as at Hawkshead he was in appearance little different from the other students.

155–65. Through the "logic of the eye" he was convinced that Nature was not a dead machine, but was pervaded by a living presence, and that this was a unity. In this is the essential difference between Wordsworth's poetry and that of Pope, which viewed Nature as a vast machine with God standing apart. Wordsworth made Nature a new thing to man by adding what the true artist must ever add, —

> the gleam,
> The light that never was on sea or land.

170. The philosophic theory of Wordsworth is founded upon the identity of our childish instincts and our enlightened understanding.

230. Arnold is the type of English action; Wordsworth is the type of English thought. — F. W. ROBERTSON.

246–55. Even this was no unimportant element in the education of a poet who would view human nature in all its aspects. Being William Wordsworth he could afford to "drift."

258–69. On a nature susceptible as his was, a residence in that ancient seat of learning could not but tell powerfully; if he had learned no more than what silently stole into him, the time would not have been misspent.

275. Remains of this mill are to be seen about three miles from Cambridge.

283. See Milton's *Penseroso.*

298–300. Of this exploit Sir Francis Doyle, in his Oxford lectures, remarks: "A worthy clerical friend of mine, one of the best poetical critics I know, and also one of the soundest judges of port wine, always shakes his head about this, and says: 'Wordsworth's intentions were good, no doubt, but I greatly fear that his standard of intoxication was miserably low.'"

312. *Surplice:* On Saturday evenings, Sundays, and Saints' days the students wear surplices instead of gowns.

322. His genius grew too deep and strong to grow fast. "He read the face of Nature; he read Chaucer, Spenser, and Milton; he amused himself and rested, and since he was Wordsworth he could not have done better." — REV. S. BROOKE. For a companion picture see Cabot's *Life of Emerson*, Vol. I., page 57.

Wordsworth's sister Dorothy, in a letter written in 1791, says: "William reads Italian, Spanish, French, Greek, Latin, and English." — KNIGHT.

462. The Revival of Learning was in the sphere of culture and art what the Reformation was in the sphere of religion and politics. The first, intellectual; the second, ethical.

473. The begging scholar was common in the Middle Ages.

476. All were connected with the Reformation and Revival of Learning.

491. He lost the shadow, but kept the substance of education.

580–81. In this miniature world he had developed in him the human element. Poetry demands God immanent in Man and Nature.

BOOK FOURTH.

1–10. On the road from Kendal to Windermere. The description is exceedingly accurate. Wordsworth's home at Cockermouth was broken up, and his sister was living with relatives; this accounts for his return to Hawkshead.

13. The ferry, called "Nab," is below Bowness.

18. *Hill* · Leading from the ferry to Sawrey.

21. Hawkshead Church. An old Norman structure built in 1160. In it is a private chapel of Archbishop Sandys.

22. The position of the church on the hill above the village is such that it is a conspicuous object from the Sawrey Hill. In tramping through this region the Prelude is the best of guides.

26. See note, line 74, Book I.

28–39. Anne Tyson, with whom the poet had spent nine years. She died at Colthouse, on the opposite side of the Vale, in 1789, at the age of 83.

47, 48. There is no trace and no tradition of the "Stone table and dark Pine" at Hawkshead. In *Peter Bell* we have, —

> To the stone table in my garden,
> Loved haunt of many a summer hour. — KNIGHT.

51. The famous brook presents some difficulties to the relic· hunter. Crossing the lane leading to the cottage we find it nearly covered with large, slate flags, giving the name Flag Street to one of the alleys of Hawkshead. The house adjoining the garden is not Dame Tyson's; hers is a few rods distant.

61. Changes had been wrought in his life of which he was unconscious, and what seemed to him a useless expenditure of time was necessary to the union of Nature and Humanity.

76. His Academical attire.

82. The cottage faces southwest, and in one of the two upper rooms the poet must have slept.

89. No remains of the ash can be found.

130. Wordsworth seems to have been well aware of the suspicions his conduct would arouse among the dalesmen.

164-71. The evening hour in the presence of Nature influenced him like the face of an old friend; strength and comfort — the sense of the majesty of human life entered his heart. Those matins and vespers were times of consecration.

191–92. The result of his University life.

280–81. "We must often reach the higher by going back a little, and Wordsworth's ' boundless chase of trivial pleasure' was a necessary parenthesis in his education." — REV. S. BROOKE.

310. At a farmhouse near Hawkshead.

323. At this baptismal hour his path must have been from some of the heights north of Hawkshead. Here he was consecrated to "truth and purity, and high unworldly endeavor."

380. The brook is Sawrey beck, on the road from Windermere to Hawkshead, and the long ascent is the second from the ferry.

387. The narrative with which he closes the book is a proof that his interest was now turning toward man. This narrative would not have been appropriate at an earlier date.

———•◦•———

BOOK FIFTH.

1–28. Wordsworth here sounds those depths and ascends those heights which are the haunts of the contemplative mind. His words are the words of a seer.

18–28. *Then also man!* We seem here to find a reason for his deliberately sacrificing this great poem during these years, when, to have published it would have meant so much to him.

29–49. Nature is the type of permanence and reality. "Man is transient and ever changing, and imprints himself only upon man." This is not the attitude of an anchorite who declares all things under the sun to be but vanity and vexation, but of the seer who knows all things to be but the shadow of what is behind the veil.

60. "I read while at school all Fielding's works, Don Quixote, Gil Blas, Gulliver's Travels, and the Tale of the Tub." — W. W.

88–92. All that is of lasting value in the intellectual achievement of the poet, according to this dream, are the books of poetry and mathematical science, but the ruin that is to engulf all else! what is it?

140. Mr. Duffield, the translator of *Don Quixote*, says, that although no criticism of the work had appeared, yet Wordsworth in the above lines has given a most poetical insight into the real nature of the Hidalgo of La Mancha; he has shown us that it was a nature compacted of the madman and the poet. The earliest criticism of the Spaniards on the work was that one could not tell whether Don was speaking, or Cervantes, or the Cid.

152. "Though this be madness, yet there's method in't." — SHAKESPEARE.

162. See Coleridge's sixth characteristic of Wordsworth, in Preface, page xxiii.

185–91. This is Nature teaching, seriously and sweetly through the affections; it is knowledge inhaled like a fragrance.

198. Wordsworth believed in the motto *non multa sed multum* as applied to reading, and Emerson is perhaps, next to Wordsworth, the best exponent of the results of such a course.

221. Wordsworth has been accused of Pantheism. If presenting a new insight to mankind and turning theology into religion be Pantheism, then he merits the accusation.

230–41. A high tribute to his early teachers, — his mother, Rev. Mr. Gilbanks of Cockermouth, Mrs. Birkett of Penrith, and the Master at Hawkshead.

257. Mrs. Wordsworth died when the poet was in his eighth year. She used to say she had no fears for her other children, but as for William, he would be remarkable either for good or evil.

264–93. Wordsworth, fortunate as he was in his birthplace, was no less fortunate in having a mother worthy of such a tribute as he here pays to her. The picture is drawn with a masterly stroke, and we feel that it is from such sources that the best part of education proceeds.

298–340. The touch of wholesome banter in this passage is exceedingly interesting, and its application is eminently judicious. He was among the first to protest against educational hot-beds. Wordsworth seldom indulges in satire, but this passage proves conclusively that had he chosen to use it, he might have attained to eminence as a satirical

poet. The Edinburgh Polyphemus might well have congratulated himself that Wordsworth preferred the attitude of haughty indifference to
his malignant criticisms.

346. In a system of education where acquirement counts for more
than culture, the spirit of egotism is fostered rather than the spirit of
self-forgetfulness.

364. Of the following description Coleridge said: "Had I met
these lines running wild in the deserts of Arabia, I should have instantly screamed out — Wordsworth!"

383–84. The frequent description of such scenes as this shows us
how sensitive was the poet's ear. He recalls not only the general
aspect of the place, but the sounds return as well. He hears no noises
in Nature; he hears voices. He often arrests our minds by the single
allusion to sound : —

> How calm, how still, *the only sound*
> *The dripping of the oar suspended.*

Again : —

> Loud is the vale! the voice is up
> With which she speaks when storms are gone.

He both observes and hears Nature.

391. Esthwaite.

392. *Churchyard:* The description here is accurate.

393. *School:* Hawkshead Free Grammar School, founded by Archbishop Sandys in 1585, was a famous classical school of the North of
England; the building is changed but little since the poet's time. It
rivals in interest and quaintness the Stratford Grammar School, and,
like the latter, is still used. There is in it a library presented by the
scholars, and an interesting old oak chest containing the original charter of the school. On the wall is a table containing the names of the
masters. The oak benches are somewhat "insculped upon," and one
of them contains the name, — William Wordsworth. This the Wordsworth Society has had covered with glass to preserve it from relic-
hunters. Over the outside door is the old sun-dial.

394. While seated in the churchyard one evening in the summer of
1886, perhaps near the grave of this boy, this scene was brought
vividly before me as a band of Hawkshead children came through the
yard from their sports upon the hill beyond.

397. *Grave:* The grave of the boy cannot be identified. Wordsworth, in a note on these lines, mentions one William Raincock, a
schoolmate who was unusually proficient in the "owl language"; but as
he was also at Cambridge with Wordsworth, he could not have been
the "immortal boy."

406–20. *May she long:* Rousseau says: "In my time children were
brought up in the rustic fashion, and had no complexion to keep. . . .
Timid and modest before the old, they were bold, haughty, and com-
bative among themselves. They made men with zeal in their hearts to
serve their country, and blood in their veins to shed for her. May
we be able to say as much, one day, of our fine little gentlemen,
and may these men at fifteen not turn out boys at thirty." — *Letter to
D'Alembert.*

421–25. The late Dr. Hudson has the following wise comment
upon education: "Assuredly the need now most urgently pressing
upon us is, to have vastly more of growth, and vastly less of manufac-
ture, in our education; or, in other words, that the school be altogether
more a garden, and altogether less a mill." — *Essays.*

441–42. *Snapped the breathless stillness:* Another allusion to sound.
See also *Fidelity:* —

> There sometimes doth a leaping fish
> Send through the tarn a lonely cheer.

491–95. The unconscious forces in education are here emphasized, —
forces which we often make so little of, and cramming with mere instruction, without waiting for any proper assimilation we expect immediate results, thus crushing out originality and the poetic spirit.

"Worldly advancement and preferment neither are, nor ought to be,
the *main* end of instruction, either in schools or elsewhere." — W. W.

507–11. *Our childhood sits:* In these lines we have the principle of
the *Ode on Immortality,* —

> Heaven lies about us in our infancy.

522–35. The picture here presented of the young imagination feeding upon the romantic and the legendary, is one which may well cause
us to tremble when we think of what the corruption of that imagination
by draughts from a "stagnant pool" may mean. We should remember
that those appetites "must have their food," and that unless we see to

it that the communion is a holy sacrament of the mind, it will be a sacrament of evil.

546–50.
> Turn wheresoe'er I may,
> By night or day,
> The things which I have seen I now can see no more.
>   — *Ode on Immortality.*

561. *Friend:* As unknown as the boy "who blew mimic hootings to the owl," unless it be the one with whom he walked "five miles of pleasant wandering" around Esthwaite. See note, line 333, Book II.

563. *Lake:* Esthwaite.

570. Passages from Pope and Goldsmith. "The first verses I wrote were a task imposed by my master. I was called upon to write verses upon the completion of the second centenary of the school (1785). These were much admired — far more than they deserved, for they were but a tame imitation of Pope's versification and a little in his style." — W. W.

586–605. *Who in his youth, etc.:* In passing from childhood to youth he was most attracted by the poets, and Nature gave him a keener appreciation and a deeper insight. Are these the momentary flashes which illumine our childhood path and then pass forever out of our sight "into the light of common day"? If so, it were better that we had not experienced them. Here the philosophy of Wordsworth (which is nothing else than his genuine common sense) helps us in our perplexity and saves us from becoming morbid. He everywhere teaches that the joy of life must come from those childlike emotions which, if not crushed out, become the most fruitful sources of ennobling the character. No one has ever taught this truth with such exquisite power as has Wordsworth. Who can read without emotion the following words of old Matthew? —

> My eyes are dim with childish tears,
>   My heart is idly stirred;
> For the same sound is in my ears
>   Which in those days I heard.

This philosophy will wear, and in all the vicissitudes of our life, in grave and gay, it will whisper to us, "Waste not." See *Character of the Happy Warrior.*

· *BOOK SIXTH.*

It will be well for us to review the first two acts in the poet's life in order that we may the better understand the third, into which the following books conduct us.

We have seen how his love of Nature was begotten, and how it was nurtured until the new element of Humanity is introduced by his University surroundings. We have been with him in those sacred moments, when — once, in the gray light of the gloaming, and again in the crimson flood of dawn — he felt that the altar-flame of his devotion was kindled, and that thenceforth he was "a dedicated spirit," a priest set apart for service in the Sanctuary of Nature. From these experiences of his we have learned something of the circumstances under which true poetry is born in all inspired souls, —

> From Homer the great Thunderer, from the voice
> That roars along the bed of Jewish song,
> And that more varied and elaborate,
> Those trumpet-tones of harmony that shake
> Our shores.

We have learned that both religion and poetry thrive upon the same elements; that they live in and die apart from human interests and feelings. We can now comprehend what Milton meant when he said that poetry must be Simple, Sensuous, Passionate. In its origin poetry is based upon the primal and universal elements of our nature; in its method it is sensuous, — flashing truth by pictures; and in its aim it is passionate, — the awakening of the slumbering sensibility in man by infusing into thought the fire of emotion.

We are now ready to follow him in his return to the University, and on his visit to the continent.

6. *Granta* and Cam are names for the same stream. Granta-bridge is the Anglo-Saxon for Cambridge.

14. *Rocky Cumberland:* —

> And now he reached the pile of stones,
> Heaped over brave King Dumnail's bones;
> He who had once supreme command,
> Lost King of rocky Cumberland. — *The Waggoner.*

23. *Many books, etc.:* Being a year in advance of his class in Mathematics, he spent his time mostly with the Classics.

24. *Disobedience:* Considering the circumstances under which he was sent to Cambridge, it would not be unlikely that his uncles would be dissatisfied with his course. It required courage on his part to preserve the " vital soul" under the routine and spiritless drudgery of his Cambridge instructors. " The flood tide of new life had not yet set in at Cambridge; she was still slumbering." — MYERS.

45-56. Many of Wordsworth's finest poems were composed before this time (April, 1804), but he was still at work on the Prelude, and had in view the remaining parts of the Recluse.

76. *A single tree:* No remains of the ash-tree are now to be seen in the college grounds. In 1808, Dorothy, on visiting Cambridge, wrote: " I sought out a favorite ash-tree which my brother speaks of in his poem."

> And each particular trunk a growth
> Of intertwisted fibres serpentine. — *Borrowdale Yews.*

90-94.
> This is a holy faith, and full of cheer
> To all who worship Nature, that the hours
> Passed tranquilly with her fade not away
> For ever like the clouds; but in the soul
> Possess a sacred silent dwelling-place. — PROF. WILSON.

Wordsworth taught that the origin of poetry was in emotion recollected in tranquillity.

99, 100. This shows that the reading of the poet was not very " vague " after all.

106. Nature, though not affording him so many facts, had yet broadened his understanding.

110, 111. Alluding to the custom of forming English verse after the model of the classics.

117. *Though advanced:* Before leaving Hawkshead he had mastered five books of Euclid, and Algebra through Quadratics.

173. *That loved, etc.:* —

> Then twilight is preferred to dawn,
> And autumn to the spring. — *Ode to Lycius.*

180. *Bard:* Thomson. *Castle of Indolence.*

189. It is this character of frankness in Wordsworth which renders the Prelude so faithful a record.

193. *Dovedale:* A rocky chasm not far from Ashburn, Derbyshire.

194-200. It was probably during his second summer vacation that he was restored to his sister, who had been living at Penrith with maternal relatives.

205. *Castle:* Brougham Castle, built by Roger, Lord Clifford, and situated at the junction of the Emont and Lowther, about a mile from Penrith, on the Appleby road. It was often plundered by Scottish bands and in the Wars of the Roses. It is now in ruins. See song at the feast of Brougham Castle: —

> Armor rusting in his halls
> On the blood of Clifford calls;—
> Quell the Scot, exclaims the lance, —
> Bear me to the heart of France
> Is the longing of the shield.

208. *Helvellyn:* One of the largest mountains of the lake region, near Grasmere and in sight of Dove Cottage.

209. *Cross-fell:* A mountain near Helvellyn.

221, 222.
> The streams with softest sands are flowing,
> The grass you almost hear it growing.

Wordsworth frequently addresses the "inevitable ear" in us, but the rush and hurry of life often unfit us for appreciating these finer tones of his music.

224. *Mary Hutchinson:* A schoolmate of his at Penrith. See note, line 62, Book I. Also see
> She was a phantom of delight.

229. *So near us:* Wordsworth married Miss Hutchinson in 1802.

233. *Border Beacon:* A hill northeast of Penrith upon which, during the Border Wars, beacon-fires were lighted to summon the country to arms. On the 21st of June, Jubilee year (1887), the border counties of Cumberland and Westmoreland were illuminated by bonfires upon the tops of the mountains, this "Beacon" hill being one. The fires extended from Castle hill, Carlisle, to the sea.

237. Coleridge and Wordsworth first met at Racedom in June, 1797. Of Coleridge, Dorothy wrote: "He is a wonderful man, his conversation teems with mind, soul, and spirit."

240. He had gone to Malta to regain his health.

251. *Etesian :* The mild winds of the Mediterranean.

> Be true,
> Ye winds of ocean, and the midland sea,
> Wafting your charge to soft Parthenope.
> — *On Departure of Scott for Naples.*

258. Poetry and Philosophy.

266–74. A blue-coat-boy at Christ's Hospital, London. "Come back into memory as thou wert in the day-spring of thy fancies, Samuel Taylor Coleridge, logician, metaphysician, bard! How have I seen the casual passer through the cloisters stand still, entranced . . . while the walls of the old Grey Friars re-echoed to the accents of the *inspired charity boy !* " — LAMB.

272. *Stream :* River Otter in Devon.

> For I was reared
> In the vast city, pent 'mid cloisters dim,
> And saw naught lovely but the sky and stars. — S. T. C.

279. *Thou camest :* Coleridge entered Cambridge in February, 1791, one month after Wordsworth had taken his degree.

281. *Student :* Coleridge, besides the Classics and Mathematics, studied Philosophy and Politics.

281. *Course :* See Life of Coleridge.

294. See Charles Lamb's " Christ's Hospital Five and Thirty Years Ago," in his *Essays of Elia.*

322. Robert Jones, a college mate, to whom the poet afterwards dedicated the *Descriptive Sketches,* memorials of this tour.

340. " We crossed at the time," wrote Wordsworth, " when the whole nation was mad with joy, in consequence of the Revolution." In August, 1789, the Nobles in the Assembly surrendered all their feudal rights and privileges.

342. " We went staff in hand, without knapsacks." — W. W.

346. July 14, 1790, when the king swore fidelity to the new Constitution; on this day trees of Liberty were planted all over France. They went from Dover to Calais.

350. They went by Andres, Peronne, and Soissons, to Chalons, and thence sailed to Lyons.

355. *Villages :* —
> By secret villages and lonely farms. — *Descriptive Sketches.*

362.   Her road rustling thin above my head. — *Descriptive Sketches.*

377. July 29, 1790.

395. *Landed :* At Lyons.

406. A singular picture of the "moody" young poet.

418–29. On Aug. 4, they reached Chartreuse, a monastery situated on a rock 4000 feet above the sea. It was founded by St. Bruno; was despoiled during the French Revolution and the inmates driven off.

430. See *Ecclesiastical Sonnets.*

436. Forest of Bruno, near Chartreuse.

439. Rivers at Chartreuse.

480. *Groves :* In the valley of Chartreuse.

484. Crosses on the Spiry Rocks of the Chartreuse, almost inapproachable.

497. From July 13 to Sept. 29.

501. *Valleys :* —
> Ursern's open vale serene. — *Descriptive Sketches.*

515. *Industry :* —
> Abodes of peaceful men. — *Descriptive Sketches.*

519. *Vale :* Between Martigny and Col de Balme.

524. *Ridge :* Col de Balme.

528–40. Compare with this description Coleridge's hymn to Mount Blanc; also Shelley's.

563. Built by Napoleon, is 6628 feet high, and connects Geneva with Milan.

619. Down the Italian side of the Simplon. See poem on the *Simplon Pass.*

624–40. The majesty of the place seized on him; its grandeur and awfulness ravished him beyond himself, and the stupendous powers of the world spoke one language to him, — he was lost in revelation.

663. The banks of Lago di Como are mountains 3000 feet high, with hamlets, villas, chapels, and convents.

665. *Pathways :* Narrow foot paths are the only communication, by land, from village to village.

670. *Verse:* In *Descriptive Sketches.*

700. *Gravedona:* At the head of Lake Como.

723. *Night:* Aug. 21, 1790.

764. They reached Cologne Sept. 28, and went thence through Belgium to Calais.

769. *Was touched:* He went to the continent bent on seeing Nature; he found sublimity in the Alps and beauty at the Italian lakes. The depths of his soul were stirred, and began to assert themselves in creation; the power of expression now begins to dawn. He had felt the call to be a poet, and he must not be disobedient to the heavenly vision, although his course might seem hardy disobedience to friends.

BOOK SEVENTH.

1. *First:* Feb. 10, 1799. See note, lines 1–10, Book I. In a letter dated Grasmere, June 3, 1805, Wordsworth says: "I have the pleasure to say that I finished my poem about a fortnight ago." Thus we are sure that the last seven books must have been written in the year 1805.

4. *Preamble:* First two paragraphs of Book I.

6. *Transport:* The Preamble.

7. *Scafell:* The highest mountain in the lake district.

11, 12. *Stopped:* It is evident that this was in 1802, otherwise we cannot account for the "years" intervening before "last Primrose-time," 1804. See note, lines 45–56, Book VI. and text.

13. *Assurance:* Coleridge, before going to Malta, urged Wordsworth to complete this work.

16. *Summer:* 1804.

31. *Will chant:* This book must have been begun, then, in the fall of 1804.

44. *Grove:* John's Grove, so called because it was the favorite resort of the poet's brother, Captain Wordsworth. It is but a few moments' walk from Dove Cottage. You pass it by the middle road

to Rydal, opposite the famous "Wishing Gate"; from it there is a fine view across the lake to the mountains beyond.

> And there I sit at evening, where the steep
> Of Sölver How, and Grasmere's peaceful lake,
> And one green island gleam between the stems
> Of the dark firs, a visionary scene! — *Poems on Naming of Places.*

52. *Excursion:* Related in Book VI.

54. *Quitted:* He took his degree, B. A., in January, 1791, and left Cambridge.

58-65. *Undetermined:* He went at once to visit his sister at Forncett Rectory, near Norwich, where he remained six weeks. The crisis of his life lay between this time and his settlement at Grasmere. He had resolved to be a poet, but poetry would not feed him unless he prostituted his talents and wrote for the crowd. "Flash" was what would pay, but he could not reconcile the "flash line" with the line of duty. In this perplexity of mind he went to London, and roamed about, noting men and things. All the time his friends were urging him to enter the church, the law, or the army.

68. *Three years:* It is evident from this that he must have visited London in 1788.

81. See *The Seven Wonders of the World.*

112. *Whittington:* A famous citizen of London, thrice Lord Mayor.

121. *Vauxhall, etc.:* Pleasure gardens, now built over; the names are applied to streets in the city.

129. See *Sonnet on Westminster Bridge.*

131. *Giants:* Gog and Magog, sometimes carried in the pageant of Lord Mayor's Day.

132. *Bedlam:* Lunatic Hospital, built in 1549.

136. *Monument:* On Fish Street Hill, erected to commemorate the Great Fire in September, 1666. It required six years to erect it; it is a fluted column 202 feet high, designed by Sir Christopher Wren.

Tower: The most celebrated fortress in Great Britain. It was built by William I., and has been used as royal residence, armory, prison, treasure-house, and seat of government. The "Chamber" is the armory in four compartments: (1) armor of Battle of Hastings, (2) of the French wars, (3) of Henry VIII., (4) of James I. and Elizabeth.

160. Referring to the custom of marking the house in which some noted man lived. 7 Craven St., Strand, has, " Benjamin Franklin lived here."

267. *Saddler's Wells :* A theatre, named from the spring in the garden. Here the plays of Shakespeare and the old dramatists were acted.

297. *Maid :* Buttermere is about fifteen miles from Grasmere. The "Spoiler" was afterwards hanged at Carlisle.

305. Coleridge and Wordsworth must have seen her when they took their tramp through the lakes. See note, line 74, Book I.

382. To Cambridge, 1787.

458, 459. All of these events lose their triviality when considered as necessary parts of the poet's education.

484. His father had set him to learn passages from the best English poets.

491. *Stage :* Parliament, when the debates were in progress on the French Revolution. He said, " You always went away from Burke with your mind filled."

498. See Shakespeare's King Henry V.

529. *Theory :* See Burke's *Reflections on the French Revolution.* It is not easy to account for Wordsworth's admiration for Burke, as recorded here and elsewhere, when we consider that their theories were antagonistic; one taking the optimistic, the other the pessimistic view.

564. *Death of Abel :* By Solomon Gesner, born in Zurich, 1730. His *Death of Abel* was translated into English in 1780. Wordsworth probably means by " the other day " the appearance of a new edition.

565. *Bard :* Young, author of *Night Thoughts.*

678. *St. Bartholomew :* Henry I. granted the privileges of holding fairs on this day; but as they had deteriorated to cheap shows, they were proclaimed in 1850.

744. See Shairp's *Poetic Interpretation of Nature,* Ch. XIV.

BOOK EIGHTH.

In the rush and roar of London, caught in the tides of her feverish life, Wordsworth seems to have been drifting aimlessly. But the poet's heart was beating in his breast all the more rapidly because of the contrast of the city's din to the quiet of his cloister life at Cambridge, and at each pulse he felt himself drawn nearer to the life of man. Until this time, Nature and God were first, and Man second; here in the centre of the great metropolis the transition was made. Now, at the beginning of the Eighth Book, he looks back and gives us an inside view of the workings of his own soul while it was being played upon by the influences of Nature and of Man. The value of Book VII., of itself the least interesting in the Prelude, is not grasped except by understanding its relation to the following, —

> " There's a day about to break,
> There's a light about to dawn."

1–20. One of these fairs is alluded to by Dorothy in her Grasmere Journal, Sept. 2, 1800. At that time Coleridge was with them at Dove Cottage. "We walked to the Fair . . . It was a lovely moonlight night, and the sound of dancing and merriment came along the still air." The annual sports of the North of England at Grasmere resemble one of these fairs, —

> Bid by the day they wait for all the year,
> Shepherd and swain their gayest colors don,
> For race and sinewy wrestling meet upon
> The tournay ground beside the shining mere.
> *   *   *   *   *
> No banner fame they boast, no high emprize;
> A brother's praise the simple meed they ask;
> The fullest guerdon of the stubborn task
> The love that lights a fluttering maiden's eyes.
> — H. D. RAWNSLEV.

48–52. From *Malvern Hills*, by Mr. Joseph Cottle (see Prefatory Note to Book I.).

70–76. Looking back, the poet sees that his love of Nature led him on to the love of Man.

78. *Gehol:* Hanging Gardens of Babylon.

98–100. His childhood, passed among magnificent scenery where man was free, was moulded by the simple life of home. The men were as sturdy and incorruptible as the mountains themselves. The beauty of his country, like that of Switzerland, was more beautiful because of the liberty of soul which characterized the people. The freedom of Nature was not marred by " man's inhumanity to man." This idea Wordsworth made central in *Michael.*

> Of shepherds, dwellers in the valleys, men
> Whom I already loved: — not verily
> For their own sake, but for the fields and hills
> Where was their occupation and abode.

128. These shepherds, living as they did so near to Nature, seemed to his young imagination but another aspect of the life of the hills. The rocks and streams were vocal, in the traditions of the dalesmen, with many a tale of suffering or heroism amid the howling winds and the driving storms which often destroyed both them and their flocks. See *Fidelity.*

129. *Saturn :* An ancient mythical king of Latium.

132. *Golden Age:* See Virgil VIII., 319.

135. *Grecian Song :* Polybius IV., 20, 21.

139. *Arden :* See Shakespeare's *As You Like It.*

142. See *Winter's Tale.*

144. *Spenser : Shepherd's Calendar* (May).

145–63. Some of the rural pastimes are still kept alive in the region of the Lakes, but the tourist, with his fine clothes, pretension, and presents, has done much to create dissatisfaction in the breasts of the rural folk. At Grasmere and Ambleside the custom of " Rush Bearing " is continued, in memory of the time when they strewed the ground in the churches with rushes gathered from the lake-side. It now occurs in August, and the rushes wreathed with flowers are used to decorate the church. It is a Children's Festival, and to see them, headed by a band of music, march through the streets, singing, —

> " Our fathers to the House of God,
> As yet a building rude,
> Bore offerings from the flowery sod
> And fragrant rushes strewed," —

suggests that the spirit of Wordsworth is still moving amongst them. Never do they forget to place an offering on the poet's grave.

170. See *The Brothers.*

175. *Galesus :* An Italian river, famous for fine-fleeced sheep.

176. *Adria :* See Acts xxvii., 27.

180. *Clitumnus :* A tributary to the Tiber, famous for its snow-white cattle.

182. *Lucretilis :* A hill near the farm of Horace. See *Ode* I., 17. The excellence of style in these descriptions, — the pulsation and thrill, the exquisite effects of metre, the graceful and natural flow of words, the art of concealing art, and the classical atmosphere pervading the whole, — show in a peculiar way the genius of the poet.

186. *Pastoral track :* At Goslar, near the Hartz Mountains. See Prefatory Note, Book I.

210. *Walls :* In the Fenwick note to *In Germany,* he says, "I walked daily on the ramparts, or on a sort of public ground or garden." — KNIGHT.

215. *Hircynian :* Near the Rhine, in Southern and Central Germany. See Cæsar, *B. G.* VI., 24, 25.

217. *Channels:* Wastdale, Ennerdale, Yewdale, etc.

223–93. Here "Nature seems to take the pen out of his hand and write with her own sheer, bare, penetrating power." In this there is the grandeur of the mountains, which by their relation to man ennoble and glorify him. The passage is unique and unmatchable; it is characterized by a profound sincerity and an exquisite naturalness, accompanied with something of the dramatic; it is the heart of the poet beating in sympathy with Nature and Man.

294–340. Thus it was that the poet gained his firm faith in the nobility of man. He did not find evil as fast as he found good in those early days, for he read his first lesson on Man from the book of Nature, and saw him in his setting of beauty and sublimity. The voices of sea, of mountain, and of forest, testified to the liberty of Man, and educated him into a republican. When the thick veil of custom, of artificial manners, of pretension and display, has obscured from our view the natural dignity of human nature, and we rate men by what they have rather than by what they are, it will do us good to listen to this singer of "humble themes and noble thought."

340–91. Although Nature was at first pre-eminent in his thoughts, yet his vision of man was growing clearer and clearer, and he began to unite the two in one picture. See *Tintern Abbey Poem.* (361) *Of tenderness:* See *Green Linnet* and *Hartleap Well.* (369) *Harmonious words:* See *The Evening Walk,* written at the age of seventeen, and *Descriptive Sketches.*

403. *Rock:* It is difficult to determine whether this alludes to Dove Cottage or Ann Tyson. If the former is meant, the rock would be on Red Bank; if the latter, it would be on the hill northwest of Hawkshead.

421. In preface to *Lyrical Ballads,* he says: "Fancy is given us to quicken and beguile the temporal part of our nature; imagination, to incite and support the eternal."

459. *Thurston-mere:* Coniston Lake, not far from Hawkshead.

468. The following eight lines are recast from a poem which he wrote in anticipation of leaving school, and which he said was a tame imitation of Pope's versification.

477. *High emotion:* Poetry written before 1805.

543. *Entered:* Probably in 1788.

562. *Antiparos:* One of the Cyclades, containing a stalactite cave. *Den:* A limestone cavern near Ingleton in Yorkshire.

619. For Wordsworth's theory of diction, see Preface to *Lyrical Ballads.*

631. From all sides knowledge of man poured in upon him, and he had the ability to grasp it, not in its narrow detail, but in the majesty and loftiness of the vast and unmeasurable power of humanity, — a power for evil as well as for good.

634. The following ten lines illustrate to what heights of sublimity his imagination was capable of rising. The analogy between Nature and Mankind here is not so far-fetched as some think. The sense of ceaseless activity of Nature showing itself in frost, in flood, and in lightning, corresponded to the rush, the passion, and the strife of this sea of humanity.

645. As he had read the face of Nature, and under its apparent frown read love, so here he looked beneath the surface and grasped the real abiding principle, and saw that manhood was even more manly when contending in the crowded marts. This was the needed sequel

to the picture of man which he had among the mountains, and it
made him sympathetic in all the struggles of life.

669. This was the thought which exalted the idea of man above all
others; the thought of Brotherhood under God, the Father of all.

677–86. Nature had been his guide to the idea of the unity of Man
and the fatherhood of God, and had developed in him love of his race;
yet he often sought in her rest and refuge from the lawlessness and
guilt of mankind.

---◦◦◦---

BOOK NINTH.

We have seen what impressions Wordsworth received from Nature,
and how, beginning at Cambridge and continuing in London, they
led him up to the study of Man.   He now loved both Nature
and Man, and his enthusiasm for humanity was growing day by day.
After spending four months, February, March, April, and May, in
London, he visited his friend Jones in Wales, and refreshed himself by
communion with the hills; visiting Menai, Conway, and Bethgelert;
enjoying the splendor of the Vale of Choyd; and upon the summit of
Snowdon beheld the "vision" recorded in the last book of the Prelude.
Yet even here in the solitude of Nature, the voice of Humanity sounding in that song of liberty allured him to the theatre of Revolution.
The Revolution was not confined to the sphere of politics: that was
only one feature of the great movement toward the goal of equal rights
to which the nations were tending.   It was a return to Nature in all
the departments of life.   This enthusiasm for Nature took form in
France under Rousseau's extravagant and diseased sensibility.   In
Germany the same feeling was manifested by Goethe, who combined
the poetic with the scientific aspect of Nature, and swelled the great
wave of feeling which was gathering force as it advanced.   In England
it had been growing into form for half a century.   The heralds of the
day arose from quarters, and under circumstances quite unexpected, —
from the sorrow and disappointment of Cowper and the untaught melodies of plow-boy of Ayrshire, — the one in his invalid nightcap, the

other in his blue bonnet and homespun. But the poet who was to conduct the heart of England to the love of rivers, woods, and hills was, in the autumn of 1791, leaving Brighton for Paris, about to plunge into the blood and furor of that revolutionary city.

28. *Year:* See comments above.

35. *So lately:* With Jones in 1790.

40. *Town:* Orleans.

45. *Mars:* In the west of Paris.

46. *St. Antoine:* In the east of the city.

47. *Martre:* In the north of the city.
Deme: The Pantheon, in the south.

51. *Tossed:* On May 4, 1789, the clergy, noblesse, and tiers état, constituting the States General, met in Notre Dame. The next day the tiers état assumed the title of the National Assembly, and urged the others to join them. The Jacobin Club began the same year. Madam Roland and the Brissotins were now in the ascendant.

52. *Palace:* Palais Royal, built by Cardinal Richelieu, and presented to Duke of Orleans by Louis XIV.

68. *Bastile:* State prison and citadel of Paris. It was taken and destroyed by the Revolutionists, July 14, 1789.

71. *Truth:* Wordsworth was a natural republican, and hence his indifference.

77. *Le Brun:* Court painter of Louis XIV.

132. They were so disgusted with the Revolution that they stood ready to join the emigrants in arms against their country under Leopold, king of Prussia, and to restore the old régime.

139. *One:* The Republican general, Beaupuis.

176. *Carra, Gorsas:* Journalist deputies in the first year of the Republic. The latter was the first of the deputies to die on the scaffold. See Carlyle's *French Revolution,* Vol. II.

182. *Flight:* See note, line 132.

214. See *Merchant of Venice,* Act II., Scene viii., second speech of Prince of Aragon.

216–17. This statement is as true now as when it was written. Ruskin, in 1876, said that he had, in his fields at Coniston, men who might have fought with Henry V. at Agincourt without being distinguished from one of his knights.

232. "Drawn from a strong Scandinavian stock, they dwell in a land as solemn and beautiful as Norway itself. And the Cumbrian dalesmen have afforded, perhaps, as near a realization as human fates have yet allowed of a rural society which statesmen have desired for their country's greatness." — F. W. H. MYERS.

265. *Posting on :* see note, line 132.

281–87. Thus it was that the Revolution touched the hearts of the young and imaginative minds of England; the light of a new heaven and a new earth seemed about to dawn on men. They believed that God was avenging the wrongs and injustice of the rulers. Coleridge and Southey were beside themselves at the prospect of a Pantisocracy, — a religious socialism.

290–321. In company with this rejected Republican, Wordsworth lived; they were kindred spirits. The description here given of a man whom the ideas of Revolution had changed from a noted gallant to a military hero illustrates the type of men whom great emergencies breed. Similar events produced the heroes of our Civil War.

321–39. Discussion of rights, based upon universal brotherhood.

340–63. The oppression and tyranny which had hindered Man's progress.

363–89. Man, his noble nature, and what must result from it. In reference to 321–389, see quotation from Senator Hoar in the preface.

392. *Rotha :* See sonnet, by Rev. H. D. Rawnsley, in the preface.

393. *Greta :* A river which flows past the home of Southey at Keswick. See sonnet to *River Greta.*

Derwent : See note, lines 270–75, Book I.

409. *Dion :* a pupil of Plato's. See the poem *Dion*, composed in 1816.

410. Both Plato and Dion tried to influence Dionysus, the tyrant of Syracuse, but did not succeed. Finally, Dion was induced to attempt the deliverance of Syracuse. See "Dion" in Plutarch's *Lives.*

412. Philosophers who assisted Dion.

413. Syracusan exiles.

416. Dion sailed with 800 troops, and took Syracuse.

451. *Angelica :* Character in the *Orlando Furioso* of Ariosto.

453. *Erminia :* Heroine of *Jerusalem Delivered,* by Tasso.

481. *Romorentin :* Capital of Sologne. "It was taken in 1356 and in 1429 by the English, in 1562 by the Catholics, and in 1589 by the Royalists." — KNIGHT.

482. *Blois :* Birthplace of Louis XII. In XVI century, court was often held there. It is one of the most interesting places in France. Wordsworth went from Orleans to Blois in the spring of 1792.

484. *Lady :* Claude, daughter of Louis XII.

491. *Chambourd :* Village nine miles from Blois, noted for its chateau and park. Francis I, Charles IX, Louis XIII, and Louis XIV held court there.

501–41. These dreams have been pronounced chimerical; yet if they are to prove so, the spirit of Christianity and its root-thoughts must be equally chimerical. It is this deep Christian feeling which is the parent of Democracy, and the creator of the idea of an universal humanity. Nothing short of Christian ideas applied to the relation of men to one another, and to the state, can solve the problem which is baffling so many at the present time.

> By the soul
> Only the nations shall be great and free.

547. *A tale : Vaudracour and Julia,* founded on a tale related to Wordsworth by a French lady who was an eye-witness of the scene described.

553. The following four lines are the prelude to the above-mentioned poem.

BOOK TENTH.

11. *Metropolis :* In the autumn of 1792 he left Blois for Paris.

12. *Fallen :* Aug. 10, 1792, the mob stormed the Tuileries and imprisoned the king and his family in the Temple. In December he was tried, and in January, 1793, executed.

18. *Mogul :* A corruption of Mongol, the name given to emperors of India.

19. *Agra and Lahore:* Cities of India implicated in the Sepoy rebellion.

20. The Rajahs were the native princes of India, and the Omlahs were their officials.

40. *League:* The supposed union of Louis with European monarchs to put down the Rebellion.

41. *Republic:* On the 22d of September, 1792, the Republic was proclaimed.

43. *Massacre:* The Danton massacres were just over; they lasted from the 2d to the 6th of September.

48. He arrived in Paris in October, 1792. The city heaved like a volcano. Robespierre, one of the "Committee of Public Safety," which believed in the imprisonment of all who did not accept the extreme views of the Revolutionists, was rising.

56. *Carrousel:* Place de Carrousel, a public square, used for festivals.

63–93. *But that night:* This passage expressing the intensity of feeling of the young poet is one of the finest in all his poetry. Although he took sides against Robespierre, yet he held fast to the principles of the Revolution. He seemed to see in all the vengeance and bloodshed the hand of God, and he felt that in the end Freedom would win.

95. *Orleans:* See note, line 51, Book IX.

111. *Jean Baptiste Louvet,* who, when Robespierre was summoned to the tribune to answer to the charge of aspiring to the dictatorship, and asked who accused him, answered "*Moi,*" and recited crime after crime, until the tyrant, who had abolished the worship of God and declared that of Reason, was cowered.

114. Robespierre got a delay of one week to prepare an answer, and by smooth speech finally triumphed.

120–90. The vein of optimism running through these lines is characteristic of a man trained as he had been. His optimism is that of one who firmly believes in the righteousness of right, and that through the eternal Love and Justice of God man would become regenerated. It was this element in his nature which made his poetry of man not only revolutionary, but Christian.

198-99. *Harmodius and Aristogiton:* Athenians who put to death the tyrant Hipparchus, and rid the city of the rule of the Pisistratidæ, much as Brutus rose against Cæsar.

222-31. Such was the fascination of the terrible city, and such was his sympathy in the great movement, that had his funds not given out, he doubtless would have "seen it out," and perished with his friends, the Brissotins. He returned to England in December, 1792.

236. *Twice:* He left England in November, 1792.

245. *To abide:* He remained in London during the winter of 1792-3, with his brother Richard. In Dec. 22, 1792, Dorothy writes from Forncett Rectory: "William is in London."

247. The movement of Clarkson and Wilberforce for abolishing the slave trade. See *Sonnet to William Clarkson.*

264-65. When in January, 1793, the Republic threw down the head of Louis XVI. as her battle gauge, and England joined with Holland and Spain against France, his indignation knew no bounds; it was a terrible shock to his moral nature. If England was to disappoint him, where was he to look for support?

283. *Rejoiced:* This is the culmination of that idea of interest in mankind outside of the bounds of England which began in the poetry of Goldsmith, was continued in Cowper, and became so intense in the "Poet of Humanity," — Wordsworth.

315. *Red Cross flag:* Union Jack. When the crowns of England and Scotland were united under James I., the red cross of St. George and the white cross of St. Andrew were ordered to be joined in one ensign.

316-30. Wordsworth, in his advertisement to *Guilt and Sorrow,* says: "During the latter part of the summer of 1793, passed a month in the Isle of Wight, in view of the fleet then preparing for sea at Portsmouth, and left the place with melancholy forebodings."

331-75. The "Reign of Terror" began in France in July, 1793. Mob rule and terrorism won the lead against the Conservatives, and the guillotine was the strong arm of the law against all who opposed the radical ideas of the "Committee of Public Safety," and the Atheistical party which enthroned the Goddess of Reason in November, 1713.

381. Madame Roland, wife of the minister of the interior under Dumouriez; his opposition to Louis XVI. caused his dismissal from office, and produced the insurrection which paved the way for the restoration of the Girondists to the ministry. The saloon of Madame Roland was the rallying-point of the Girondist leaders. The Jacobins were bent on the death of M. and Madame Roland, and she was beheaded on Nov. 8, 1793. When upon the scaffold, turning to the statue of Liberty, she said, "O Liberty, what crimes are committed in thy name!" Her husband committed suicide.

383. *O Friend, etc.:* The result, given in the following lines, was not a strange one on a nature like Wordsworth's. The eclipse of his fair idol of the rights of man was almost total.

430. The love of Nature had been superseded by the love of Man, and now that the second love was weakening, the crisis was near at hand.

436–80. In his most passionate moods, temperance was at the centre, and prevented the flame of emotion from consuming him. When he looked deep into the roots of the Revolution, he saw that God was educating the nation by the punishment of evil, and that the "Reign of Terror" was a natural sequence of the greed and tyranny of the *noblesse.*

491. With Jones in the vacation of 1790.

496–7.
> Jones! as from Calais southward you and I
> Went pacing side by side, the public way
> Streamed with the pomp of a too credulous day,
> When faith was pledged to new-born Liberty.
> — *Sonnet composed near Calais, 1802.*

498. *Arras:* A town one hundred miles from Paris, celebrated for its tapestries. The birthplace of Robespierre.

512. The reaction from the "Reign of Terror" had set in; all parties combined against Robespierre, and he was executed by his former supporters, July 28, 1794.

513. *The day:* The winter of 1793–4, Wordsworth spent in Cumberland, at Keswick and Penrith. This journey must have been in August, 1794.

515. Over the Ulverston sands, where the waters of Windermere find their way to the sea.

525. Ulverston is not far from Hawkshead.

534. At Cartmell, where the Rev. William Taylor, master at Hawkshead School, 1782–6, was buried. Just before his death he sent for the upper boys of the school (amongst whom was Wordsworth), and took leave of them with a solemn blessing.

> The blessing which to you
> Our common Friend and Father sent.
> — *Address to the Scholars of the Village School.*

536. Besides the inscription are the following lines from Gray : —

> His merits, stranger, seek not to disclose,
> Or draw his frailties from their dread abode, etc.

552. The writing of poetry was imposed as a task upon the boys of the Hawkshead School. See lines *Written as a School Exercise Anno Ætatis, 14.*

576. Another star of hope was now to be seen above the horizon of his fears, and enthusiasm was rekindled in his bosom by the thought that the world would now recognize the laws of righteousness.

596–98. On his way to Hawkshead from Furness Abbey and Conishead Priory. See note, line 102, Book II.

BOOK ELEVENTH.

1. *Time:* The "Reign of Terror" ended with the death of Robespierre.

11. *In the people:* How deep was that faith which could still trust in the conscience of the masses! It shows what an influence the honesty and sincerity of those companions of his, the shepherds, had had upon his young life.

53–73. The dread of Revolution in England was in consequence of there being many supporters of France there. The habeas corpus was suspended, and some Scottish Whigs were ordered to be transported.

98. *I began :* He was now to use his intellect more than his heart, and to study man as a citizen; the result was that he was led to take a greater interest in political and national questions than any poet of his time.

105-44. These lines first appeared in the *Friend*, Oct. 6, 1809. They were written in 1805, and, as he looked back on the dream which was now becoming fulfilled, it added new enthusiasm to the cause of Humanity, and made him the champion of the rights of man. It also furnished him the impulse to write that philosophical poem, *The Excursion*.

175. In 1795.

206. In this act his last hopes of liberty suffered eclipse, and he was overwhelmed with shame and despondency; yet his hatred of oppression became stronger than ever, for he believed that in this movement all the darkest events of the old *régime* were combined. He uttered his indignation in that remarkable series of sonnets on liberty.

223-320. He now set about the analysis of right in the abstract, and in this operation even the grounds of right disappeared. This was the crisis of his life. He now plunged into the nether gloom by the use of this critical faculty. He grew sceptical of faith, which could not be demonstrated by logic. He fell under the absolute despotism of the eye; "all things were put to question," and he began to think that this power of seeing was nobler than the power of feeling, and to judge that all his life had been conducted upon a wrong principle. We see this experience repeated again and again at the present day. The thraldom of sense is supreme, and true love of Nature has no resting-place. The scientific spirit dries up both heart and conscience; a complex worldly life is creating a worldliness of the eye.

333-48. *Then it was:* In the winter of 1794 he joined his sister at Halifax. He had not seen her since 1790. She had always been his better angel, and in this sickness of his soul she knew what remedy to apply. She visited with him many of the most interesting districts of their native Cumberland, and amid the freshness and beauty of Nature his feverish spirit was soothed and healed; he was brought back to his true self; wandering around among the rural people, he partook of their joys and their sorrows; and in this occupation his own joy returned. The world has loved to view the picture of the devotion of Charles and Mary Lamb in their lives of sadness; the companion picture of William and Dorothy Wordsworth is not less interesting and touching. Mr. Paxton Hood says: "Not Laura with Petrarch, nor Beatrice with Dante are more really connected than Wordsworth with his sister Dorothy." See *Dorothy Wordsworth; or, Story of a Sister's Love,* by Edmund Lee; also *Tintern Abbey.*

360. In 1804 Buonaparte summoned the Pope to anoint him emperor of France.

376. Coleridge was living in Sicily, whither he had gone from Malta. See Vol. IX., Knight's edition of Wordsworth.

379. *Timoleon :* A Greek who reduced Sicily to order. He refused all titles, and lived as a private citizen. See Plutarch's *Lives.*

418–23. See sonnet on *Departure of Sir Walter Scott for Naples.*

434. *Empedocles :* Philosopher of Agrigentum.

435. *Archimedes :* Geometrician of Syracuse.

437. *Theocritus :* Pastoral poet of Syracuse. See Burns' poem, *Pastoral Poetry.*

444. *Comates :* See Theocritus, *Idyll,* VII., 28.

450. At Dove Cottage. See note, line 74, Book I.

BOOK TWELFTH.

1–43. Healing had been ministered to a mind diseased, and he now looked upon the face of Nature with the imaginative delight of childhood yet with a fuller appreciation of the sources of her beauty. The experience through which he had passed had strengthened, matured, and disciplined his mind, so that it became the fountain from whence issued much of what was high and unworldly in the thought of the following generation. The harmony of thought and language in this passage is hardly surpassed by that of the Tintern Abbey poem; the notes are as joyous as those of his own skylark, —

> With a soul as strong as a mountain river,
> Pouring out praise to the Almighty Giver.

44–74. In this review of his struggles he is more minute in his delineation than heretofore, and shows us to what extremes the tyranny of sense had driven him.   He came to look upon the heroic in Man as of little advantage unless it could be demonstrated to have proceeded by logical processes; hence the Epics as well as the Lyrics were useless, and all study and enjoyment of them a mistake.   His was no longer the spirit of the artist, but that of the art critic.

88–151. He transferred his observation and analysis now from Man to Nature, and put her under the malignant spell; and the result was the denuding and unsouling of all natural scenes and objects. Nature became a laboratory instead of a garden.

151. *And yet I knew a maid, etc.:* The reference here is not to his sister, but to the first meeting of Miss Hutchinson, who afterward became his wife.   Next to the blessing of that sister, who conducted him from the region of despair and spiritual death to that of assured hope and enlargement of soul, stands that

> Creature not too bright or good
> For human nature's daily food.
> A perfect woman nobly planned,
> To warn, to comfort, and command.

The simplicity of her manner, and her soothing and sustaining influence is celebrated in many lines of the poet's later works.   In the companionship of two such appreciative and home-hearted women, he was blessed beyond most of his brethren in song.

174–207. Once he worshipped without criticising, and enjoyed without dissecting; but the miserable carping spirit, which he now possessed, kept him continually on the lookout for the *how* and the *why,* — a sort of malignant motive-hunting.

208–25. Here we have the ground idea of the great *Ode,* — the power of redemption possessed by the recollection of early impressions. Looking back to that imperial Palace whence we came, we get nourishment and recreation for the business of life.   It is this element in Wordsworth's poetry that gives it its unwithering freshness, its power to make us see beauty in the commonplace, and to help us idealize the real.   Thus Wordsworth's philosophy is not a theory; it is a *life.*   It had saved him from despondency and spiritual death; it will recreate all of those who will but put themselves under its influences.

253-61. *It was in truth, etc.:* For similar thought, see text, 364–391, Book VIII.

261-71. *When, etc.:* The spiritual freedom which sets the poet's imagination into action seldom fails to centre it upon solid foundations. In this he differs so much from Coleridge, whose imagination seems to wander through the mazes of every new association, regardless of any focal point. In lines 426–432, Book VIII., Wordsworth dwells upon these differences and says: —

> I had forms distinct
> To steady me.

272-86. The child spirit is immortal.

> But for those first affections,
> Those shadowy recollections,
> Which, be they what they may,
> Are yet the fountain light of all our day,
> Are yet the master light of all our seeing.
> — *Ode on Immortality.*

287. *One Christmas time:* This was evidently 1783. His father was then living at Penrith, and the *led palfreys* would go by Kirkstone Pass and Ambleside. From Ambleside to Hawkshead there are two roads which meet within about two miles of Hawkshead village; here there are two crags, either of which would answer the description.

311-35. Wordsworth in this passage corroborates what has already been said of his susceptibility to sound; he is always listening, and when he afterwards recalls the scenes, he blends sights and sounds, the latter often being the most prominent. In early life his imagination was too masculine and severe; the terrible pleased him more than the tender, and he was blind to the sweetness of character, and the repose of the landscape. Through the humanizing influence of his sister he was softened; she gave him a·

> Heart, the fountain of sweet tears,
> And love and thought and joy.

BOOK THIRTEENTH.

1–10. The power with which Wordsworth illustrated this truth makes him one of the greatest teachers and benefactors of his age. He is no less the poet of contemplation than the poet of passion, and the lesson was taught him by Nature. It is only by calmness in the midst of passion that the highest beauty in poetry is attained. All of Wordsworth's finest poetry is the result of emotions recollected in tranquillity.

> They flash upon the inward eye,
> Which is the bliss of solitude.

11–47. Returning now from the study of Science to the beauty and sublimity of Nature, he found in her the "image of right reason," which he could take with him into the world of man.

48–119. His emotion being now under regulation, he determined to find out the truths of human life, and what were the elements of permanence in human feelings. He gave up his sanguine schemes for the regeneration of mankind, and turned to the abodes of simple men, where duty, love, and reverence were to be found in their true relation and worth. Here he found that human heart, —

> The haunt and main region of song.

130–141. His wounded heart was healed as he experienced the "love in huts where poor men lie."

> He wandered far; and much did he see of men,
> Their manners, their enjoyments, and pursuits,
> Their possessions and their feelings; chiefly those
> Essential and eternal in the heart.

141–60. From the terrace-walk in the garden of the Cockermouth home can be seen the hill here referred to, and the road running over its summit. The road is now only a foot-path, but was then a public way to Isel, a town on the Derwent.

160–85. The riches which he gleaned from these mines of neglected wealth made him the singer of "simple songs for thinking hearts," and essentially the poet of home. He learned

> How verse may build a princely throne
> On humble truth.

186–220. Wordsworth here touches the core of our modern artificial life and thinking, and he teaches us that unless we estimate life by other terms than those of matter and flesh, we are but hastening the crisis when class shall be arrayed against class, — we are sowing the germs of another Revolution.

220–78. This passage is the finest in thought, and the most perfect in expression, of any of the Prelude. It illustrates the courage of the man who dared thus, in an age of superficiality and pride, to fly in the face of all the poetical creeds, and make the joys and sorrows that we encounter on the common high road of life the subjects of his song. Hence you will never find the man who passes his life in society take any interest in Wordsworth's poetry; it breathes an atmosphere too bracing for such characters. Frederick Robertson says: "A man whose object is to have a position in what is called fashionable life is simply *incapable* of enjoying the highest poetry."

314. *Sarum's Plain:* In 1793 he wandered with his friend William Calvert over Salisbury Plain.

353. *Unpremeditated Strains:* The *Descriptive Sketches*. Coleridge happened upon these when an undergraduate at Cambridge, 1793, and wrote of them: "Seldom, if ever, was the emergence of a great and original poetic genius above the literary horizon more evidently announced."

361. The poets did not meet until 1797.

BOOK FOURTEENTH.

1–10. In the summer of 1793 he visited his friend Jones in Wales.

35–130. Of this vision of the transmuting power of imagination, Stopford Brooke says: "It is one of the finest specimens of Wordsworth's *grand style*. It is as sustained and stately as Milton, but differs from Milton's style in the greater simplicity of diction." Here is established the harmony between God, Man, and Nature. In this experience is the completion in Wordsworth of the marriage of Mind to the Universe and to God. In this, too, he found the guide and anchor of his being. Eor an illustration of this result upon his poetry see *Stanzas on Peele Castle in a Storm* and *The Yew-Trees of Borrowdale;* there is nothing like it in English poetry. The rapture which he feels in the presence of the life of Nature, when the soul of man receives her inflowing soul, is a deep religious consciousness — it is love and worship. Such poetry cannot live upon appearances; it dies in an atmosphere of Positivism and Agnosticism, for "all great art is the expression of Man's delight in the work of God."

168–69. *By love:* No great poet has been content with mere outward Nature; he must pass through it to the soul of man. Wordsworth never rests in what appears to the outward eye; he rests only in the aspirations caused by what the senses reveal.

188–92. Even the love between man and man must rise by imagination of what we are to become, or else it is not spiritual; it does not rise above natural affection. We must

> Look abroad,
> And see to what fair countries they are bound.

Unless imagination can look to the celestial mountains, and see them, not as floating clouds, but as solid substance, spiritual love must pine and die, and there can be no

> Blessed consolations in distress.

253. See *Sparrow's Nest* and *Tintern Abbey.* "What was once harsh in Wordsworth was toned by the womanly sweetness of his sister; and with a devotion as rare as it was noble, she dedicated to him her life and service." — EDMUND LEE.

266–68. Mary Hutchinson. See *She was a Phantom of Delight,* second stanza.

281. Wordsworth said: "He and my sister are the two beings to whom my intellect is most indebted."

311. See Advertisement to this work, page 1.

353. After leaving London, 1793, he went to the Isle of Wight, the valley of the Wye, and later visited with his sister the scenes of his youth in Cumberland and Westmoreland.

355–69. *Calvert:* Raislay Calvert, a young man much in the same position of life as Wordsworth, who, although he did not write verses, could appreciate genius, and believed that Wordsworth possessed it. In January, 1794, while Wordsworth was unsettled in his plans for life, and while he was waiting for a reply to an application for a position on a newspaper, Calvert was taken sick, and Wordsworth went to take care of him at Penrith, remaining with him until his death. It was found on opening his will that he had left Wordsworth £900; this enabled him to share a home with his sister, and, in 1795, they settled at Racedoun Lodge, in Dorsetshire. It was here that Coleridge visited them two years later.

396. See prefatory note.

404-7. *The Idiot Boy* and *The Thorn.*

419. In the spring of 1800 their brother John, who was captain of an East Indiaman, came to their new home at Grasmere. He thoroughly appreciated his brother's poems, and predicted their ultimate success. He remained with them about eight months, and in the fall he started upon the voyage which he intended should be his last, as he desired to live with his brother and sister. He often said that he would work for them while they were endeavoring to do something for the world. In February, 1805, his vessel was wrecked off Portland, and all on board perished. There are touching allusions to him in *Elegiac Stanzas, Character of the Happy Warrior,* and *Lines suggested by seeing Peele Castle in a Storm,* all testifying to his refined taste, true nobility of character, and devotion to his brother and sister.

430-54. The concluding lines of this "anthem of a beautiful and holy life" show his conviction of the high calling of a poet. In the following sonnet to Haydon, the artist, he has given expression to this ideal : —

> High is our calling, Friend! Creative Art
> (Whether the instrument of words she use,
> Or pencil pregnant with ethereal hues)
> Demands the service of a mind and heart,
> Though sensitive, yet in their weakest part
> Heroically fashioned, — to infuse
> Faith in the whispers of the lonely Muse,
> When the whole world seems adverse to desert, etc.

The grand determination with which, abandoning professional life and giving himself to counteracting the "mechanical and utilitarian theories of his time," he stood up against ridicule and obloquy, cannot

be matched in literature.   Mr. Edwin P. Whipple, in his admirable
review of Wordsworth, says: "Wordsworth never will be a popular
poet so long as readers do not distinguish between being passionate
and being impassioned, and who prefer strength of convulsion to
strength of repose; readers who will attend only to what stirs and
startles the sensibility, who read poetry not for its nourishing but for
its inflaming qualities, and who look upon poetic fire as properly consuming the mind it animates.   Wordsworth is not for them unless they
go to him as a spiritual physician in search of 'balm for hurt minds.'
Placed in a period of time when great passions in the heart generated
monstrous paradoxes in the brain, he clung to these simple but essential
elements of human nature on which true power and true elevation must
rest; and, while all around him sounded the whine of sentimentality
and the hiss of Satanic pride, his mission, like that of his own beautiful
blue streamlet, the Duddon, was 'to heal and cleanse, not madden and
pollute.'"